THE 40-Day Reset FOR WOMEN

Realigning Your Mind to the Power, Peace, Purpose, and Promises of God

SARA SINGH

40-Day Reset for Women: Realigning Your Mind to the Power, Peace, Purpose, and Promises of God

Copyright © 2022 Sara Singh

All rights reserved. No part of this publication may be reproduced, distributed, or transmitted in any form or by any means, including photo-copying, recording, or other electronic or mechanical methods, without the prior written permission of the publisher, except in the case of brief quotations embodied in critical reviews and certain other noncommercial uses permitted by copyright law.

Scripture quotations taken from the 21st Century King James Version®, copyright © 1994. Used by permission of Deuel Enterprises, Inc., Gary, SD 57237. All rights reserved.

Scripture taken from The Message. Copyright © 1993, 1994, 1995, 1996, 2000, 2001, 2002. Used by permission of NavPress Publishing Group.

For permission requests, write to the publisher, addressed "Attention: Permissions Coordinator," at the address below.

Published by: HigherLife Publishing & Marketing
PO Box 623307
Oviedo, FL 32762
AHigherLife.com

40-Day Reset for Women: Realigning Your Mind to the Power, Peace, Purpose, and Promises of God Sara Singh — 1st ed.

ISBN 978-1-954533-41-7 Paperback
ISBN 978-1-954533-42-4 eBook

Library of Congress Control Number: 2021916255

Printed in the United States of America.

10 9 8 7 6 5 4 3 2 1

DESCRIPTION OF STUDY:

The Bible repeatedly mentions the important time of reflection of forty days:

Noah was in the ark during the flood for forty days. Moses was on Mt. Sinai for forty days to get the commandments. Elijah went forty days without food or drink while fasting. Jesus fasted for forty days before his ministry began, and there were forty days between the resurrection and ascension of Jesus.

The number forty in the Bible always refers to a time of reflection, realignment, and mental reset needed to strengthen and deepen our faith. Contemporary Christian women can take these following forty days to reset their mind and hearts to the purpose, destiny, promise, and power that God has given us as women.

This study dives into many modern-day topics that women face in their everyday life, including:

drama, social media, clap back culture, change, joy, social activism, anxiety, depression, New Age beliefs, purity, modesty, racism, feminism, perspective, overcommitting, inner peace, worry, mothering, S.Q.U.A.D. goals, and marriage.

By

Sara Singh

THIS BOOK IS DEDICATED TO:

My Children: Kevin, Aliyah, Kaidan, and Avianna. Thank you for all you are. You have taught me just as much as I have taught you. I pray that you always choose God, live kingdom over culture, and stand apart and proud of your faith. Remember, even in seasons where you feel buried, you are just planted; let your roots go deep, and you will bloom in God's time. I love you four with all my heart. Thank you for your patience with your mommy.

#FAMILY #BFFs

My Husband and Best Friend: Kevin. Thank you for all that you do for our family as a provider and father daily. Thank you for the constant encouragement and pushing me to complete this work of my heart. You are truly my best friend and my equal partner mentally and emotionally. You are my only true love. I am proud of your growth and faith. I love you for always. Thank you for being my best friend and we really are a perfect team.

CONTENTS

Description of Study:	*iii*
Dedication	*v*
Acknowledgments	*ix*
Introduction: Welcome, Sisters	*1*

DAY 1	Eve: Fallen Yet Redeemed	7
DAY 2	Kingdom over Culture	13
DAY 3	Change Is Growth	21
DAY 4	Part One: Worldly Feminism vs. God's Value System	27
DAY 4	Part Two: Feminism	35
DAY 5	Peace, Be Still	43
DAY 6	The Weapon Will Be Formed, But It Will Not Prosper	49
DAY 7	Esther: From Beauty Pageant Winner to Courageous Queen	57
DAY 8	Anxiety: How to Breathe and Be at True Peace	63
DAY 9	Joy: It's Not an Emotion — Make It a Lifestyle	69
DAY 10	Living Unoffended and Unaffected (Forgiveness)	75
DAY 11	The Woman at the Well	81
DAY 12	I Feel Unbalanced	87
DAY 13	Generational Traumas and Curses & Blessings	93
DAY 14	Meekness Is Not My Weakness	101
DAY 15	Agape Love vs. Conditional Love	109
DAY 16	Old-Fashioned or Keep Up with the Times?	115
DAY 17	Overcommitted and Stressed Out	123

DAY 18	Delilah: Woman of the World vs. Woman of God	129
DAY 19	Social Justice Activist or Woman of Action?	137
DAY 20	New Age Mentality	145
DAY 21	Victim Mentality	155
DAY 22	Validation Is for Parking Stubs Not Your Self-Worth	163
DAY 23	Worry is a Waste of Time!	169
DAY 24	Happy Wife, Happy Life?	175
DAY 25	Clap Back and Cancel Culture: Where's the Grace?	185
DAY 26	Is Your Squad S.Q.U.A.D.?	193
DAY 27	"Why Fit in When You Were Born to Stand Out?"	201
DAY 28	What Kind of Mother Are You?	211
DAY 29	Ruth: Loyalty and Faith Lead to Abundance	219
DAY 30	God Will Take You Down to Lift You Up	225
DAY 31	Rahab: From Prostitute to Hero	233
DAY 32	Racism and Our Biblical Response to It: Part 1	241
DAY 33	Racism and Our Biblical Response to It: Part 2	249
DAY 34	I Have No Support for the Things God Called Me To	257
DAY 35	Sarah: God Is Faithful Even in Our Disbelief and Impatience	265
DAY 36	Keep Growing, Even When It Hurts	271
DAY 37	Mary: Faithful, Gentle, and Normal Mother	277
DAY 38	No More Drama	283
DAY 39	Perspective: There Are Three Sides to Every Story	291
DAY 40	Time Is of the Essence	299

Conclusion	307
About the Author	309

ACKNOWLEDGMENTS

My wonderful husband, Kevin. You have taught me SO much along this journey. Thank you for your love, encouragement, and patience during this process. Love you forever.

To my amazing in-laws (Mom [Sybil], Dad [Dave]). Thank you for allowing me to grow and loving me all the while, even if you didn't quite understand me. You are an important part of my heart, and you have filled in a space, long empty. You both are a blessing, and I appreciate you and I love you both always.

My grandparents (John and Joyce), thank you for taking me in and raising me to know Jesus. You set a strong foundation of faith for me.

To our pastor Gary Howell and Glad Tidings Church. Thank you for your time and love. Your feedback on these subjects is priceless, and I appreciate your time and guidance. Thank you for all you have poured into our family while shepherding us. You are anointed, and you are appreciated.

To my group of kingdom women. You all know who you are. Thank you, a million times, for your love, friendship, encouragement, prayers, and grace. Thank you for teaching me, pushing me, and covering me and this project in prayer. God brought you all into my life to push me to the next kingdom level and I will always do the same for you. Y'all are truly kingdom S.Q.U.A.D. goals, and you are all seen, loved, and appreciated.

Cristina, my priceless BFF. I love you more than words can say. I'm so proud of the strong woman, dedicated wife, and amazing mother you have become. It's been an honor to watch you blossom from high school until now. Thank you for being an encourager of this book and my biggest cheerleader in life. I love you forever!

INTRODUCTION: WELCOME, SISTERS.

ACCORDING TO A RECENT study executed by the Anxiety and Depression Association of America (ADAA): "Women (10.4 percent) were almost twice as likely as were men (5.5 percent) to have had depression."[1] There is a realistic, tangible stress and constant pressure felt by all people — but especially by modern-day women.

Society says we are supposed to be cool girlfriends; loyal wives; sexually and physically attractive; perfect, doting moms; empowered; spiritual, but not too religious; free-spirited, but modest; independent and assertive; easygoing and polished; work full-time and still have a spotless home; drive the best car; cook like a chef; be skinny; have perfect makeup; be on the PTA; keep up with the trends; stay young; be fit; drink water; be fun; have a social life; and be perfectly organized.

Whew. With this never-ending list, it is apparent why women today have plenty of mental health issues, stress, depression, and anxiety.

We are overwhelmed, mentally exhausted, and constantly seeking value and validation from the other human beings around us, who often fail us. We have Facebook and Instagram, and we take four hundred selfies just to get the perfect one, so complete strangers can tell us we are beautiful. Yet, we scream, "Women's Empowerment!" and "I am not my looks!"

---

[1] "Women and Depression." Anxiety & Depression Association of America, accessed October 2, 2021, https://adaa.org/find-help-for/women/depression.

Today the entire world's society and culture is based on contradictions. Contradictions create confusion, and without a firm and strong, unshakable foundation, we will never be steady and sure in who we are and what we are supposed to accomplish.

To all this instability, confusion, pressure, stress, and depression, there is ONE solution that has been proved for thousands of years:

God.

God designed and desired for us to live in constant peace, and His peace is a perfect peace that surpasses human understanding. People are on a never-ending search for "their inner peace," not even realizing "peace" is a gift given as a seed at salvation, and we can nurture it to grow. This peace is one the world cannot understand or take away from you. It is a peace the world will sometimes think is sheer blind ignorance. It is a peace that confuses the world and makes them think you are not "woke," when in fact, as a believer, you often see things much deeper and clearer than society sees them. But it is an amazing peace, and I have begun to feel sorry for those who do not have it, instead of justifying my peace to them. Stop debating them and trying to win them over to your belief — they must have their eyes opened by God only when their hearts are ready.

"She remembered who she was and the game changed." —Lalah Deliah

We are the daughters of the Most High King. We are princesses with royal blood. The God who created this world and put the planets into orbit desires for *you* to change this lost world. Yes, you!

You are a world-changer, a giant-slayer, and a chain-breaker with the Holy Spirit empowering you. That isn't just a marriage; you aren't just raising kids; that isn't just a job; that isn't just a business, or a book, or a play, or a song you are writing or producing — that is your ministry, and it is how *you can change the world*. It is how you can share God's love, peace, and joy with the world. Remember, no topic in this study is written to judge, condemn, or accuse anyone of any sins or previous or present choices or beliefs. I cannot judge sin, and only God can judge what is a sin and what is not. One of my biggest personal beliefs is free will and individual liberties. I want you to understand that I believe that everyone is free to live their life and their lifestyle

INTRODUCTION:

without judgment. Judgment does not bring people in and win souls for the kingdom; it ostracizes and isolates the unsaved. Our job is to speak truth and attract them with our actions; the Holy Spirit's job is to convict them to change any unrighteous ways. Our job is to love them where they are and to serve as a positive witness.

Sisters, I am not speaking in any self-righteousness intent; I am humbly sharing truths that I have discovered in my painful journey. I believe these truths can bring light, hope, peace, power, and love to your journey. If you follow the book's page on Instagram (@40day_reset), you will see that I blog about many of these issues that I am still being convicted on and still personally working on. We all are growing and learning in our faith, and nobody is better than another. Join us on IG to be part of a supportive group of kingdom women who can pray, encourage, and cover each other!

Conviction is NOT the same as condemnation. Conviction is the pull of the Holy Spirit giving you a chance to GROW, whereas condemnation implies you are always going to be stuck where you are. Please know the intention of this study is to set our hearts and minds to kingdom mentality and that will naturally clash with earthly mentality. Please keep an open mind and open heart in every subject covered. We must begin to think kingdom-minded and start to separate from worldly thinking.

Remember our GOD is a GOD of progression, and He is always convicting, growing, and propelling you onward and upwards. God calls us each to run our individual unique race, in our own way, with free will. When we stand before the throne, we will be judged on OUR individual decisions and lives. We will not be judged on our friends', social circles', spouses', political parties', families', or neighbors' choices of lifestyle. We were created as individuals, and we are responsible for our own choices, beliefs, and subsequent decisions or actions. We need to focus on our race, and stay in our lane, not looking around to the runners beside us, ahead, and especially behind us, who will only slow us down.

These are some complex and even controversial topics I notice are really affecting the peace and kingdom productivity of the women of Christ in today's age. I do not mean it to be controversial or divisive.

Instead, I mean it only to reset my sisters' perspective in heavenly things to spread peace and steadfast joy.

This book is ideal for women who are believers and are struggling (or desire) to have a strong and unshakable foundation that the world cannot erode or move. It is for women who have a basic understanding but want to dive deeper into the Bible to really grasp what God wills, expects, and promises in our lives as women. God has really opened my spiritual eyes to some secrets to real biblical inner peace and a more happy and stable life as a believer. I believe they can help empower us to unplug from some worldly issues, distractions, and conflicts and plug into the true peace and joy that only comes through Jesus Christ. I want to share some of the secrets I have found to this heavenly peace with you, my sisters.

Let us spend some time on our true mental health. The world tells us about mental health days and timeouts, so let us take a few moments every day to learn what God really requires, instructs, and promises us as modern-day, capable, and Holy Spirit-powered women. If we can go back to the basics of the Bible, in a modern-day explanation, we can realign our outlook, mindset, balance, and purpose in this world. Sometimes we think the Bible is full of old stories we all know, and we do not apply it to our everyday issues in life. The amazing truth is EVERY situation and issue in the modern world has an answer in the Bible. I will share powerful promises and lessons that I have found with you.

These precious minutes of your day for the next forty days will be focused on realigning your mindset and perspective with the Word of God. I believe it will be life-changing, perspective-altering, and that it will propel you into a deeper spiritual journey into your calling as women of God. We cannot believe in and invest in the measure of a value system by the world's beliefs; we need to reset our belief systems in the ONLY undisputable and steadfast Word of God. This is what will bring us REAL inner peace and a strong belief foundation to build our lives on.

God desires you to have peace, joy, and fulfillment from an endless source: Him. The world cannot satisfy you, nobody in this world can meet all your needs. Jesus tells us He is the well of Living Water, who

INTRODUCTION:

will never run dry. Come on, sister, let us dive into the endless ocean of God's love and peace and learn how we can dwell in that true inner peace everyday of our lives. In the middle of every raging storm, you can reset your mindset to remain in perfect peace.

Day One

EVE: FALLEN YET REDEEMED

"I am fallen, flawed and imperfect. Yet drenched in the grace
and mercy that is found in Jesus Christ, there is strength."
ADAM YOUNG

YES, WE ARE GOING to start with "that" woman. The woman with a past. The cursed woman. The one who caused all the pain in her life because of her choices in the past. I mean, what was she thinking? What could have made her make that choice? Why on earth would she think that was a good idea?

It sounds a lot like, "How could she wear that?" or "How could she date him?" We have all talked about or silently judged women like Eve before.

I dream of all the biblical figures I will get to sit and talk to when I get to heaven. For Abraham, I'd ask him what he thought when God almost made him sacrifice Isaac. For Esther, I'd ask her what it felt like to save her people so bravely. For Eve, I'd ask her was that fruit *really delicious*? Because since that error in judgment, we all have suffered so many things as women. Did you think twice about your decision, and how did you deal with your guilt after? But alas, in heaven the only thing we will be doing is praising the Lord, so whatever issues I had with Eve needed to be worked out here in my mind and heart on the earth.

But one day, God reminded me, sadly, we have ALL been Eve at one time. We all have fallen short, we have sinned, and sometimes we did wrong, knowing it was wrong and dealt with the consequences. Why am I more deserving of forgiveness and grace for my mistakes than she is? The answer: we are not more deserving, as we are all equal in our sins.

There is more to Eve's story than she gets credit for, and there is courage, grace, hope, mercy, and redemption in her story that mirrors the loving grace shown to Mary, the mother of Jesus. In Genesis, when Eve received the curse of her sin, it was as follows: "Then God said to the woman, 'I will cause you to have much trouble when you are pregnant. And when you give birth to children, you will have much pain. You will want your husband very much, but he will rule over you'" (Gen. 3:16 ERV).

We have all heard this and thought the curse was just about the pain in childbirth, the general physical pain of being a woman, and the "curse" of submission to our husbands (which isn't really a curse, but a source of strength, as we will discuss later on). But we overlook the verses before, beginning in Genesis 3:15, where God cursed the serpent/Satan as well. So the Lord God said to the serpent, "I will make you and the woman enemies to each other. Your children and her children will be enemies. You will bite her child's foot, but he will crush your head" (Gen. 3:15 ERV).

There is something in that curse that stood out to me: "You will bite her child's foot, but he will crush your head." Even though the serpent would bruise our heels as women, we, with our seeds, would have the strength to crush the serpent's head.

That is powerful. Satan can bruise you; he can knock you down, but he does not have the authority to take you out. Satan can *only* bruise you, and all bruises heal with time — but *you* have the authority from God to *crush* his head. Also hidden in this curse to the serpent was a generational promise to Eve that from her seed one day Mary would eventually come. Mary would produce, in the future, the Messiah,

Jesus, who would deliver an eternal crushing blow to the serpent's head. That there was grace and hope in her sin and finality in Jesus's forgiveness.

You see, that is the exact definition of God's grace.

The "bruised heels" could be a paradox for unhealthy childhoods, abuses, rapes, teen pregnancies, failed relationships, mistakes, bad decisions, sexual immorality, mental abuse, bad teenage decisions, unhealthy outlooks, generational curses, adultery, being hurt, or fears. We can have bruised heels in any area of our lives, but they can still crush the serpent's head. We still have "spiritual empowerment" when we realize all those previously mentioned things have *no* power over the bright future God has written for us.

There is a *but* here: Eve had to *do something* for her promise to come to life. She had to take a *step* of *real action* — not just talk about the action. Eve had to start producing heirs for her seed to produce the line of David and, ultimately, the Messiah who would deliver the crushing blow to Satan and extend us all eternal life once again. See, even in her *huge mistake*, she had *faith* that God had a *greater plan*. Eve had to step out, even though it would be painful for her seeds to grow. She knew it would hurt her, it would bruise her, but only through her faithfulness to God's will could the Messiah ever come to save us.

We must see ourselves as Eve, once flawed, once broken, and recognize that through the blood of Christ, we can hold our heads high and walk fully knowing we are women who are set free, redeemed, restored, and faultless before our Heavenly Father. We have the power to crush the enemy's head with the seeds we plant in life: whether that is our ministry, our marriage, our projects, our family, our jobs, our influence circle, or our physical children.

Allow your scars to tell the story of where you have *grown* from, not the pain of a sordid history you must relive over and over. Society is constantly encouraging people to dwell and rehash their past losses. While looking back is important for healing, we cannot just stay in our pasts reliving our pain and victimhood. We must decide at a certain point to stand up and take *action* to bring out the message in our past mess.

The world loves to tell believers, especially us women, "Who are you to tell us about Jesus? Your life hasn't been perfect." Or, "Look at your past, and you want to preach about Jesus." Those are lies from the pit of hell and from Satan himself. They mean for those insults and accusations to stop us, to judge us, to disqualify us.

I would like to submit to you that the scarred past you have is what qualifies you to testify about Jesus's redemptive love that forgives all and washes away our past sins. I dare you to believe that God does not call the qualified; He qualifies the called. I dare you to let go of your past Eve mistakes, but hold on to those lessons, and use them as your testimony, of where you were and what God has grown inside of you. God brings us all through different battlefields, so we can testify to His grace and our growth in different ways.

Listen — show me a "perfect" Christian, and I will show you a hypocrite. Nobody is perfect, and no one is perfectly qualified to minister. We all have sinned and fallen short, but it is God's redemptive forgiveness and grace that allows us to be bigger than our past. You cannot build a testimony without some substantial tests, and you can't have an impactful message without some messes.

There is power in this. *This* is your true power as a woman. There is power in Eve. There is substantial power in the story of a once flawed woman who has been redeemed through the Blood of Jesus. God sees you through the blood; He does not see your past mistakes and flaws; He sees you as His redeemed and righteous child. *You are equipped, anointed, redeemed, and worthy.* Walk in this truth today!

DAILY QUESTIONS:

1. What are your flaws, or Eve mistakes, in your past? Is there anything you need to forgive yourself for?

_____

_____

_____

_____

EVE: FALLEN YET REDEEMED

2. Is there a dream that you have been talking yourself out of because of your past shortcomings? How can you begin planting new seeds?

_____

_____

_____

_____

3. Have you ever judged "that woman" without seeing her through the grace of God? How can you repent and make that right?

_____

_____

_____

_____

DAILY PRAYER:

"Father, I forgive Eve, and I forgive my inner Eve, who is flawed. I thank You for Your son. I thank You that I have been redeemed, forgiven, and SET FREE. I thank You that I have the power to crush the serpent's head, even with bruised heels. My heels are bruised in the way of ___ _____. God, I know You have righted my wrongs, and I am new creation in Your life. Please help my seeds to grow. I have been planting seeds in _____. I know I need to plant more seeds in _____ ____. It will be painful, but I trust you to make my seeds a powerful force in the kingdom. I give You my life and my seeds to use for Your glory. In Jesus's name I pray. Amen."

DAILY FOCUS:

1. Forgive your inner Eve, who has made mistakes in the past. Embrace your past mistakes and allow them to be your testimony of God's redemption.
2. Forgive the flawed Eves in your life. Every woman has a past, so do not judge other women in a way you do not want to be judged. Give the same grace God has given you. Remember, even bruised heels have been given the power to crush the head of the enemy.
3. Consider your seeds. What is your promise? If you have been planting them, nurture them to grow. If you have not been planting them, start! There is *no* time like today. God promised if we produce, our seeds would be blessed. To fulfill this promise, we must begin to produce what He has placed down inside of us, even if it is painful.
4. Remember whose you are, not who you once were. You are forgiven, chosen, adored, loved, and valuable. Walk in that truth today. You have power over the devil; he can bruise you, but you can crush his head. Live and walk in that authority.

Day Two

KINGDOM OVER CULTURE

> "A man has to accept culture will no longer define him.
> God will define him and everyone else has to adjust.
> You will bring your faith into the culture and
> not be defined by the culture."
> DR. TONY EVANS, *KINGDOM MEN RISING*

THERE IS A COMMON underlying theme in this study of "kingdom culture over earthly culture." I want to take a day to dive into what this means because it will set the tone for all the days to come, so our human perspective and mindset can be truly and firmly aligned with heaven.

To live truly *kingdom* culture over *earthly* culture does not mean we have to completely abandon or forget our earthly culture. But we must find a way for you to carry KINGDOM culture into YOUR personal culture. You were placed in every position you find yourself in for a specific purpose. Our earthly culture heavily influences and dictates how we view others and build our value system and perspectives. Today we are talking about a KINGDOM MINDSET that can be a new filter for your viewpoints, perspectives, mindsets, and values.

The kingdom of God is based on the Bible alone. There is no substitute for the gospel to set our mindsets and perspectives on.

2 Corinthians 5:17 says, "When anyone is in Christ, it is a whole new world. The old things are gone; suddenly, everything is new" (ERV).

When we become Christians, we should take on the *first* culture of heaven, kingdom, and God. We can still be unique in our earthly cultures, customs, and skin color, but that can no longer be our first immediate mindset or identity. We must begin to view the people around us, our families, our situations, our hardships, through the lens of the kingdom instead of society's views. This will give us a clearer path to live daily, reach others, and react the way Jesus did.

Remember sisters, Satan comes to divide and destroy. The less labels and divides we live by, the more kingdom-minded we will be. The church was not designed to ever allow division because anything divided *cannot stand strong*. The church is assigned to take the kingdom into the culture, not allow the culture to erode at our beliefs and values.

As society's culture changes daily, the kingdom of God is steadfast, never wavering. We must be careful that the gospel of Jesus never becomes inundated by worldly theory and becomes a watered-down Christianity. This was never the intention. God told us in Romans 12:2, "Do not conform to the patterns of this world" (NIV). That is very clear. If we are living kingdom-minded, we must aim to be completely kingdom-minded, not lukewarm.

We need to begin to view others as individuals instead of trying to label them in an earthly group-think way. When we get to heaven and they look in the book of life for our name, it will be by individual souls, not earthly minority labels. They are not going to say, "Sara Singh, Indian woman section." No. God doesn't see us that way. We are told by Jesus to begin living here on earth as it is already in heaven.

Jesus was a Jew, because He was born from Jewish parents and a long line of Jewish kings dating back to King David. But He did not require everyone who believed in Him to leave their earthly culture completely. The disciples thought people had to convert to Judaism to become Christ-followers. They, on their own, were telling people they had to conform to Jewish traditions, like circumcision. Jesus corrected them on this point.

Jesus dressed and acted Jewish from all accounts. But Jesus often put His earthly culture behind Him to further His ministry. Like when He talked to the Samaritan woman, when He touched the lepers, and when He talked to the Gentiles (those who were not accepted by the "chosen" people of Jews). Jesus was our example of being perfectly kingdom-minded and perfectly living in His earthly culture of being Jewish at the same time. He celebrated Jewish holidays; He observed Jewish customs. However, He did not place His identity of being Jewish over His identity as being kingdom-minded.

Jesus often told people not to just follow Him from town to town after performing miracles. He often told them to go back to their hometown and tell the others in their own communities the good news. He knew if they all abandoned their culture and society to follow Him, their specific culture and society might never hear the good news. He wanted them to share their testimony with those in their society, who could relate to them, so that their encounter could be told from a witness and be much more relatable. Cultures must take their experiences and blend it with the gospel, to make the gospel relatable to that community, while keeping the message 100 percent biblical.

This does not mean that the gospel ever changes, but the way it reaches each community is different. A modern-day example of this is the variety of Christian music that carries the gospel message into different segments of the world. For example, there are artists in various genres: country, R&B, rap, Spanish, and gospel. Their message goes into their corresponding cultures to reach lost souls with the gospel. They may have different languages, styles, and tastes, but they all tell of the story of Jesus and the gospel in a way that connects with the people in their cultures.

We need to stop viewing other believers as "black believers," "white believers," "traditional believers," "contemporary believers," "Pentecostal believers," etc. We are designed to unite to all be equal brothers and sisters in the family of Christ. There is not supposed to be one over the other or one group more respected than the other. In

God's eyes, we are equal. We were all created from dust, and we will all return to dust.

Others may have a different way of praising or teaching or celebrating Jesus, but if they are still teaching the gospel, we are all one Body of Christ. This perspective can open the door for true kingdom unity. Remember, any label or divisive thoughts are an attack from Satan. God unites; Satan divides. We need to see all things in life as spiritual attacks on earth. Stand firm against division and unite as the Family of God and the Church of Christ.

I have realized that the more labels that are placed on us, the more isolated and closed off we become. I personally refuse to use earthly labels to limit or isolate myself. We need to identify ourselves as Christians first and the rest after. Remember, the ways, values, and beliefs of society change nearly every day, but the Word and kingdom of God are steadfast and infinite. God is never wavering, never failing.

Sisters, this is our entire goal for this study, to realign our hearts and minds to kingdom culture over society's culture. We cannot be wavering like the world around us, floating from one social issue to another. We need to resolve to change the world around us daily with Christ's love and light.

Are you more concerned about earthly society's issues or kingdom issues? The Bible tells us living everyday kingdom-minded will start to resolve every earthly issue. The world today is struggling with hate, division, injustice, anger, anarchy, murder, and prejudice. These are the opposite traits of kingdom living. These are Satan's way of infiltrating humankind's relationship with God. Love, joy, peace, patience, kindness, self-control, and godliness are all fruits of the Spirit and are exactly what society needs today. Fruits of the Spirit only come from a relationship with Jesus. When the kingdom invades culture, then society will begin to heal. Stop following the earthly trends, sis. Jesus was the ultimate trendsetter, not a bandwagon follower.

DAILY QUESTIONS:

1. Have you ever been confused about the "kingdom over culture" mindset? What do you understand now?

_____

_____

_____

_____

2. Are there any personal beliefs you may want to readjust to have a more kingdom/biblical view?

_____

_____

_____

_____

3. How can you transform your mindset to bring kingdom into YOUR culture?

_____

_____

_____

_____

DAILY PRAYER:

"Lord, thank You for allowing me to understand and reset my mind to kingdom of God. Help the kingdom mindset to take first position and place in my life over the culture around me. Lord, the society we live in is forever changing and shifting, but I know that You are the solid rock on which I can build my life. Lord, I pray that You continue to strengthen me to bring kingdom light and love into the society around me. God, help me to see the world around me with kingdom perspective. Help me to spread Your gospel into my community while standing firm and unwavering in the Word of God. Lord, I love You. Thy kingdom come. In Jesus's name. Amen."

DAILY FOCUS:

1. To live truly "kingdom culture over earthly culture" does not mean we have to completely abandon or forget our earthly culture. But we must find a way for you to carry kingdom culture into your personal culture. Our culture heavily influences and dictates how we view others and build our value system and perspectives. These are the things that we are focusing on – not the food, music, language, or arts of your culture.
2. When we become Christians, we should take on the first culture of heaven, kingdom, and God. We must still be unique in our earthly cultures, customs, and skin color, but that can no longer be our first immediate mindset or identity. We must begin to view the people around us, our families, our situations, our hardships, through the lens of the kingdom instead of society's divisive views.
3. Remember, any label or divisive thoughts are an attack from Satan. God unites; Satan divides. We need to see all things in life as spiritual attacks on earth. The spirit of division is not from God; anything that causes us to point fingers and divide is an attack from Satan. Stand firm against division and unite as the Family of God and the Church of Christ.
4. Choose to invade culture today, spread joy, share peace, and give kindness. Begin living as a warrior woman who INVADES the culture to share her fruits of the Spirit: love, joy, peace, patience, kindness, self-control, and godliness. Stand firm, beat Satan back, and

invade some space around you today for Jesus. Be salt and light, and you will begin living kingdom-minded.

Day Three
CHANGE IS GROWTH

Being a Christian demands constant progression, not perfection. One of your superpowers as a Christian woman is embracing continual growth and allowing God to reposition and stretch you. Many of the people around you constantly struggle with change. There are many people who are afraid of change, and any kind of change gives them severe anxiety and stress.

GOD CREATED A WORLD that is ever changing. He created a world that has changing tides, changing seasons, changing weather. From the moment you are born your body is constantly maturing and changing. Change is a part of the way God designed the earth, and we need to learn to embrace it as a joyful part of our journey. The more adaptable we are to the changes in our life, the more peace we will keep. We must learn to accept that change is an inevitable part of life, and we will become more adaptable and peaceful when it comes around. Half of life is not what happens to you but how you choose to react to it.

Change is good, change is maturity, change is progression, and change is success. Elevate your perspective and vision of change, and it will transform your feelings toward it. We were created to grow, and we can have a healthy outlook about every change in our life bringing us new blessings. Inner work is the hardest unseen work. Nobody may see it, but they will see the fruit of that change.

The Bible is full of characters who adapted to change with faith, and their faith was greatly rewarded. Sarah adapted to having a child after being long barren in her old age. Esther was propelled from an orphan girl to a brave and powerful queen who saved her people. Hannah went from being barren to having a blessed child who was destined to be one of the greatest prophets. Ruth went from gleaning leftover wheat in the fields to owning the fields. Mary, who was a virgin, had to adapt to the news that she would conceive the Messiah. How these women adapted to change in their lives changed the world and the story of our faith.

As believers, we are called to constantly change, learn, and grow. Most of the time we get stuck in what's comfortable, and we get stuck in ruts — in our faith, our career, our friendships, our calling, our marriages. We tend to fight change, when change is actually God trying to push us to a new level of growth. However, while it is easier to stay comfortable than to do the hard work to change who we associate with, anything that stops growing is slowly dying.

It can be a scary thought, but God calls us to keep moving forward and upward. Change is part of transformation, and transformation is an integral part of Christianity. We must always be striving to be better and be more Christ-like.

Acts 3:19 says, "So, you must change your hearts and lives. Come back to God, and he will forgive your sins" (ERV).

To go to the next level, you must change the way you are thinking and acting. God is always working, and He is always moving. You need to lean into the movements of God, embrace the changes, and have faith He is taking you to new heights. Change is a part of life you cannot escape, but when you ask God to change situations in a divine way, you need to expect drastic change. He is not a God of inaction — He is a God of sudden action. He is not a God of slow and evolutionary-like progress; He is a God of decisive action. In fact, many of the stories in the Bible begin with "suddenly." The Bible says Jesus will "suddenly" return. The angels "suddenly" appear to the shepherds; the storm "suddenly" appears when Jesus is sleeping on the boat.

CHANGE IS GROWTH

We cannot pray for our lives to change and then be surprised when suddenly life changes. We need to be prepared and adaptable to change. It is such a great coping skill to have and cultivate. So, while change is inevitable and often uncontrollable, you can change your reaction to it and the power it holds over you.

After all, if God was to leave us in our comfortable places — jobs we have had for years, friends we have had for years — we would never grow to our full potential. Growth only comes through change, and God needs us to keep growing and keep learning so we can conquer new territory for the kingdom. People struggle with so many things in life that could be overcome with a changed mindset. It is such a power to learn how to seek the messages in the messy moments and to search for the lessons in the losses. Living with this mindset is a way to cultivate lasting peace. Let go and lean into the work of God in your life, embrace change, and view it as an opportunity to learn and be better. Life can be simple if we stop overanalyzing every little thing. Many issues or problems can be avoided if we stay rational and stop reacting with our emotions.

You need to make sure the people around you can grow as well. You need to surround yourself with people who understand your heart, your intentions, your goals, your value systems, and where you are going. You need a tribe who can edify your values and build you up. You cannot go to the next level God has set for you still holding on to heavy baggage from your past. You need people around you (even if it is one person) who see your growth and your value and see what God has done in your life as a testimony. Do not be afraid to change who you hang around with. You do not have to deal with dysfunction. If it is not building you up, it is draining you and tearing you down. Be wise and surround yourself with healthy people who can contribute to your growth.

This has been the hardest part of my growth — to stop craving validation, support, and understanding from those who are not meant for this portion of my journey. We tend to give full-time positions to people who can only fulfill part-time hours. We tend to expect seasonal people to last a lifetime.

We need to vet your circle. Can you lovingly rebuke me when I am wrong? Can you hold me accountable for mistakes? Can you pull me back when I've gone too far? Can you force me to level up? Do you push me to be a better wife, mother, friend, person?

If they do, those are kingdom friends.

As in the parable of the prodigal son, the worldly friends will encourage you to keep damaging yourself. They will encourage you to forgo responsibility and forget God. They will add to your demise, then abandon you when you lose your worth, leaving you in a literal pit of pigs.

The coolest thing is — just like that parable — your Father is always home, waiting and ready to forgive. When you shed the negative worldly company, God will send kingdom people, and your life will increase tenfold in happiness, joy, contentment, and peace.

We cannot move to the next level of our destiny lugging around all the baggage, drama, issues, and heartaches of our past. I think sometimes God has more blessings ready for us to claim, but our hands, hearts, and minds are so full of our past that we do not have the room or the capacity to handle the new blessings.

Imagine you are climbing up a ladder. Climbing takes effort and strength, so you cannot maintain an upwards direction looking backward or being weighed down by the past. Sisters, we have got to aim to keep moving. If something or someone is no longer pushing you forward or growing with you, we must be confident enough to leave it behind. Not in hate, not in anger, but in peace and meekness. God has to strengthen our capacity, so we can handle the new level of blessings God has for us.

There is peace in moving forward. There is a weightless, freeing peace in leaving the old behind and soaring to new heights. Sometimes we will choose what is familiar, comfortable, or normal instead of embracing faith in pursuing God's full favor. If we refuse to move from what is comfortable, we will never grow to our full potential. This decision of choosing comfort is a literal growth blocker.

Rahab was a perfect Old Testament example of this. Even though she was a prostitute in her past life, she made a choice to change her life, ended up saving the Israelite spies, and later married one of them. She even became a princess of a prominent Israelite tribe — the Tribe of Judah. She was the mother to Boaz and an ancestor of King David. From her embracing a changed life, she is one of only four women mentioned in the genealogy of Jesus Christ. Sisters, change is powerful, and it can build an amazing generational legacy.

DAILY QUESTIONS:

1. Have you ever had an unhealthy reaction to change? If so, when?

_____

_____

_____

_____

2. Has your perspective on change shifted throughout the years? How?

_____

_____

_____

_____

3. How can you transform your reaction to change to keep your peace?

_____

_____

_____

_____

4. Do you need to vet your circle to help bring about kingdom change?

_____

_____

_____

_____

DAILY PRAYER:

"Lord, thank You for creating a world that is ever changing and maturing. Thank You for creating us with the ability to mature and transform. Thank You that I am not who I once was. Thank You for my past, which is now my testimony, and for my future, which is bright. Lord, I ask that You transform my thinking about change. Help me to see it as a new opportunity to conquer. Help me not to get stuck being comfortable. I do not want to become stagnant. Lord, guide me and protect and enable me to embrace every season of change as a gift of a new beginning and a new level of life in You. In Jesus's name, I pray. Amen."

DAILY FOCUS:

1. God created a world that is ever changing. He created a world that has changing tides, changing seasons, and changing weather. From the moment you are born, your body is constantly maturing and changing. Change is a part of the way God designed the earth, and we need to learn to embrace it as part of our journey. The more adaptable we are to the changes in our life, the more peace we will keep.
2. You need to make sure that the people around you can grow as well. You need to surround yourself with people who understand your heart, your intentions, your goals, your value systems, and where you are going. You need a tribe who can edify your values and build you up. You cannot go to the next level God has set for you, still holding on to heavy baggage from your past.

Day Four: Part One
WORLDLY FEMINISM VS. GOD'S VALUE SYSTEM

"We don't need feminism to define who we are as women. God's original definition is totally and completely sufficient."
GIRLDEFINED.COM

I AM GOING TO SAY this up front: I am not a feminist. I am an individualist — meaning that every individual has seeds of divine capacities to be the hero of their own story, whether they are men or women. There is a new wave of feminism that is becoming a major danger to our families, marriages, children, and our communities. I know that is not a popular statement, but it is biblically true. Just as you cannot worship two gods, you must pick ONE belief system and build your life upon it. We cannot have our feet in two worlds and expect to live a kingdom life.

I want you to understand that I believe that women can do anything they are called to do. Women are important, equipped, strong, and capable, but so are men. We are ALL equipped to do what we are called to do. Genesis tells us that all humans are made in the image of God and one gender is not more important than the other.

Genesis 1:27 says, "God created humans in his own image. He created them to be like himself. He created them male and female" (ERV).

From the very beginning, Eve was created to be a helpmate and companion for Adam, and she was created to fulfill that role before the fall. Meaning, being her husband's helpmate was not a result of the first sin and this role was not created as a punishment. The resistance and resentment of this role is a result of the fall of humanity. It is something we must fight against to realign ourselves with the kingdom perspective.

We are all equal souls to God — both men and women. We have different roles to fill in life, but we are equally important and valued by God. I tell my daughters they are not victims of anything in their lives — that they can do and be anything they want. We are only victims of our life choices. You cannot live in your bright and blessed future fighting ancient beliefs and battles of the past you are told about.

Sisters, the world today is so focused on reliving, refighting, and righting the atrocities of the past. We simply cannot move ahead looking backward. We must learn from the hardships and struggles of our sordid and amazing history and use those lessons and resilience as a strong foundation to build a brighter future for ourselves. We do not forget the people who went through hardships or fought for different causes in the past. But we must not stay there idolizing them and bemoaning their struggle; we must keep moving and build upon those lessons. That is what they fought for, for us to keep moving and accomplish more than the last generation. Every generation must heal a bit more, accomplish a bit more, and learn a bit more.

We need to free ourselves from thinking we are somebody's victim, which assigns them prolonged power over us and our circumstances. Assuming the role of a victim negates our accountability for our own choices and decisions. We are not victims. We are victors with Christ Jesus, and our mindset matters.

I teach my sons the same thing I teach my daughters. I do teach my daughters about modesty and purity, because that is a biblical value God gave to us as women for our lives' enrichment. I am not a feminist, but that does not mean I am a doormat — nor am I weaker, limited, or less able than a man. We are to have the Word of God as the foundation of our beliefs, values, and lifestyle, and then we are to go into the world with a strong foundation. We are not supposed to allow the culture of the world to eat away or change the foundation of our beliefs. We are the salt of the earth. If salt is diluted, then it loses its flavor. We must live in the world but not be of the world. We cannot just pick up whatever cause the culture is hyped about and jump on the bandwagon if it is not furthering the kingdom of God and the way He intended us to live. That is a harsh but necessary reality.

We read about how God created the world, and He created it in systems. He created night and day, He created water and land, and He created the sun and moon. He created everything in systems, and when a system breaks down, it is detrimental to the adjoining systems alongside it. God created a system for our faith, our lives, and our families. But He allows us to have free will, meaning we can choose to operate in the systems God placed us in, or we can choose to go off the path, and God allows us free will to choose the way we want to live. In marriage, the role of a wife being a helpmate or companion comes with the result of the encompassing peace of submitting to God's way.

God created us all with equal souls. God created Adam, then saw it was not good for the man to be alone, and He created Eve as a helpmate or support for him. God created them to coexist and help each other to cover each other's weaknesses.

There are strengths that men have where women are weaker, and there are a lot of strengths that women have where men are weaker. There are natural things that I can do better than my husband, and there are natural things my husband does better than me. When you embrace those strengths and differences as mates and begin to cover each other's inadequacies with grace, that is when you can maintain a truly healthy relationship or marriage.

God created us to live in family units. It is His design. When He put women and men together, it was to help each other survive and advance. There is nothing belittling about saying women were created as a helpmate for men, or that men were created to provide and care for women. Men feel the most accomplished in this role as a protector and provider. They may never tell you, but man was created with a need to provide and protect his family. When you take that job away, it emasculates and ultimately depresses him.

First wave feminists had a goal of wanting women to be recognized as equal citizens who have the right to own property, work, vote, and be in the political arena. This was a recognition of personal dignity, and it was a right. We should have and we do now thankfully have these rights in most western countries.

Second wave feminism was wanting women to be recognized as equal to men in the workplace and life choice rights, meaning we do not have to marry or have children and have the freedom to choose our lifestyle. Yes, we should be able to choose a career over family if we want or feel called to, or vice versa. We should get paid the value of our work, education, and experience. We should be thankful for the women and men who fought against social norms in the past to allow us to have these rights, and we should honor them by living to our fullest abilities and accomplishing our callings and passions.

Third wave feminism, however, has tried to establish no difference between men and women. It has become hateful and detrimental to men. It seeks to elevate women above men, because in history men have been "above women." But as much as the world tries to blur facts, there are differences — vast differences — between men and women, and they are our strengths. They should be celebrated. This wave of feminism also believes in the notion that women should be valued over men, just because past generations had it wrong. Just because others were wrong in the past, that doesn't mean we have to overcompensate in the other direction to make up for it. Quite frankly, the men alive now should not be punished for the sins/mistakes their ancestors made. They are already gone, and God holds each soul accountable for life choices.

Also, this wave of feminism is focused on sexual freedom and immodest appearance as an expression of women's freedom and independence. Women are publicly selling themselves short and cheaply to prove they are "equal and free." It is a culture full of contradictions, and contradictions leave people confused and constantly searching for validation. How can women yell, "Don't judge me for my appearance," but then dress as sexy and provocative as possible, posting pictures on social media for the public to see?

How can we say we are free and independent thinkers and then proceed to degrade ourselves by allowing menial men, with little to no commitment to us, access our most sacred physical and mental parts? How can we preach about equality yet not hold the men we interact with in a dating scene up to the same spiritual, mental, and value level we are living on? Why are so many women selling themselves short, not requiring marriage and real commitment from men? How can we say we are "valuable" but not require a man to marry us before we bear a child, who may be our sole responsibility? This is all completely contradictory.

In today's society, why are famous women allowing themselves to be displayed as (and profiting from being) over-sexualized female figures? This is what confuses many kingdom women most about modern feminism. Why are these types of women the loudest voices and wearing the least clothing? If you have so much to offer, why offer the cheapest, most basic version of yourself? If "sex sells" is the reason these celebrities degrade themselves, then maybe they should stop seeking fame and wealth and start seeking virtue and value.

I say enough. These kinds of "celebrity women" can't speak for me. They can't influence me or my family. We must be discerning of the women we follow or idolize. We must remember the enemy is sneaky. Many famous women are selling the new age "religion" of spirituality. We must measure any women we consider following with how they measure up to kingdom standards.

I am valuable, not just because of my face and body, but because of my intellect, heart, and faith. Also, because my Father in heaven said I am valuable and validated. I have more to offer than a magazine "perfect" figure; I am not cheap and ordinary. I was created to be priceless and valuable.

Therefore, I dress, carry myself, and speak as such. We are daughters of the King of kings — the ruler of the universe. Modesty is *not* old-fashioned. It is carrying yourself with timeless and priceless worth, grace, and royalty. Hold your head up, girl. Dress like royalty, stay modest, and be the fierce woman of God you were created to be. You are not of this world — you are a princess of heaven.

DAILY QUESTIONS:

1. Have you ever labeled yourself a feminist? Do you reconsider this now?

_____

_____

_____

_____

2. Has anyone ever told you the Bible has a low view of women? How has this view changed for you now?

_____

_____

_____

_____

3. What are some biblical truths about women?

_____

_____

_____

_____

4. Do you need to reconsider any earthly women you follow or idolize?

DAILY PRAYER:
"Lord, thank You for creating me as a woman. Thank You for the strength and dignity that You have assigned to me as a woman. Help me to separate myself from the worldly ideas and causes that want my allegiance. Help me to pledge my allegiance first to the kingdom. Lord, please help me to stop seeking my worth from what the world says and help me to focus on what the Bible says. Give me discernment to determine what I should think and believe. Help me to hold me head high and carry myself as the princess of heaven that You have created me to be. In Jesus's name. Amen."

DAILY FOCUS:
1. Women are important, equipped, strong, and capable, but so are men. We are *all* equipped to do what we are called to do. Genesis tells us that all humans are made in the image of God, and one gender is not more important than the other.
2. Third wave feminism, however, has tried to establish no difference between men and women. It has become hateful and detrimental to men. It seeks to elevate women above men, because in history men have been "above women." As much as the world tries to blur facts, there are differences, vast differences, and those differences are our strengths, and they should be celebrated.
3. Also, this wave of feminism is focused on sexual freedom and immodest appearance as an expression of women's freedom and independence. Women are publicly selling themselves short and

cheaply to prove they are "equal and free." It is a culture full of contradictions, and contradictions leave people confused and constantly searching for validation.

Day Four: Part Two
FEMINISM

> "Eve was not taken out of Adam's head to top him, neither out of his feet to be trampled on by him, but out of his side to be equal with him, under his arm to be protected by him, and near his heart to be loved by him."
> — MATTHEW HENRY

NOW THAT WE HAVE established that our worth and dignity as women is not assigned by anything on earth (but rather as part of our creation by our Heavenly Father), let us explore what our current society is experiencing today.

Third wave feminism has a culture of "men are trash" or "I am independent and don't need a man for anything" mentality. These thoughts are detrimental to not only our chances of having a godly marriage, but they are also breaking down our family unit and values. A family without a strong leadership team means open ground for Satan to infiltrate our children's beliefs. This is the danger of any worldly theory that seeks to destroy the nuclear or traditional family. When you destroy the family unit, you weaken the next generation's ability to be steadfast and grounded.

All this trend does is weaken and damage men. We need strong and powerful men to be the heads of our households. That is how the Bible set up the family system. A man who feels appreciated and valued will grow and blossom in faith, grace, and love. Men need this support. They have hardwired pressures that women do not have to provide and be strong most of the time. Men are not trash — men were created to be strong leaders. If they are constantly knocked down, belittled, and demeaned, they will naturally shut down and be the opposite of what they were created to be. Are some men evil or sinful? Of course — just as some women are.

Many feminists look with disdain at Christian women, as poor, sad souls with no backbone. They see our godly submission, forgiveness, and grace to our partners as weakness. But Christianity is full of strong, meek, and powerful women.

We have Sarah, who God made a promise to that He fulfilled. We have Esther, who was beautiful, meek, graceful, and determined, and she saved her entire race of people. We have Ruth, who was loyal and faithful and became a powerful woman in a foreign country and became King David's great-grandmother and heir in the lineage of Jesus. We have Hannah, whose womb was closed, and God granted her desire in her heart and gave her Samuel, who was one of the greatest Old Testament prophets. We have Rahab, who was an impoverished prostitute, but took a step of brave faith and married into one of the most powerful Israelite families and is mentioned in the lineage of Jesus.

The New Testament Bible gives us the stories of Mary, Elizabeth, the Samaritan woman at the well, Mary Magdalene, Abigail, Joanna, Tabitha, and so many more. Women who were flawed and imperfect yet were redeemed by God and did powerful things for the kingdom.

Jesus was way ahead of His time in how He reached, interacted, and spoke to women. Have you noticed how men had to hike up mountains and go to temples and fast to "seek" God's presence? Have you even noticed Jesus came to the women He interacted with and touched their lives right where they were? He knew they were busy, so He went to them. He sought them out and called them where they were.

Jesus sat with Mary Magdalene. He visited Mary, taught her, and spoke to Martha as she was busy cooking and cleaning. He validated the Samaritan woman at the well and said her future could be anything she decided in a time when those two races did not interact or speak. Jesus gave grace and stood up for the woman who was to be stoned. He appeared first to the women at the tomb and allowed those women to tell the disciples He had risen. The greatest news on earth was shared by a woman.

Jesus made sure even on the cross that His mother had John to look after her, as He was dying. He valued women, praised women, stood up for women, interacted with women, and He included women in His ministry. He did all this ahead of the time, for in His day women were not allowed to do all the previously mentioned things. He even called strong and powerful women in the early church actively spreading the gospel. Jesus believed women were daughters of the King, and He included them in His mission.

In many marriages, I see the wives are constantly trying to fight for power, dominance, and to demand obedience and allegiance, and they are unhappy. We must let go of this mentality and move past this. We must embrace the unique qualities of women and the unique qualities of men. Silently fill in the spaces where your husband is weak. Do not mock him for his inadequacies and do not insult or put him down — especially not publicly.

He should also support you in your weak areas without insult. Others do not need to know the areas you cover for him. God sees it, and God will validate and reward those silent sacrifices. Every human praise for an action you receive here on earth means you have already been rewarded for it. I would rather God reward me for eternity for my sacrifices than just get a fleeting like on social media.

I have personally gained so much more in my marriage by forgiving, being meek, and giving grace than I could ever get with condemnation, nagging, and hate. The kingdom of God is run on opposites, love those who hate you, bless those who curse you, and forgive those who accuse you. Take those principles and apply them to your relationships and marriage.

You will have more power in submission, and you will have more peace in forgiveness. You will have more joy in giving grace, and you will have more agreements in staying quiet and respectful than in being degrading, insulting, and arguing. It is a concept the worldly feminists will never understand because the kingdom of God is not easily understood and not natural to our human condition. The kingdom is the exact opposite of the world. Good advice is to always strive to do the opposite of what is trending or popular in society.

We are not entitled to anything just because we are women. We are not more valuable just because we are women. We should not be listened to just because we are women. We are all equal, we are all valuable, and we should all be listened to — because every soul is valuable to our Lord. We must value every person placed in our life in the role God assigned to them.

Women today are desperate for validation and to find their identity and establish their earthly worth, but sisters, we were validated on the cross. In the Bible, God tells us our worth — we are priceless, and our identity is more than conquerors in Christ Jesus. Set yourself apart, stand firm in the belief that you are capable, strong, beautiful, anointed, forgiven, and redeemed, and so are our male counterparts.

Carry yourself like you are a part of a royal priesthood. Your Father is the King of kings, so walk like a princess and carry yourself with kindness, calmness, grace, and love. We are daughters of the King, and we must realign our perspective and mindset with the Bible and God's system of the kingdom. God established your worth, He has set your inner peace, and He has established your identity. We are not lost drifters like the world. Our lives are built on a solid foundation.

As Christians, we are empowered only through the Holy Spirit. We are not empowered in our own selves. We are not empowered by others. Be careful with any doctrine or trend that teaches "self-reliance," "self-love," and "self-empowerment." We must discern if anything we are following or listening to is taking away from the starring role God must play in our life. We are empowered by the Son of God, who loved us enough to die for our sins and then rise victorious.

Embrace that power, but remember, God gave us grace in our sinful nature. He gave us forgiveness when we did not deserve it. He gave us love so strong He would lay down His life for us, and He gave us mercy when we did not deserve it. We, in turn, need to mirror those qualities and be women of God to a lost, hurt, and confused world.

We cannot join in their hurt, anger, and confusion when we have the answer to it all — Jesus Christ.

As women our value, self-worth, and validation were set in stone when Jesus died for us. Nobody on earth can add or take value away from you. Nobody on earth can limit your God-given capabilities and anointing. Take your emotional power back and stop fighting invisible and sometimes non-existent enemies. We should not need a "Women's Day" or an "empowerment movement" to validate our value, strength, abilities, or goals as women.

Our strength, talents, abilities, and worth are not earthly things that need to be valued. They are eternal things that are valued by our Heavenly Father. We need to find our value and our confidence *only* in Jesus. If our confidence is based on shifting, earthly things, and people, then it is corruptible; if our confidence is founded in Jesus, then it is never-ending and eternal. You are anointed, called, capable, strong, equipped, and worthy because Jesus validated you on the cross.

Sisters, let us try to reject worldly stress, labels, and divides. Be an individualist, and plant seeds of hope in ALL people. Speak life to all people. Support all people and love all people — the way *Christ died for all people.*

You cannot cling to your worth in ONLY being a woman — you must choose to cling to your worth in being who JESUS created you to be. Let us try to be set apart and not follow the culture and society's trends. It is so hard but being set apart is where the peace of Jesus is.

DAILY QUESTIONS:

1. Have you changed your beliefs in secular feminism? If so, how?

_____

_____

_____

_____

2. What is your value system, and what do you believe about being a woman?

_____

_____

_____

_____

3. Have you ever realized the Bible was so full of powerful and anointed women? Who is your favorite and why?

_____

_____

_____

_____

4. Is there anything you need to change in your life to more closely match biblical modesty?

_____

_____

_____

_____

FEMINISM

DAILY PRAYER:

"Father, I want to align my belief system with Your kingdom, not this world. I want to grow as a Holy Spirit-powered woman of God in the way You have called and anointed me to. I want to carry myself like I am a daughter of the King of kings, and I want to reach the world around me. Please help to grow my grace, love, kindness, and forgiveness as a witness for You. Set me apart from the lost women of the world. Remind me daily of my identity in You and my worth to You. God, help me to know that whether we are women or men, we are all valuable to You. Please help open my eyes to the deceit of the world that does not align with the kingdom of God's values. Lord, help me not to jump behind what is popular culture and forsake my kingdom culture. I place You and Your desires first, Lord. I love You, Lord. In Jesus's name. Amen."

DAILY FOCUS:

1. In many marriages, the wives are constantly trying to fight for power, dominance, and to demand obedience and allegiance, and they are unhappy. We must let go of this mentality and move past this. We must embrace the unique qualities of women and the unique qualities of men. Silently fill in the spaces where your husband is weak. Do not mock him for his inadequacies; do not insult or put him down, especially not publicly.
2. Do not pick up the values and victimhood of the world. That is a stress and mental pressure that Jesus Christ died to save you from. You are not a victim. You are a victor with Christ Jesus. You are a conqueror. Do not support a cause, just because it sounds right; weigh it with the Word of God.
3. Try to think about the things you purchase as well. Girls' clothing that says, "Girls Run the World," "The Future Is Feminine," "The World Belongs to Girls," "Girls Rule, Boys Drool" — those messages are not reaching the world for Jesus. That is telling half the population they do not matter as much. Every choice we make should edify the kingdom.
4. Stand tall as the Bible says we women are Holy Spirit-empowered, strong, capable, anointed, called, graceful, beautiful, wonderfully created, and heirs to the kingdom of heaven.

Day Five

PEACE, BE STILL

> "God's peace is not the calm after the storm.
> It's the steadfastness during it."
> UNKNOWN

THE ENTIRE WORLD SEEMS to be searching for peace. What is peace, and why does it seem the entire world is searching for a source of "inner peace"? Random people are even trying to help us search for peace. I saw a yoga advertisement that claims to help cultivate inner peace. Now, do not get me wrong, if you love yoga, that is great. But there is a reason the Bible refers to Jesus as the "Prince of Peace." True peace comes from one source and one source alone — Jesus Christ.

Colossians 3:15 says, "Let the peace that Christ gives control your thinking. It is for peace that you were chosen to be together in one body. And always be thankful" (ERV).

Philippians 4:4 says, "And the peace of God, which surpasses all understanding, will guard your hearts and minds in Christ Jesus" (ESV).

The word "peace" appears approximately 420 times in the Bible. So, it would appear peace is important in God's eyes. Biblical peace, in the original Hebrew, can be translated as "shalom," meaning, "fulfillment, wholeness, harmony, security, and wellbeing."

There was a meme going around social media some time ago that read: "Girl — you can eat all the kale, buy all the things, lift all the weights, take all the trips, trash all that doesn't spark joy, wash your face, and hustle like mad, but if you don't rest your soul in Jesus, you will never find peace and purpose." WOW. Can I get an amen?

There is a peace that we as believers have that the world thinks is just crazy. There are crazy times in life when only Jesus can give your soul and heart such peace that the people around you can think you are naive or strange. Dare I say it, but sometimes our peace really surpasses human understanding. Remember, the philosophy of heaven looks ridiculous through an unbeliever's eyes. Peace is something that is internal. It is yours, and it is yours to lose. We need to weigh whether certain situations are worth losing your peace over.

Peace is a fruit of the Spirit, which infers that the more we are full of the Holy Spirit, the more peace we will cultivate. Jesus is our single and most potent source of peace. Yes, yoga, exercising, and dieting can add to our peace or help us calm down, but our ultimate source of steadfast peace is our faith and belief in Jesus Christ Himself. Jesus has promised that He will provide us with peace that passes human understanding. This does not mean you will never have trials or hard times, but staying in *peace* helps your perspective of having and maintaining faith even within the storms.

This became so apparent to me through the COVID-19 quarantine of early 2020. The whole world was engulfed in this pandemic with dread, fear, and worry being all that the media and social media was spreading. Meanwhile, my family and I were literally having the time of our lives. You see, we saw that time as a blessing and a literal reset. Yes — we were safe. Only one person went to the store, only one person went to work, four kids homeschooled (then transitioned into in-person learning), but we embraced it as part of God's plan. We turned off the negative news and surrounded ourselves with joy and God's Word. We chose to stay in peace because peace is not dependent on your situation. It is an outlook, a mindset, a perspective. We were even mocked and berated for not being worried or scared enough by some family and friends. Inside the walls of our home, we knew that this peace of God just could not be understood by the scared world.

I remember a youth pastor once stating, "The fact that a boat is in water doesn't cause the boat to sink. A boat can survive being surrounded by water. It is only when the water gets into and overfills the boat that the boat begins to sink." That is a powerful and poignant example of how we should be in the world.

Yes, stress comes, and finances, work, and children can contribute or add stress. Only when we allow that stress into our hearts and minds does it overtake our faith. That's when we really begin to drown in hopelessness. Other trends that are peace-killers are overanalyzing, unnecessary anger, and worrying. Many people are getting angry about things that don't really matter and are overanalyzing drama, instead of dealing with issues directly. We must filter these behaviors out of our lives!

Peace is not a destination. Peace is a mindset to have during the entire journey. We cannot go through life hoping to one day reach peace, and we must be steadfast in maintaining our peace in our everyday lives. That means if our thinking isn't aligned to the kingdom, we will never have true biblical peace. Therefore, we must continue to be a witness for the gospel. It is not really true love to know the answer for people's search for peace hidden in our hearts and never be bold enough to share it with them.

Peace should be our goal, peace should be our new normal, and peace should be what we are aiming to maintain. We have already been given peace as a seed by the Father at salvation. It needs to be in fertile soil, it needs to be watered and cultivated, and it is up to us to not let the world we are surrounded with steal our peace. We need to protect our peace. If people are not adding to your peace, you need to distance yourself. We are in this world, but we are just passing through. Remember, this world is not our home and not our final destination. We are here to fulfill the purposes that God has assigned us to reach the world and win souls for the kingdom. We are not made to submerge ourselves in the culture of this world, we are to always immerse ourselves in our heavenly culture. Remember, kingdom over culture.

DAILY QUESTIONS:

1. What is something that seems to steal or tries to steal your peace?

2. Like the analogy of the boat, what are you surrounded with that you need to keep out?

3. Has there been a situation in which your peace really passed others' understanding?

DAILY PRAYER:

"Lord, thank You for reminding me that You are the Prince of Peace.

Thank You for gifting me with supernatural peace. I ask that You always keep me in the palm of Your hand. I ask that You help me to remember my peace is more than the world can understand, and that is only sourced from You, through my relationship with You. God help me to be like the boat, surrounded by problems and stress, but not allowing them to get inside of me, where my peace is. Help me to keep my focus and my aim to always be peaceful. Thank You, Jesus. In Jesus's name. Amen."

DAILY FOCUS:
1. Jesus is the Prince of Peace. He is your lone source of peace. Do not look to the world to provide you with peace. It will be false peace.
2. Remember the boat; it is surrounded by water. Only when water overtakes it inside does it begin to sink. You can be surrounded by the stress of everyday life and still maintain your peace.
3. Don't try to explain your inner peace to others. It is your own. Others cannot or will not understand it, especially if they are not believers. Allow your personal inner peace to cultivate a lifestyle of joy that can be shared with others.

Day Six

THE WEAPON WILL BE FORMED, BUT IT WILL NOT PROSPER

> "The enemy is not after your money or your stuff.
> He wants your mind, your attitude, your heart, your faith,
> your peace. Understand that you're not being attacked over
> the tangible things in your life. The enemy is
> fighting you over the things not seen."
> UNKNOWN

I USED TO VIEW SPIRITUAL attacks as demon possessions or exorcisms you saw in the horror movies. Many of us probably still do think of it this way. But Satan utilizes many common, everyday spiritual attacks, and I think we do not recognize them for what they truly are. Anything that makes you doubt the Word of God; anything that destroys your peace; anything that contradicts the things God says about you; anything that keeps you stressed, worried, or depressed is an attack from the enemy.

Sisters, we are not supposed to just be on constant defense from Satan, counter attacking his primary attacks and constantly cowering in fear. No! We are created and called to be Holy Spirit-powered and on the offense to cut him off before he can launch an attack in the first place. Satan has been given no power over you. Sometimes recognizing the attack is all you need to overcome, overpower, and rebuke it. You have power over every scheme of the devil.

We cannot physically fight, kick, punch, and "clap back" the enemy. You must use spiritual weapons. Recognizing demonic attacks, engaging in praise and prayer, quoting Scriptures, listening to uplifting sermons, and edifying our minds with what God says about us and our power through the Holy Spirit is how we fight. We fight by recognizing what is an attack from the enemy, standing firm in our knowledge that we have power over it and using the weapons God has given us to push the enemy back.

Common attacks are: fear, anxiety, needless arguments, anger, low self-esteem, self-doubt, worry, sadness, frustration, resentment, insomnia, pessimism, and ungratefulness. Sisters, any feelings that are not of your Heavenly Father's nature come from the enemy.

Ephesians 6:10-11 says, "Be strong in the Lord and in his great power. Wear the full armor of God. Wear God's armor so that you can fight against the devil's clever tricks" (ERV).

We are not supposed to be constantly running away from Satan; we are called to stand firm. You have been given the armor of God to protect you, the Word of God as your weapon, and the faith of God as your strength. You are equipped to fight. You are a victor, not a victim.

Remember our enemy does not come to us with his pitchfork and red horns, he comes to us disguised as the things listed above, to shake the core and demean the foundation of our faith. Satan rejoices in the small battles he wins through our small decisions, when we pull away slightly from God. He does not push us straight to demonic behavior. He is a cunning, shrewd, slow-moving enemy.

That means every decision we make, no matter how insignificant it appears, is a battle and it matters. Even following a few New Age beliefs (which we will discuss further in a later day) or human secularism just a little is a small way the enemy tries to draw us away from our Father.

Bob Sorge, in his book, *Glory: When Heaven Invades Earth*, says, "The nature of the enemy's warfare in your life is to cause you to become discouraged and to cast away your confidence. Not that you would necessarily discard your salvation, but you could give up your hope of God's deliverance. The enemy wants to numb you into a coping kind of Christianity that has given up hope of seeing God's resurrection power."[2]

We need to always be living with an end goal of healing and wholeness and stop just coping and recovering. That is not living in God's fullness. Jesus died to give you complete victory over Satan and every one of his attacks. Remember what we learned about Eve — Satan can bruise your heels, but those bruised and painful heels still have the power through Christ to crush the head of the enemy. We must have this truth so ingrained in our mind, that we never doubt our power over the enemy. You were created to heal and thrive, not just cope and survive!

Remember Job? Satan could not bring any hardship to him without God's permission. Satan cannot bring anything to you unless it has passed by God; that means you are equipped to fight every attack from the enemy. You are not powerless, you are not scared, and you are not a victim. Stand up, have a strong footing, and fight back. When you realize the true power that your Heavenly Father has given you over every attack of the enemy — you will be a force to be reckoned with.

2 Corinthians 10:4-5 says, "The weapons we use are not human ones. Our weapons have power from God and can destroy the enemy's strong places. We destroy people's arguments, and we tear down every proud idea that raises itself against the knowledge of God. We also capture every thought and make it give up and obey Christ" (ERV).

We all wished we were able to be a superhero when we were kids, because we wanted to be able to do something "powerful" or because we wanted to have a superpower nobody else had. Maybe it is not about the power you have; it is about the power you can plug into. Jesus is a source of power we can tune into, plug into, and draw from for every attack from the enemy. Listen, suit up, superwoman! You are

---

[2] Bob Sorge, *Glory: When Heaven Invades Earth* (Grandview: Oasis House, 2000).

equipped and able to fight off every attack of the enemy. Your superpower is that you have the Word, perspective, and knowledge of God in your mind and heart.

This means God has given you discernment, the ability to see things for what they truly are. That means when someone is rude to you in a store, you recognize that this is just an attack from the enemy to steal your joy. That means when you get stuck in traffic, you recognize this is just an attack of the enemy to steal your peace. That means when someone is judgmental, gossips about you, or is mean, you recognize that this is just an attack of the enemy to steal your confidence. That means when your spouse is rude or grumpy, you recognize it is an attack of the enemy to steal your agape love. That means when you do not get a job, promotion, or a coveted business deal, you realize it is an attack of the enemy trying to steal your faith. Choose to win.

There is a spirit mentioned in the Bible, in Isaiah 27:1, who is described as the "Master Twister" also called Leviathan. This is a powerful, world-ruler spirit that is responsible for most twisting of the truth, manipulation, gaslighting, mind-control on a mass level, and narcissism. His goal is simple division. He siphons his power from the amount of division and contempt he can incite. This spirit is running rampant in society today!

In Job 41, he is known as a "creature of the swamp or sea," almost crocodile-like. Many of the verses describe the jaw and teeth of the spirit, which tells us he is a spirit who can control the mouth. When a crocodile snatches its prey, it spins and pulls it into their realm and then dismembers it. This is symbolic of twisting words, distorting the meanings and intentions, and creating division and drama in our lives. Job also describes him as a spirit of pride, where people are not going to be teachable if it is controlling them, because pride makes them unteachable.

Leviathan is described as a spirit that "stirs up the pot and makes the depths of the sea churn." Our world is in a time where many people are passionate, angry, and even led to violence in the name of political, ideological, and personal convictions and beliefs. There is a tangible spirit of twisting the truth to fit specific narratives, pitting friend against friend, even family against family. When the Holy Spirit

THE WEAPON WILL BE FORMED, BUT IT WILL NOT PROSPER

grants you discernment, you will be able to discern truth from manipulation, properly identify the spirit, fight it, and ultimately rebuke it. Much of the twisting, churning, and inciting we see in today's culture is really a spiritual battle against the church. This is the manifestation that is driving the evil spirits crazy and causing hateful chaos among humans.

Remember, feelings of division, hatred, and angry violence do not come from our Heavenly Father. Toxic thinking is straight from Satan himself. If you discern and recognize Leviathan, you must pull away from the emotional connection; it is essential to deescalate the emotions, and pray against it, so God Himself can bind it. It is a strong and manipulative spirit.

Choose to see every attack for what it really is, so you can maintain your peace, joy, agape love, confidence, and faith. You are an overcomer, a soldier in God's army, and a warrior woman of God. Fight the enemy back and win the battles. The weapon will form, but your Heavenly Father has promised it will not prosper.

DAILY QUESTIONS:

1. Have you ever thought of disappointment or struggle as an attack from the enemy?

___

___

___

___

2. How can you grow in your discernment to recognize spiritual attacks?

_____

_____

_____

_____

3. How has your perspective about spiritual attacks in everyday life changed?

_____

_____

_____

_____

4. Leviathan is a prominent spirit in today's world. After today's explanation, can you think about anytime it may have been rising against you?

_____

_____

_____

_____

THE WEAPON WILL BE FORMED, BUT IT WILL NOT PROSPER

DAILY PRAYER:
"Father, I thank You for creating me as an overcomer and not a victim. Please help my discernment grow, so I can sense and realize every attack of the enemy. Help me to keep on the offense, so I can defeat every attack of the enemy. Help me to never be scared but remember Your Holy Spirit is powering me to FIGHT. Lord, please guide me in being able to fight the enemy at EVERY attack. Lord, I pray that I would sense every stress and anxiety as a spiritual attack from the enemy. Help me to choose joy and peace instead of giving into anger or frustration. Lord, help me to discern spiritual attacks and evil spirits like Leviathan, so I can rise against them. In Jesus's name I pray, amen."

DAILY FOCUS:
1. Anything that makes you doubt the Word of God; anything that destroys your peace; anything that contradicts the things God says about you; anything that keeps you stressed, worried, or depressed is an attack from the enemy.
2. Stop coping and recovering. That is not living in God's fullness. Jesus died to give you complete victory over Satan. Remember what we learned about Eve— Satan can bruise your heels, but those bruised and painful heels still have the power through Christ to crush the head of the enemy.
3. You are created to overcome every attack and trap the enemy has set. You were not created to be overcome by the enemy — you were created as an overcomer. Your superpower is that you have the word, perspective, and knowledge of God in your mind and heart.
4. Leviathan is described as a spirit that stirs up the pot and makes the depths of the sea churn. Our world is in a time where many people are passionate, angry, and even led to violence in the name of political, ideological, and personal convictions and beliefs. There is a tangible spirit of twisting the truth to fit specific narratives, pitting friend against friend, even family against family. When the Holy Spirit grants you discernment, you will be able to discern truth from manipulation, properly identify the spirit, fight it, and ultimately rebuke it.

Day Seven

ESTHER: FROM BEAUTY PAGEANT WINNER TO COURAGEOUS QUEEN

"Be an Esther, bold and courageous enough to stand for the truth, to voice your opinion and fight for the good of others, even when it means to sacrifice yourself. If God has put you in a position, it is for a purpose. Never be afraid to heed that inner voice."

APOSTOLIC ENCOURAGER

THE STORY OF ESTHER is sometimes an overlooked story of a strong woman's courage, meekness, and determination in the Bible. Here is a summary of the story: The King of Persia sought a new wife and desired to marry the most beautiful woman in the land. A young and beautiful Jewish orphan, Esther, was chosen by way of a historically described "beauty pageant." However, she was careful and deliberate to keep her Jewish ethnicity secret, because her uncle, her only living family, suggested she keep it quiet. She was obedient, and it was part of God's divine plan.

Mordecai, Esther's uncle, offended a high-ranking official and confidante to the King called Haman, by not bowing before him. Haman then decided to kill not only Mordecai but hatched a plan to slaughter all the Jews in the Persian empire. Esther prayed and fasted, God built up her courage to approach her new husband, and she was successful. Esther, with God by her side, turned the tables on Haman's evil plan. She pleaded with the king, and her husband was incredibly angry. Haman was horribly punished — hanged on the very gallows he had built for Mordecai.

The Jewish people in Persia were saved, and by a woman no less. The annual festival of Purim commemorated the courage of Esther and the triumphant deliverance of the Jews.

Esther's story teaches of divine appointments, which we still have today. Not only did God place Esther exactly where she needed to be, He ordained her as queen. She was not in line to be queen, and she wasn't born into royalty, but God placed her there in a time of need. He knew the Jews would be persecuted, and He knew she had the faith to walk the courageous path He gave her. You see, she was placed in the right place at the right time, with the right physical attributes, and the right mindset to allow the king and his court to accept and adore her and not investigate her ethnicity.

God ordains moments in our lives; He has Spirit-led moments, moments that are a divine appointment for things to fall in place. If we are praying and faithful and have the courage to walk, even frightening paths He sets us on, we will reach every divine appointment at the exact correct time. You are never too late, and your opportunity is NEVER missed. What is appointed to you will find you in God's perfect timing. Stop wasting your time regretting "missed opportunity." Sister, if you "missed" it, then it was not meant for you.

Before Esther approached her husband, she prayed and fasted, and she prepared herself. As we women nowadays would say, she got her hair done, took a long bath, got her nails done, got the perfect outfit and the perfect accessories and shoes. She paused, she prayed, she calmed her mind, and THEN she went. She did not rush in unprepared; she had true patience. She took a process in preparing not only her physical appearance but her heart, her courage, and her approach. This reminds me of Jesus in the Garden of Gethsemane. Jesus did not rush to the cross, He stopped deliberately and prayed so earnestly He sweated drops of blood. He prepared His mind and built up His courage for what was ahead of Him.

Sometimes, in the urgency of needing something done now, we rush, we skip the praying, and approach things in our own way. Rushing to react is often what causes fights and arguments. If we would slow down and be still, we could approach situations in a calm and loving manner. When we slow down and pray and seek God, He gives you a path to follow, He gives you the calmness to assess situations, and He will give you even the right words to say. God will place you in the right room, with the right people, and give you the right words they desire to hear. God is a God of the supernatural, not humanly possible. His ways are always higher than ours, and His ways are always better than ours. We need to stop, take time, be still, pray, and let God lead us in our reactions and our approaches in everyday life.

Esther had the courage to call out the wrong about to be done with humility. She did not adopt a high and mighty attitude of a person who was wronged. She also did not approach him as a troubled victim. She did not approach the king haughtily or pridefully; instead she demonstrated a character of meekness and humility (which we discuss further later). We have all heard the saying, "You attract more bees with honey." This is a true mentality; you cannot expect grace if you do not give grace.

We all need to be meek when we deal with ALL difficult or problematic situations in life, not weak. Remember, meekness is not weakness; meekness is power in control. Esther knew who she was, she knew what she looked like, but she knew and played her position with wisdom. She came giving respect and left held in more respect, she came adored and left loved, she came unprotected by the king, and she left vindicated and protected. When you assume a position of meekness, God will vindicate you; if you try to vindicate things yourself, you take God out of the situation. I would rather God fight my battles than me, because the Bible says vengeance belongs to the Lord. He can see more than I can, and He alone can turn hearts and minds around. Let's strive to keep our hearts and minds pure and let God deal with injustice and wrongdoing.

Here is an example of God's vengeance—Haman was hanged on the gallows he prepared for Mordecai, Esther's uncle and only family. That is God's vindication. Let me explain something, Mordecai refused to bow in front of Haman on the street. Haman got mad and was in a position of power to sully the king's mind against a made up "Jewish uprising" (yes, politicians made false narratives even back then). Mordecai was not wrong; he was standing firm in his faith, and Haman was full of pride and thought he should be worshiped. Haman left two things out of his grand plan, a praying woman and a vindictive God. When we pray, God goes to battle for us; it is not our battle anymore, it is God's battle. When we are Christians, every battle belongs to the Lord.

Sisters, we cannot try to do it all by ourselves. Someone will always be stronger, more capable, more powerful, and more knowledgeable than us, but they are not stronger, more capable, more powerful, and more knowledgeable than our God. Take a step back, and watch God begin to fight on your behalf. Doors will open, opportunities will fall into place, God will place you in rooms you are not qualified enough to enter, yet you are invited into those rooms, because God went ahead of you and prepared a place for you. Just like God put Esther in the right place at the right time.

Sisters, you have been placed where you are. That marriage is not an accident, those kids did not get randomly selected, that job is intentional, that calling is divine. You are qualified, and you are equipped to stay in your lane and run your race. Do it with meekness and quiet confidence, do it by prayerfully seeking God in every reaction, and do it by letting God fight your battles for you.

God knows who is for you and who is secretly plotting against you. It is not your job to figure it all out; the Bible does not say, "figure it out." The Bible says, "God will provide you and protect you." God is making a way for you, He is bringing opportunities to you, you do not have to campaign for them, and if you need to force something into your life, it was not meant for you. Stop trying to knock the door down; God will open the door FOR you. Stop trying to force them into your life; God will invite the right people in and give them a desire to stay. Be an Esther in today's world: courageous, meek, obedient, calm, collected, humble, confident, prayerful, powerful, and kind.

DAILY QUESTIONS:

1. Did you ever consider the humble strength of Esther?

_____

_____

_____

_____

2. What speaks to you most about her character?

_____

_____

_____

_____

3. What does this story inspire you to model or reconsider?

_____

_____

_____

_____

DAILY PRAYER:

"Father, I want to thank You for the story of Esther. Thank You for the model of quiet strength, meekness, courage, and prayerfulness. Lord, help me to seek You first in all situations as Esther did. Help me to listen to Your voice and walk the paths only You direct me to. Keep me in the lane You have assigned to me, keep me in the opportunities You want me to be in, and help me to know what Your desire for me is. Lord, help me to remain humble and meek. Help me to approach every situation today in prayer and follow Your lead. God, cultivate in me humility and meekness, so I can be a shining light of faith in this dark world. In Jesus's name I pray. Amen."

DAILY FOCUS:

1. Esther is a regal example of meekness being strength in control. She is strong, courageous, yet meek and prayerful. She is a wonderful example of how God puts us in the right place at exactly the right time. She did not have to campaign, force, or coerce her destiny — she was placed there. We do not have to force the things meant for us in life.
2. Esther was prayerful and took her time in her actions. She did not rush unprepared into the biggest trial of her life. She took her time, sought after God through prayer, prepared her mind and her courage, and put her best foot forward appearance-wise. We can model this same procedure and reap the same positive results. Slow down. Seek God, and all the rest will be added.

Day Eight

ANXIETY: HOW TO BREATHE AND BE AT TRUE PEACE

> "The root cause of anxiety is a failure to trust all that
> God has promised to be for us in Jesus."
> JOHN PIPER

PLEASE KNOW, IF YOU *have a medical condition, you need to seek help. This is a biblical view of anxiety as an attack of the enemy, and it is not intended to substitute for professional or medical help.*

So many women suffer from anxiety in today's world. Anxiety is defined as "a feeling of worry, nervousness, or unease." Anxiety to some people can be completely crippling, mind-consuming, and can become a real handicap. Anxiety leads to depression, insomnia, stress, anger, rage, and pushing others away. Anxiety really stems from fear; it is the worry or the fear that something can or will go wrong or issues do not work out. Anxiety is a real issue. But the Bible says it differently. Did you know we are commanded, "Do not be anxious"?

Philippians 4:6-7 tells us, "Don't worry about anything, but pray and ask God for everything you need, always giving thanks for what you have. And because you belong to Christ Jesus, God's peace will stand guard over all your thoughts and feelings. His peace can do this far better than our human minds" (ERV).

In Psalm 139:19-22, David is anxious and stressed about those who are putting wicked thoughts and gossip in Saul's ear and causing Saul to be so angry that Saul wants to kill him. David's first phrases in this psalm are anxious and stressed and plainly angry. "You murderers, get away from me! God, kill those wicked people — those who say bad things about you. Your enemies use your name falsely. Lord, I hate those who hate you. I hate those who are against you. I hate them completely! Your enemies are also my enemies" (ERV).

Then, he suddenly realizes the key to his anxiety and his outlook, and his focus shifts to what really controls his anxiety. He goes on to say, in Psalm 139:23-24, "God, examine me and know my mind. Test me and know all my worries. Make sure that I am not going the wrong way. Lead me on the path that has always been right" (ERV).

Can you believe that this is the same psalm? What a switch from telling God every wrongdoing, every gossip, every malicious act that was done, every bit of drama, and then tells God, "Search me." Because in truth, anxiety begins to form and fester inside your own mind. You can control your thoughts; it is hard, but they can be conquered.

Here is the reality: It is not what is happening that gives you anxiety, it is how YOU are thinking about it, or reacting to it, that causes anxiety. You are not anxious because of your career, marriage, friends, or parents; you are anxious because that trigger has contaminated your inner peace. A boat does not sink because it is in the water; it sinks when the surrounding water gets into it. Just because drama, stress, anxiety, and problems are around you does not mean they have to get into you. Now, this is not to condemn you, but to remind you that you have authority over any attack from hell.

In every situation, if you were to remember God has numbered the hairs on your head and He has promised to satisfy all your needs — if you were to truly believe that, what is there to really worry about? If we really trust Him, do we need to worry about our jobs, kids, and marriages? I am not suggesting that you stop caring about these things. I am talking about actionless worry and anxiety, just crazy, undisciplined thoughts running through our minds at 5,654 mph.

I used to suffer from severe anxiety, I used to worry, stress, and wonder, and I used to stay up at night to overthink. One day, I heard a sermon and realized that *this is an attack from the devil himself.*

2 Timothy 1:7 says, "For God has not given us a spirit of fear, but of power and of love and of a sound mind" (NKJV). This verse describes a sound mind and says God has given us all a sound mind. Sound means "peaceful." If God gave me a peaceful mind, who gave me a worried anxious mind?

Once I knew it was an attack from the devil, I learned I had the power over it. Satan can attack you, but you have been given power over his attack. You have been given authority over the enemy by Jesus Christ Himself. The enemy cannot bring anything to you, until it has passed through God first. Nothing is a surprise for God, and that thought alone gives me immediate peace. There are actual demons or spiritual attacks that cause many of the mental anguishes we face, and anxiety in one such attack. Anxiety and worry are ways that Satan steals our peace and sound mind, and we are equipped to fight his attacks.

So how can you fight off anxiety when it does rear its ugly head? One way is by turning your worry into worship. The devil cannot hear the name of Jesus. As worried as you are, even praise and worship can chase away any demon trying to attack you. If your mind is filled with praise and your thoughts are focused on God, you will not even have room in your mind for worry and anxiety. Praise brings the presence of God, and in the presence, there is no room for anxiety or worry. It will literally be pushed out of your mind. Put on praise music or simply sing it out loud. Where light is, darkness cannot be. Praise is a way to FORCE Satan to flee.

Another way is prayer. I find myself worrying and then mentally say, "Nope, Satan, not today. I have too much to do to let my mind be taken over by you and worrying. I rebuke these thoughts in Jesus's name." It took a lot of practice, but now it has become a habit. They say it only takes twenty-one days to practice something before it becomes a habit. Let us start making this a habit today. Recognize the anxiety and battle it with prayer, instead of giving in to it.

Another powerful way is to turn off the noise. Stop watching the news twenty-four/seven, stop reading drama, stop comparing your looks or life or job to other people, stop reading celebrity gossip. Turn it off. Our minds can be too busy sometimes, and we can begin fighting battles we do not need to. I have seen people arguing on social media with a stranger in Turkey about a celebrity. What a way to open the door to needless anxiety. Stop! The devil's playground is our mind. If he can control our mind, he can control the direction of our lives. Take your mind back. Take your energy back. Those things add to anxiety, and they are battles you are not meant to fight.

Remember any thought that does not calm you, soothe you, or encourage you is an attack of the enemy. Satan is the one who brings anxiety, worry, and stress into your mind. We need to learn to discern these voices so that you can fight the right battles and obey the right voices. You have power over your anxiety; you have the authority of Jesus upon you. Remember, Satan can bruise you, but he cannot take you out. Take authority over any anxiety today. Leave room in your mind for God to move and direct your life. You are an equipped, chosen, and strong woman of God who was created with a sound mind. Walk in that truth today.

DAILY QUESTIONS:
1. What makes you anxious?

_____

_____

_____

_____

ANXIETY: HOW TO BREATHE AND BE AT TRUE PEACE

2. What is your specific plan to fight anxiety?

_____

_____

_____

_____

3. Have you ever realized you had power over anxiety?

_____

_____

_____

_____

DAILY PRAYER:

"Father, I want to realign my mind with Yours. I realized that anxiety is Satan attacking my mind to keep me from what You have in store for me. I ask that You keep reminding me that I have the absolute power over the enemy. Satan, you have no authority over my mind. I will train my mind to focus on You, God, and not everything crazy going on around me. Please help me to remember that anxiety may come, but I cannot stay in that anxiety. Please give me Your peace that passes all human understanding. I trust You that my life is in Your hands. I reclaim my mind and my life for Your purpose. In Jesus's name I pray. Amen."

DAILY FOCUS

1. Realize anxiety is an attack. It is real. But it is a spiritual attack from Satan to derail you from your purpose and calling in life.

2. Realize you have been given authority over Satan; he has NO power over your mind if you do not allow him to influence you.
3. Consider your anxiety. How can you control it? When does it appear? How can you rebuke it? Have a plan that you can execute quickly.
4. Live in your authority. Live above all the mindless drama and problems, and keep it all out of your boat, so it is around you but not inside of you.

Day Nine

JOY: IT'S NOT AN EMOTION — MAKE IT A LIFESTYLE

> "Joy is not necessarily the absence of suffering.
> It is the presence of God."
> SAM STORMS

IN RECENT YEARS, I have realized joy is a lifestyle choice. Sounds strange, right? But a big mistake people make is thinking joy is an emotion, but our emotions change minute-by-minute; emotions are dependent on our feelings, situations, and reactions.

Imagine your day starts out: You can wake up happy, spill your coffee, then become mad, then leave for work feeling rushed, get stuck in traffic, and become frustrated, you get cut off in traffic, and become angry again. Now you get to work, search endlessly for a parking spot, then get nervous you will be late, then clock in and your boss is rude, then you become sad and disappointed. That dynamic roller coaster of emotions can happen in thirty minutes.

If joy was as fickle as an emotion, then joy would not be included as a fruit of the Spirit. The fruits of the Spirit are the evidence and the outward display of the Holy Spirit's work within a human. Joy is deeper than happiness; it is an outward and inner peace that is rooted in God, and it comes from God. It is unshakable. Joy is a serene outlook and much more stable than worldly happiness, which is fleeting and fickle. As believers, joy must become an outlook; it must become a constant choice. When you truly have joy, nobody can take it away from you. Joy is keeping your outlook joyful, no matter how upsetting your circumstances are around you.

I painted this picture for my daughter one day: Imagine each day you start the day with joy, just in a small vial, like precious, priceless perfume. Would you go around dumping it out on people who are rude to you or treat you badly? Of course, she answered with a solid "No." Joy is that precious, priceless perfume. Every time someone makes you upset, is rude or disrespectful to you, do not dump your joy on them. Instead, walk around all day sprinkling your joy on the people around you who need it. The sweet smell of your joy will last and linger after you are gone.

It is a realistic picture. God desires that we live our lives with an outlook of joy. An outlook of joy creates consistent emotional stability. I operate an extremely high-stress business, and after living my life with a true outlook of joy for the past few years, it has opened so many doors to tell my testimony. I do not say a word about God or the Bible, but people ask, "Aren't you worried? Why are you still happy?" It allows me to share my faith in a casual manner. Joy will draw people to you; it will open doors for you to testify about the kingdom.

As believers, seeking joy in everyday moments can tip the balance of a pessimistic outlook. When you begin viewing the small issues in life with joy-colored glasses, it will completely change the way you see negative experiences. Having joy does not mean you're smiling like a crazy person at a funeral; it is not an oblivious or socially awkward happiness. It is finding joy and hope even in your sorrow, it is having peace in your storm, and it is staying in peace while God guides you through the trouble. It is knowing nothing can come against you that has not already been seen by your Father and having a joyous outlook even through your sadness, disappointment, or anger. Joy is literal inner peace.

JOY: IT'S NOT AN EMOTION — MAKE IT A LIFESTYLE

Joy is a conscious choice. It means that we have set our mind beyond earthly mishaps, and we have set our mind on the grace and goodness of God. Joy is seeking the lesson in the losses and the messages in the messes. It is a choice to tune out the negative and focus on the goodness in every situation. It is choosing to look beyond the negativity and concentrating your mind on the positive aspect of a situation and keeping hope alive even in a negative situation. Joy is a state of mind, a perspective, and a mindset. Joy is also a gift that we receive at salvation. Jesus is the Prince of Peace. Peace is gifted as a seed when you trust and believe in Jesus and accept Him as your personal savior, but it is up to you to water it and cultivate it to an abundant bloom.

Be warned, people may mock you for this different outlook, think you are not "woke," or criticize you, but remember 1 Corinthians 3:19 says, "For this wisdom of this world is foolishness in God's eye." And 1 Corinthians 4:3 tells us, "I care very little if I am judged by you or by any human court; I do not even judge myself" (NIV).

Find peace in this, even if others judge you for your beliefs, God sees it all. Let us, as God's warrior women, start to cultivate joy in our everyday lives. Let us begin to show joy outwardly to a hopeless world. You will stand out, and they will see something different in you. That is our job, to be light in the darkness and salt to a flavorless world.

DAILY QUESTIONS:

1. Now that you realize joy is not an emotion, how can you cultivate an outlook of joy?

___

___

___

___

2. Like the priceless perfume analogy, how have you been wasting your precious joy?

___

3. What are specific trying instances in which you can plan to keep your joy?

___

DAILY PRAYER:

"Lord, please help me to begin to cultivate and grow into an outlook of joy, in every hard, painful, sad, and trying situation. I give You my outlook and emotions, and I ask that You give me a calm, serene, and stable emotional disposition. Lord, I ask that You help me curb my emotions to remain joyful even on my hardest days. I trust You as my source of strength and joy. Thank You for the gift of joy; help me to form and grow it until it affects every aspect of my life. I love You, Lord. In Jesus's name. Amen."

DAILY FOCUS:

1. Realize joy is not emotion. Take it out of your choices of emotions or feelings. Assign joy as an outlook or perspective of your life.

2. Choose joy constantly — every day, every hour, every minute. Take a breath, and search for a continual source of joy. God hides them all throughout your day, and when you begin looking for them with spiritual eyes, you will discover hidden sources of joy throughout your day.
3. As we are led by the Spirit, He will guide you and give you peace and joy. Claim that promise today and begin walking in it.

Day Ten

LIVING UNOFFENDED AND UNAFFECTED (FORGIVENESS)

> "Resentment is like drinking poison and then
> hoping it will kill your enemies."
> NELSON MANDELA

IT IS QUITE EASY to accept an apology from someone who is terribly sorry and begging for forgiveness, but what do we do when someone won't even admit they are wrong, let alone say sorry? It is so hard to look past someone offending you, even insulting you, especially if they think they are right and remain prideful. It is so tough to offer forgiveness freely to people who do not even ask for it, let alone admit they were wrong.

Our focus today is the following verse: "And whenever you stand praying, forgive, if you have anything against anyone, so that your Father also who is in Heaven may forgive you your trespasses" (Mark 11:25 ESV).

It does not say forgive them after they bought you roses and gave you a humble and sincere apology and admitted they were wrong.

It simply says "forgive" with no prerequisites. You see, there is an old saying, "Holding a grudge is like you drinking poison hoping it will hurt the transgressor." When we harbor anger or resentment, it silently takes away from our emotional strength, subconsciously or consciously. Keep in mind that forgiveness doesn't mean you have to continue tolerating disrespect. You can forgive people and distance yourself from a constant unhealthy relationship with them.

Forgiving is not for the other person; it is for us, for our maintenance of peace. We sometimes think forgiveness is a gift we give the other person, but forgiveness is truly a gift we give ourselves of peace and freedom. We literally leave their offense at the throne of God and exchange it for peace so that God will handle it, defend us, and vindicate us. Forgiving means keeping our hearts and minds pure even when we were wronged.

We as women need to learn to let things go, to weigh if that rude answer, short quippy response, or lack of respect is worth it. We need to weigh if these things really matter in the long term of life. If they do, pursue fixing it in a calm, collected, and respectful manner, but, if it really does not matter, we need to forgive and move on, for our own preservation of peace.

I know forgiveness feels like we are giving people a free pass, but in a kingdom perspective it does not give them a free pass. We can still calmly and lovingly say, "The way you spoke to me hurt my feelings." God wants us to live our lives in transparency, to openly share our emotions and feelings, but we should not allow issues to fester. In allowing the festering of an issue or fight, we are allowing Satan to possibly use that painful issue as a weapon in the future. If we communicate in a direct manner, with grace and love, we nip it in the bud and cut off a source of hurt Satan could have used against us. God does not ask us to be a doormat, but we need the fruit of the Spirit in gentleness and self-control to make sure we are addressing the situation from a calm and collected place. Be led by facts, not your emotions when dealing with issues.

We do not need to curse, yell, argue, and be hysterical; that is not the true fruit of a Christian. You are called to be like the eagles, soaring high above the everyday drama and mess of the ordinary chickens on

LIVING UNOFFENDED AND UNAFFECTED (FORGIVENESS)

ground level. Eagles were created to soar high above the ground level that chickens live on. Remain calm. If the other person is not able to listen and receive your message, walk away.

I have even written notes before, handed them to people, and walked away. "Hi. The issue we had the other day was unfortunate. I feel _____ about _____ that was said to me. It hurt my feelings, and I found it _____. I hope when we are calm, we can discuss it and move forward. With Blessings, _____." Simple and concise. Not every issue needs an all-out verbal attack. Let God work, give it time, and get yourself out of an immediate argument.

We can communicate in love and grace so that our feelings are known, but the mistake is in harboring a grudge that is kept until they apologize in a way that pleases us. We need to realize that these grudges, no matter how insignificant they are, can be a blockage to the blessings God has in store for you. We must forgive, so that we can be forgiven, or like I tell my children, "You get what you give."

Some people will never realize their words were inappropriate, some people will never see their errors, and some people will never apologize. Those are toxic people, or worse yet, they may be a spiritual attack sent to distract and upset you. In this case, we need to weigh if issues are worth our time or energy. Sometimes we need to forgive people (even if they do not deserve it) and move on and let go. Some people are limited by their generational pitfalls or the environment they are in, and they cannot understand or meet your needs or expectations. We need to free people from our expectations and needs and allow God to meet all our needs. This will allow us to forgive people and move on without an apology needed.

God wants us to live in peace. We cannot live in peace if we are harboring ill feelings toward the people around us. We need to realize that grudges and anger and resentment can hold us away from the abundant blessings God has for us. We need to be able to walk away from an argument, forgiving them for the things they are saying, even if they never admit they are wrong, and we were right. Remember God said, "Whatever you do, work heartily, as for the Lord and not for men" (Col. 3:23, ESV). You are not forgiving them for them; you are forgiving them because God commands you to. You are forgiving them to free yourself from anger, and because you are thankful God constantly forgives you too.

In Matthew, Jesus says that church members should forgive each other "seventy times seven times" (18:22), a number that symbolizes endlessness. Jesus was not limiting forgiveness to 490 times, a number that is, for all practical purposes, beyond counting.

The Old Testament hints at forgiving others three times, and Jewish law and rabbis suggested forgiving others up to three times. Seven was the number of completion of cycles in the Bible, so Jesus was telling Christians to have forgiving hearts, to have no limit to the number of times they forgive those who sin against them. We are to continue to forgive others with as much humility and grace the five hundredth time as we do the very first time. Christians are only capable of this type of true forgiving because they are empowered by the Holy Spirit who dwells within us. Only God alone can provide the ability to offer grace and true forgiveness over and over, just as God forgives us for our shortcomings over and over.

Sometimes, we expect people to have the same heart or mind as us, so we expect them to apologize and know when and why we are upset. They do not have this ability. We need to realize that we cannot go through life emotionally dependent on other people's behavior. We need to move past hurts and disappointments, and we need to forgive them even if they do not know that they have done anything wrong or know how we feel, so we can regain our emotional stability and peace.

Remember, you are not living your life for the world to validate you. You have been called, anointed, and chosen by the King of kings. Forgiving others will take the weight off you; it will release you and lighten the load you carry around every day. Live positively in that today. Let go of anything weighing you down, and soar to the heights God has called you to. Forgive anyone who has done you wrong and set gracious boundaries for your peace in the future.

LIVING UNOFFENDED AND UNAFFECTED (FORGIVENESS)

DAILY QUESTIONS:

1. Are there any grudges you need to let go of, even if the perpetrator does not deserve it?

_____

_____

_____

_____

2. Now that you realize forgiveness is for you and not the other forgiven person, what can you release?

_____

_____

_____

_____

3. Do you need to be humble enough to ask for forgiveness from anyone?

_____

_____

_____

_____

DAILY PRAYER:

"Lord, please help me have the strength needed to forgive those who have wronged me, even if they are prideful and arrogant. Help me to learn how to let go and give my burdens to You. Lord, help me to learn to identify the fights I need to walk away from and the calm way that I can express my feelings, but help me to have the strength to just let it go and let You fight my battles. Lord, forgive me for my sins as I forgive all who have sinned against me. Lord, I give You the hurt of _____. Help me to let it go, and I believe You will vindicate me. Please cleanse my heart of resentment or anger, Lord, and create a new forgiving spirit in me. In Jesus's name. Amen."

DAILY FOCUS:
1. Identify the grudges you are holding. Make a list of them. Pray earnestly and leave each one of them to God. Let go of the unnecessary weight.
2. Train yourself to walk away from arguments or disagreements that do not matter. Train yourself to forgive people, even if they do not ask. That is true power over your own emotions.
3. Forgive people for your own peace, not theirs. Learn to be the bigger person God has anointed you to be.

Day Eleven

THE WOMAN AT THE WELL

> "Like He did for the woman at the well, Jesus gently
> turns our gaze from the sin of the past to the
> hope of our future in Him."
> MANDY PAGANO/UNGRIND.ORG

WE ALL KNOW THE story, but I but I will quickly summarize it: Jesus and the disciples are traveling through Samaria to another city. It is about noontime, the hottest part of the day. Jesus is sitting on a well, and a Samaritan woman comes to the well to draw her daily water. Most women came early in the morning or in the evening when it was cooler, but she came when no other women were there — maybe because the other village women were a bit petty about her past.

Jews and Samaritans did not get along and did not normally even speak to each other, and men did not speak openly to women in that day as well. Jesus speaks to her, and she is startled. She basically asks, "Are you talking to me?" and their conversation draws out. He tells her He has a well that will give her water, so she will not thirst anymore; she thinks He literally is going to give her thirst-quenching water and jumps at the chance to not have to lug a heavy water jug all the way to the well every day anymore. He instructs her "to go bring her husband," to which she replies, "Sir, I have no husband." Jesus begins to tell her all about her life.

I want to focus on one thing that is not always mentioned. That is the unconventionality of this encounter. It was not the social norm for that day and age. Samaritans and Jews did not speak, not cordially, and men and women did not have open dialogue. Jesus broke a lot of social norms, but this was a double up. His ministry would not have reached this woman and this city in a conventional way.

She was not a Jew, and she would not have received His message without Him telling her own life story. Jesus knew this and, therefore, stepped out of the "normalcy" to reach who really needed the gospel and changed her life. Sometimes our callings and ministries will not fit into the social norm, and we need to have the courage to step out from what is normal and acceptable to reach those we are supposed to reach, standing firm on the biblical belief of the gospel.

Sometimes, we as Christians get very hung up on traditional verses, contemporary churches, services, or worship, and judging why one is better than the other. Jesus broke every religious and social norm; He did not put the importance on the appropriate way of presenting His ministry. He cared about reaching the lost. We need to consider letting go of "stigmas" or "rigidity" of theology and denominational hang-ups and focus on the message. Is Jesus the focus? Are we teaching the basics of Christianity? Are we telling people the truth of the Bible, or are we teaching denominational doctrine? Are we following the rules and political correctness of the current culture, or are we choosing to remain 100 percent biblical? Are we telling them that Jesus is the only way to the Father? Are we teaching salvation only comes through Jesus? If so, then it is spreading the gospel. Sis, you cannot win the lost by isolating them or expecting them to understand advanced theology, and you cannot help them grow in baby faith by not teaching the truths that the Bible says about everyday issues.

Remember, the Bible addresses sin; we do not have to accuse or judge. Just tell them what the Bible says and let the Holy Spirit do the convicting. My children love Christian hip-hop. It reaches them, they understand and get the lyrics, and it speaks to them. They love the music, and I love the message of artists like: FaceDaZoe, Bryann Trejo, Monica Trejo, Zee, Youngbro, Kingdom Muzic, Sevin, Bizzle, Datin, and Stefanotto (God Over Money). They love the beat, and the words go deep. It is contemporary enough to speak to them in a way they understand.

It may be unconventional to me, but I prefer that blasting on the car speaker than the vulgar, secular hip hop of today. If it reaches them and spreads and strengthens the gospel in their hearts, then I find it edifying. If it glorifies Jesus above anything, we need to let people be reached in this way, right where they are.

There have been times pastors and popular bishops have fallen prey to the division Satan sets in the world and begin dividing the church, while Christian rappers have been promoting unity and seen the situation more biblically. This was apparent in 2020, as the world and many churches were dividing racially, economically, and politically, the Christian rappers were the ones standing up the strongest for 100 percent biblical truths and unity of the church. Use your discernment when following influencers and popular leaders, because they may be modeling their movements after the world and not the kingdom. Remember Jesus was not a trend-follower, He was a trendsetter. Start taking a stand to be unconventional.

Secondly, Jesus tells the woman at the well her own past and life story. Can you imagine meeting a stranger and him telling you about your life? She had been married five times and was currently living with a boyfriend — sin in the Bible. Yet Jesus sat on this well at this time of the day to arrange a divine appointment to speak with this woman. Jesus revealed to her directly that He was the Messiah (John 4:24-26). The woman immediately thinks He is a prophet because He told her about her sins, but He corrected her by revealing He was in fact the Messiah. However, He proves He is unfazed by her past sins; He knew her past, and He still outstretched a hand to her.

The time that she came to the well is an indication that other women may have treated her badly; we all know what it is like to be an isolated woman. Imagine her surprise when Jesus told her about her past life, with no condemnation and no accusations. She quickly ran back to the city and told everyone she could find about the "prophet" at the well, who she was convinced was the "Messiah." They all came out, and Jesus delayed His trip and spent two days in Samaria teaching the gospel and making many disciples, who reached many more of the Gentiles, or non-Jewish people.

If Jesus had stuck to all the acceptable social norms for a Jew in that day, Samaria would have never been reached. He would have walked right past "that city" and "that woman" and "those people" and focused on only "His" people. This is where we sometimes can fall in our ministries. We cannot just focus on our race, or socioeconomic equals, or even just our gender. Jesus told us, "Go into all the corners of the earth and spread the gospel." Sister, it is easier to reach those who look like us, think like us, worship like us, and agree with us, but if it is that easy — then it is not the mission God gave us. God's mission always requires sacrifice and a stretch. Embrace differences.

This study is for all women — Black, White, Indian, American, Asian, European, new Christians, seasoned saints — all of us can grow and elevate our minds. Yes, our cultures impact our thinking. Yes, our cultures matter. Yes, our cultures are special and prized, but we have a new culture when we become Christians, and that is kingdom culture. Let that be your first culture and then the rest will fall in place. Remember a great motto is "kingdom over culture." Let the kingdom invade the culture, not the other way around. EVERY person must hear the gospel, every person deserves to see your light, and everyone must be able to see your fruit. We need to reach out to the "undeserving" and "untouchable" people around you. Let the Holy Spirit guide you to all your "Samarias" and find all "those women at the well"; reach them, because only you can.

THE WOMAN AT THE WELL

DAILY QUESTIONS:

1. Now that you realize how unconventional Jesus's ministry was, how can you begin to live an unconventional life?

_____

_____

_____

_____

2. Who are the "women at the well" or "Samarias" that God has placed within your reach?

_____

_____

_____

_____

3. How can you change your view on doctrines/stigmas so that you can have a wider reach for Jesus?

_____

_____

_____

_____

DAILY PRAYER:

"Lord, thank You for including us all in Your ministry. Thank You that You came to redeem and forgive all of us, no matter our past sins and mistakes or our cultures or standings. God, You are an all-inclusive God, who gives us all the chance to choose You. Lord, help me to go beyond social norms and reach every 'Samaria' You have assigned to me to reach. Lord, help my fruit to be visible to all around me. Help me to keep my testimony focused on You as the only truth and way. Lord, guide me and help me to accept Your truth, even if it looks different than my norm. Thank You. In Jesus's name. Amen."

DAILY FOCUS:

1. Focus on the unconventionality of this encounter. It was not the norm for that day and age. Samaritans and Jews did not speak, not cordially, and men and women did not have open dialogue. Jesus broke a lot of social norms, but this was a double up. His ministry would not have reached this woman and this city in a conventional way.

2. He went into the city of the people the Jews despised and involved them in His mission. He did not only come for the "chosen" people; He came for all the people. He found the one woman they all judged, isolated, and condemned and allowed her to be the introduction to His mission. God can use anyone; even if the world has counted you out, God is waiting for the perfect opportunity to use you to further the kingdom.

3. We cannot just focus on our race, or socioeconomic equals, or even just our gender. Jesus told us, "Go into all the corners of the earth and spread the gospel." Sister, it is easier to reach those who look like us, think like us, worship like us, agree with us, but if it is that easy, then it is not the mission God gave us. God's mission always requires sacrifice and a stretch. Embrace differences.

Day Twelve

I FEEL UNBALANCED

> "Never underestimate the influence of the people
> you have allowed in your life....
> 'Bad company corrupts good morals.' 1 Corinthians 15:33."
> CYNDISPIVEY.COM

THERE ARE PEOPLE DRAWING from you daily, drawing on our emotional energy, physical energy, and our mental energy. Our spouses, our children, our coworkers, our siblings, our parents, our friends. But what happens when you have too many withdrawals in your bank account and not enough deposits? Your account would be unbalanced. That is how our emotional life can become eventually.

In today's world, we are overcommitted, overburdened, and overstimulated. We can watch videos of people tripping and falling for hours, we can find any recipe, or design and craft ideas, or we can lose ourselves in watching TV twenty-four hours a day. Technology is a great invention, but it can become overstimulating to our mind, especially when we should be at rest. According to Facebook, on any given day 1.4 billion people log into or use Facebook or other social media apps. Today, we have "friends" we do not really know, and we have lots of "followers" but less substance and fewer healthy relationships. We are striving for the likes, followers, and comments, instead of tangible relationships and healthy friendships. Do you realize this is also drawing from your emotional energy and leaving you less emotionally equipped for the people God assigned to you?

It is not healthy to have so many people in our lives, space, and business. We need to consider putting people who are not part of our kingdom assignment out of our lives, in a healthy and loving way. We live in a culture, now especially with social media, where we have too many people liking, criticizing, or commenting on our life, decisions, relationships, and actions. We were not created to have so many people interfering, spying, contradicting, or demeaning our lives and choices. In the past, only our family or close friends had the ability to give advice or comment about our life; social media has made communication easier, but it has caused us more pressure, stress, and anxiety. We are trying to impress and please hundreds of people that do not really matter, and some we do not really know or interact with in real life.

Psalm 55:22 says, "Cast your burden on the LORD, and he will sustain you; he will never permit the righteous to be moved" (ESV). When we are operating in God's will for our life, things will just naturally flow and fall into place. When our minds are tired, this is one huge way that Satan has gained a strong hold on our minds and is stealing our peace. Now, in cutting down the numbers of needless or hurtful people in our business, we do not need to make it a big deal, make a public social media status, or tell people anything to hurt or demean them. A lot of people do not even realize they are making emotional or mental withdrawals from you. It is important to stay meek and become less "available" or "convenient" and never aim to cut people off severely. We always want to walk in love but still hold our standards high for those in our inner circle. We need to make sure that those we choose to invest our time and energy in are good kingdom investments.

In God's Word, we are told we are more than enough, but we are equipped enough only for the things and people that God has designed and assigned for us. We are designed and fully equipped to handle our spouses, children, families, and the assigned people God sent us. The stress comes when we start to overcommit and start to handle issues and people that were not even assigned for us to deal with. We need to connect on a real level with healthy, real people in our lives.

Begin to weigh if missing a few birthdays, get-togethers, dinners, holidays, or visits is worth the time and stress of an overpacked schedule. Weigh if winning arguments, proving your points, or vindicating insults are truly worth your time and mental energy. There are people in life who will never be satisfied, even with our best efforts. How much does that really matter in the long run? We need to learn how to balance our lives, because often, the people who make the most withdrawals in our lives are the people who make the fewest deposits. When was the last time you balanced your life budget? Learn to say, "I can't," or "I would love to, but the reality is I can't."

This unbalance leaves us feeling inadequate, stressed, anxious, and not enough, but God does not desire us to live in this manner. We are a limited resource; it is simply impossible to be there for everybody. Only in Jesus do we have the ability, strength, and passion to care for and be there for those who are assigned to us. We need to get back to a lifestyle of quality over quantity. We may not be enough for everyone, but our God has promised us He is more than enough and more than able.

We need to let go of the guilt in not being "there" for everyone. We need to realize only God can be everything for everyone; only He can be omnipotent and everywhere every time. It is not your responsibility to be there for everyone and everything. There is tremendous peace in letting go and moving forward in a positive way. FOMO, or fear of missing out, is not a real fear; it is a desperation to be involved with anything "important" going on. This is a way Satan can use to keep us overcommitted and over involved and too busy to fulfill our real kingdom callings.

Do not overextend yourself. Take inventory of what you have and take a count of your limitations. When you realize what you do not have and you use your time and resources wisely, that is when God will step in to multiply what you have and provide you the extra you need. You must take care of yourself before you can help others; you cannot pour from an empty cup. Sis, God has called you to certain things, and you are equipped for great things, so take all those things that are not part of your anointing off your plate.

DAILY QUESTIONS:

1. Who do you think makes more withdrawals than deposits in your life?

_____

_____

_____

_____

2. Now that you realize you do not have to be there for everyone, what is your plan to stop?

_____

_____

_____

_____

3. What are the things/people/events that you need to de-commit or step away from?

_____

_____

_____

_____

DAILY PRAYER:

"Lord, please help me discern who You have assigned to me. Lord, please help me to take an honest inventory of the people and demands in my life. Help me to weed out the things that are overstimulating or overwhelming me. Help my life to become clutter free, so I can concentrate my ability and strength on the things that You have assigned to me. I am anointed and called and equipped to handle everything that You have called me to. Lord, I ask that You rebalance my life and priorities, so I can have quality over quantity. Help me to make a difference for the kingdom, not the clout or likes. In Jesus's name. Amen."

DAILY FOCUS:

1. If people are making more withdrawals than deposits in your life, you will be unbalanced, and unbalance leads to stress and anxiety. We need to reevaluate the commitments we have and refocus on the priorities.
2. Realize you are not an unlimited resource for others. Start practicing saying, "No, I can't." Stop giving everyone your time, attention, and focus. We need to prioritize and focus on only the things God has assigned to you.
3. Stop letting people and their opinions and advice into your circle. Social media can be used in a healthy way to spread the gospel to the world. Stop soliciting advice and recommendations on social media. Do not publicly ask for parenting advice, marriage advice, or work advice; instead, have a group of like-minded faithful friends (or even one or two friends) who you can ask for advice or prayer. The more you keep private, the less worry about judgments you will feel.

Day Thirteen

GENERATIONAL TRAUMAS AND CURSES & BLESSINGS

*"It ran in your family until it ran into you. God says,
'You've been anointed to break the cycle.
Generational curses stop with you.'"*
UNKNOWN

EVERY SINGLE ONE OF us has "generational curses" or traumas that we must overcome. I consider them "generational pitfalls," or something negative that runs in our families and nobody in our family has overcome yet. Generational curses could be alcoholism, drug use, teen pregnancy, divorces, pretentiousness, hypocrisy, high school dropouts, laziness, lying, gambling, emotional blackmail, sarcasm, jealousy, depression, or suicide.

These are not characteristics of a godly kingdom life, and remember if it did not come from God, then it is a trap of the enemy. Generational curses are recurring problems and issues that are passed down through the generations.

Personally, my family had traits of pretentiousness, hypocrisy, sarcasm, and condemnation. I grew up believing that it was okay to judge, condemn, or belittle others and that it was normal to not have a filter, sometimes making others feel inadequate or demeaned. Only when I grew in my personal relationship with God and was convicted by the Holy Spirit (not condemned or called out) for these traits could I recognize them as ungodly traits.

To be honest, I still struggle with them sometimes. As far as I have come, I am still breaking these curses, and I am killing any hold or foothold if they may show up in my children. I figure stopping it while they are little will set a different mindset for them. These traits will not defeat me, and they will not go one more generation. They will die when I kill them. The family I grew up with have not chosen to recognize these traits in themselves and still live under this curse. But, as for me and my house, we will defeat it and serve the Lord.

Maybe your grandparents and parents did not handle the issues in a way you think they should have; we need to stop blaming them. They may not have had the discernment, knowledge, spiritual maturity, or mental strength to deal with it. We need to forgive past generations and stop blaming parents or ancestors for not dealing with or conquering these issues. Living in the shortcomings of our family history is only reliving the painful past; we cannot move forward while looking backwards. Stop blaming others and start changing yourself. We need to resist Satan in our life and deal with the deep root of the issue that we can discern. We need to realize if it still exists, then it is our responsibility to break every chain. Blaming, resenting, and hating our family for not dealing with issues previously are diversions Satan uses to keep us from overcoming and breaking those generational issues.

My sister, through the victory in Jesus Christ, you are an overcomer. You are a chain breaker. You are a giant killer. You can set a new normal for your family. Sisters, you can be the first in your family to overcome these generational shortcomings, to break the chains of bondage, and set ALL your future generations FREE. Once you set a new normal, you have broken any power the enemy had over your family.

Negative choices, bad company, blame, and denial are what can activate negative generational curses. Even though the New Tes-

GENERATIONAL TRAUMAS AND CURSES & BLESSINGS

tament gives hope to our individual choices, I want to look back at the Old Testament to see how God first viewed ancestral sin. In the beginning of the Bible, God said He "keeps faithfulness for thousands, who forgives wrongdoing, violation of His Law, and sin; yet He will by no means leave the guilty unpunished, inflicting the punishment of fathers on the children and on the grandchildren to the third and fourth generations" (Exod. 34:7, NASB).

It is thought this verse could mean the sins of the forefathers would make the obstacles in the children's lives bigger because of these generational curses. Yes, it is a negative thought, but let us focus on the blessing part of the verse above. If you decide to start a heritage of blessings for the generations to come, God has promised those blessings will travel down thousands of generations.

Later in Ezekiel 18:20 and Ezekiel 18:3-4, God says, "The child will not share the guilt of the parent, nor the parent share the guilt of the child [NIV].... As surely as I live, declares the Lord, you will no longer quote this proverb in Israel [NIV].... The soul who sins is the one who will die" (NLT).

Then later we see how God showed favor to King Solomon because of the love and favor he had for his father David. I believe that consequences, not curses, are what we pass down through our family. Yet, the power of Jesus on the cross overcomes anything in our past or our family line. We do not have a "soul" connection with our ancestors; we do not inherit sins from our parents and get stuck with it. If a detrimental lifestyle runs in our family, the curse really is what we think is normal. Our family habits, traits, environments, and what we consider "normal" is what can be detrimental. Once we recognize and begin to fight it, we will win over any obstacle. Through Jesus Christ we are made new. Though we all are all sinful humans, we all take our individual journeys based on our personal choices to become more righteous.

As Christians we have the direction, history, and the lessons in the Old Testament, but we have added the redemptive and forgiving power of the New Testament. The New Testament teaches that each person must choose salvation for themselves, and they will be judged for their individual choices and deeds. This means any curse is already broken in Jesus's name, you just must make a conscious choice to live in a "new normal."

The first step is recognizing negative mannerisms, trends, and habits. If you grew up with an emotionally manipulative family, then you do not even recognize when you are doing it to your spouse, friends, or children. If you grew up around alcoholism, then it becomes your normal, and you may not realize the negative effects it creates. If you grew up around teen pregnancy or failed marriages, then you do not even view it as "abnormal" or morally corrupt.

Satan has a way of making our generational curses and sinful pitfalls our normal, and we do not even realize how they are detrimental to the people around us. The hardest part of trying to overcome a generational curse is identifying and admitting it is there. We need to set our mind to live biblical principles, and we will recognize any unhealthy family traits.

John 8:13-36 tells us that when we accept Jesus as our savior, we receive His ultimate freedom. He was the sacrifice that set us free from every burden, and every sin, and any ongoing curse. We do not have to live the motto, "Like father like son," or "like mother like daughter." God believes in individualism. You can choose to be different. You are set apart. This powerful redemption can become reality when you realize that these ancient issues passed down and began in the spiritual realm as distractions from the Enemy to hold us all back from our full potential.

The power Satan has through generational difficulties can be totally overcome through the decision and strength of Christ and one person — YOU. You must make up your mind that YOU will be the last one to deal with it. The most powerful thing about generational curses is with each generation it overcomes, it grows in strength and becomes more "normal," but the minute you break it, it is done. You begin a new normal for every other generation to come after you. We need to identify them and then develop a plan to stand up to them and develop new healthy habits to take their place.

You can identify any negative family line traits, and you can start today. It can be completely overcome by you. Wouldn't that be an amazing legacy to start now? Forget the past and the hardships gone,

GENERATIONAL TRAUMAS AND CURSES & BLESSINGS

forgive all your past generations who did not solve it, and embrace your new blessings and your new healthy normal that you are going to build for all the generations that come after you.

Stop blaming history and start changing and overcoming. We need to resist Satan in our life and deal with the deep root of the issue now. We need to realize if it still exists, then it is our responsibility to break the stronghold. Maybe nobody in your ancestral history had the strength, capability, or spiritual maturity to break the curse. We must stop blaming them for their shortcomings and realize you are enough and you are destined to break every chain.

DAILY QUESTIONS:

1. Do you have a generational pitfall or curse that you can see in your family history?

___

___

___

___

2. Is there a different belief or view you have on this now?

___

___

___

___

3. How can you overcome this generational pitfall or curse? List specific goals and plans.

_____

_____

_____

_____

DAILY PRAYER:

"Lord, thank You for power You have given us over any attack of the enemy. God, please show me and generational curses or pitfalls that are in my family line, even if I thought they were normal before. Lord, open my spiritual eyes to any unhealthy emotional, social, and personal beliefs or habits. God, I ask that You cleanse me and change me. Lord, help me to identify and overcome this so that nobody else in my family line must fight this. God give me the direction, strength, and determination that I need to defeat this. Lord, please help me have real change, and I ask that You give me guidance and stability and the mental clarity I need to fight this. Lord, help me to forgive my (parents/grandparents/ancestors) for this battle. Lord, I am so sorry for any pain that this caused in their lives. Help me to free all of my children and children's children from this battle. Thank You for making me more than a conqueror. In Jesus's name. Amen."

DAILY FOCUS:
1. Maybe your grandparents and parents did not handle the issues in a way you think they should have; we need to stop blaming them. They may not have had the knowledge or spiritual maturity or mental strength to deal with it. We need to forgive past generations and not continue to blame our parents or ancestors for their ineptness to deal with these issues.
2. Stop blaming and start changing. We need to resist Satan in our

life and deal with the deep root of the issue. We need to realize if it still exists, then it is our responsibility to break every chain. Through the victory in Jesus Christ, you are an overcomer. You are a chain breaker. You are a giant killer. You can set a new normal for your family. Sisters, you can be the first in your family to overcome these generational shortcomings.

3. The most powerful thing about generational curses is with each generation they overcome, they grow in strength and become more "normal," but the minute you break them, they are done. You begin a new normal for every other generation to come after you. This can be your legacy.

Day Fourteen

MEEKNESS IS NOT MY WEAKNESS

> "Meekness is the opposite of weakness; it is absolute power under control."
> UNKNOWN

TODAY'S SOCIETY LOOKS AT meekness like a real weakness. If you are not loud and proud, then you are weak and clueless. Meek is defined by Webster as, "deficient in spirit and courage; not violent or strong."[3]

I would take the liberty of saying meekness is a positive attribute of one's nature. It has synonyms of righteous, humble, teachable, and patient under suffering; willing to follow even difficult gospel teachings; and an attribute of a true disciple. That is a little more positive, right? I find it interesting that today's dictionary's definitions of both "submissive" and "meek" are putting forth negative narratives or views of these positive biblical characteristics.

---

[3] "Meek," Merriam-Webster.com Dictionary, last modified June 13, 2021, https://www.merriam-webster.com/dictionary/meek.

Psalm 37:11 says, "But the meek shall inherit the land and delight themselves in abundant peace" (ESV).

You have read the verse, but do you realize what meekness leads to? Peace. Do you see what the meek are rewarded with? Victory. Meekness is strength that is disciplined and controlled. Remember when we spoke of Queen Esther? She took the time to pray and seek God, and she went to the king meekly. The world wants all issues handled now and here and immediately. Even Jesus's disciples had some spoken and unspoken issues with His ministry because it was not here and now enough. They wanted Him to overthrow the oppressing government and wage war to free them, but He was not here to free them in an earthly governing way. Jesus was here to free them mentally and spiritually. Jesus was our ultimate example of meekness; He had the strength to remove Himself from the cross, but He stayed on it out of agape love for us. He knew the bigger picture beyond dying on the cross, and He knew He had to endure it to secure eternal victory for us all.

We need to begin to see beyond the human "here and now" mentality. There is a big picture, and there is a greater plan. We are called by Heaven to be meek, be teachable, be advisable, and to keep growing. People today are full of pride, and pride is what stunts your growth. A prideful spirit results in a person who is unteachable.

How much more could we learn if we listen, not just hear, but truly listen, beyond words into the message people are giving us? Stop listening just to try to find the one thing they say wrong, not politically correct, or negative. If you decide to harden your heart and call them on it, you may have just missed your kingdom message in choosing to dissect and judge their delivery. Jesus spoke in parables so others could understand the message, not just the words. He wanted them to think deeper and discern the true meanings in the story, not just to be told the message in one sentence, comprehending but not hearing.

Current culture desires us to talk and have others hear what we are saying. Whereas meekness is intentional communication for others to understand us, our heart, and our intent. The world wants to debate and "clap back" until people agree with us, whereas meekness is knowing what you believe and living out your truth quietly.

In the middle of an argument where everyone is yelling, nobody is using active listening to comprehend and understand what others are saying, so why waste your energy trying to make a point right then? Meekness is the ability to have self-control to realize nobody is communicating effectively and saving it to communicate your intention and heart in a calm, collected, and concise way later.

God desires us all to live as meek women, and we are all in different places in this journey. Some of us are just getting convicted to change our attitudes, and some of us have already been doing hard inner work to become meek. But in order to understand why being meek is an important attribute of a kingdom woman, we must understand the opposite of a meek woman. One powerful biblical example of a prideful woman who refused to honor God was Jezebel.

There is a sinister spirit of Jezebel that is rampant on the earth right now. It is full of independent, self-empowered, manipulative, sweet-tongued, politically correct, attractive women who are twisting and exploiting others, demeaning other women who have more traditional, biblical views, and entrapping and dominating the Ahabs — or the weak men around them.

They are popular and worldly, accepting of anything, floating from one cause to another, easily camouflaging their true intentions to become whatever is needed at the moment to manipulate the specific group they are targeting. They are even infiltrating the church. (Once culture is viewed before kingdom — it's already worldly doctrine and completely non-biblical.) Jezebel spirits use covert and hidden manipulation, at any cost, to get the wanted results, when biblically, we are told to stand strong on firm foundation and speak loving and bold biblical truth regardless of the pushback.

Jezebel spirits operate on fear, persuasion, guilt, and control. They hate those who will not cower, agree, and bow to them. They portray themselves as tolerant, but only if you fall into line, agree, and ultimately do as they say. They seek to demean, cancel, and destroy any person who dares to think or live differently. Jezebels project their shortcomings and inadequacies onto others and are pretentious and narcissistic in nature, while gaslighting anyone who stands against their plots. They are constantly trying to compete and overcompensating.

Jezebel spirits always deal in the drama, are led by emotions, and thrive on the spirit of offense, overthinking trivial issues and dwelling in continual problems. They live in perpetuated victimhood and doom and gloom and dismiss any notion of hope, facts, peace, faith, or positivity as ignorant or uneducated. They hate anyone who is a free thinker or believes in self-reliance or the limitless, God-given individual potential. Jezebel spirits will do anything for the attention, likes, clout, or followers — even degrading their morality for the little bit of attention.

We, as kingdom women, need to be able to discern difficult truth versus popular lies. False kindness versus true intentions. True goodness versus virtue-signaling. Convenient explanations versus real motivations. Biblical truth versus earthly theory. We must strive to see Jezebel spirits for what they are and remain meek even in their midst. We must recognize many earthly celebrities/idols as Jezebel spirits and not as people we should follow or support. We must be able to discern these spirits and still love them while resisting their pull.

Jezebel looks innocent, when, in true discernment, the innocence is a mask to hide sinister intentions. Jezebel is easily accessible, popular, immoral, reckless, beautiful but immodest, free-spirited, a spirit of convenience, self-serving, and constantly switching. Meekness requires us to be relatively guarded, modest, upright, steadfast, morally prideful, humble, gentle, kingdom-minded, cautious, righteous, caring, and self-sacrificing. They are complete opposites.

Let us begin to discern Jezebel spirits around us and aim to begin living a meeker life. Here are some practical examples of simple ways to begin being meeker. Start having the self-control of walking away from an argument, even if you are right. Maybe the justification is not worth the sacrifice of your peace, or because you are using grace to cover their errors, and just let it go.

Meekness is having the patience to keep listening to the underlying message your spouse is expressing, even if their delivery and word choice are not pleasing. Meekness is grace in letting people have the last word, because looking at the larger picture, it does not even really matter. Meekness is forgiveness, knowing others are gossiping about you, and still greeting them with love and overlooking their hating. It is choosing to smile and say "have a great day" when people are rude to you instead of being rude back.

Jesus knew Judas was going to betray Him, yet Judas was invited to the last supper, and he ate with them too. Meekness is having the fruit of the Spirit on full display through your actions. It is showing the fruit of the Spirit, sometimes without saying a word. It does not mean you are blind or victimized; it means that you realize not every situation deserves the emotional energy of your reaction. Meekness may be unseen to the world, but it is promised in the Word to be rewarded by God Himself, who sees all.

Colossians 3:12 says, "Put on then, as God's chosen ones, holy and beloved, compassionate hearts, kindness, humility, meekness, and patience" (ESV).

We are commanded to be meek, not weak. We are commanded to be compassionate but not taken advantage of. We are commanded to be humble but not subservient. Now, if others are not edifying your value, ween yourself away from those individuals. It does not need to be a public or personal announcement of, " I am done with you." Meekness is a change that is slow and silently withdrawing your time away from them. Meekness is following the commandment of, "Peace, be still," and not trying to solve everything yourself and make others understand and validate you. Sometimes meekness just means you need to walk away and stay quiet until God shows you a way to grow past an issue. Meekness doesn't require closure for forgiveness.

When you plug into what God desires you to be, you will find balance. Life is about balance, and when you are unbalanced, you will always be shaky and uncertain. True personal balance comes from when you know that earthly matters do not matter more than kingdom matters. Does it matter what other humans think of your stance on things, or does it matter more what God knows your heart position is? Free yourself from having to debate, argue, justify, and prove your point to other humans, embrace the freedom of a meek spirit, and realize God does not want you to take on arguments and debates that are not kingdom matters. Meekness is strength under complete control, not weakness.

DAILY QUESTIONS:

1. Have you been allowing society's way to take precedence over God's way?

___

2. Have you considered meekness as a negative attribute? If so, how has that changed?

___

3. Have you ever encountered a Jezebel spirit?

___

4. How can you discern and come against Jezebel spirits in the future?

_____

_____

_____

_____

_____

5. How can you demonstrate meekness in the future?

_____

_____

_____

_____

DAILY PRAYER:

"Lord, please help me to seek to be meek. Lord, meekness is looked down upon in today's world. But, Lord, You set us apart, to be different than the world. Give me the strength and endurance I need to cultivate meekness in my life. Help me to develop emotional strength and patience and self-control so I can decide to become meek. Lord, help me to realize You know our hearts and minds and that not every argument requires my input to justify my positions. Jesus, help me to be silent when I need to be and help me to take pauses to gather my thoughts and emotions. Lord, help me to be a meek woman who pleases You with my love and grace. In Jesus's name. Amen."

DAILY FOCUS:

1. Meekness is a positive attribute of one's nature. It has synonyms of righteous, humble, teachable, and patient under suffering; willing to follow even difficult gospel teachings; and an attribute of a true disciple.
2. Meekness is not sacrifice without reward; it is sacrificing with a promised reward.
3. The world wants to talk and have others hear us, where meekness is communication, so others understand us and our intent. The world wants to debate, where meekness is knowing what you believe and living out your truth, quietly. In the middle of an argument, when everyone is yelling, but nobody is using active listening to comprehend and listen to what others are saying, why waste your energy?
4. Jezebel looks innocent, when in true discernment, the innocence is a mask to hide sinister intentions. Jezebel is haughty, prideful, easily accessible, popular, immoral, reckless, beautiful but immodest, free-spirited, a spirit of convenience, self-serving, and constantly switching. Meekness requires us to be relatively guarded, modest, upright, steadfast, morally prideful, humble, gentle, kingdom-minded, cautious, righteous, caring, and self-sacrificing. Remember, kingdom mentality is the opposite of earthly mentality.

Day Fifteen

AGAPE LOVE VS. CONDITIONAL LOVE

> "Agape Love is...profound concern for the well-being of another, without any desire to control that other, to be thanked by that other, or to enjoy the process."
> MADELEINE L'ENGLE

THERE ARE MANY TYPES of love that exist. There is love between lovers, or a sensual love. There is love between family and children. There is genuine and heartfelt love in a caring and friendly sense. One of the most noble, strongest, most resilient, and toughest types of love is agape love. It describes a deep, selfless, and unconditional love. This is the type of love that describes how much our Heavenly Father loves us. Agape love is a godly, kingdom kind of love, not a human, earthly love; it takes great intention and purpose. This is the type of love that is needed to have a thriving kingdom marriage.

1 Corinthians 13:4-8 says, "Love is patient, love is kind. It does not envy, it does not boast, it is not proud. It does not dishonor others, it is not self-seeking, it is not easily angered, it keeps no record of wrongs. Love does not delight in evil but rejoices with the truth. It always pro-

tects, always trusts, always hopes, always preserves. Love never fails" (NIV).

Sometimes we can love someone as much as we can but not the way they may need. Agape love describes love in the way God loves us. God's love is unconditional and sacrificial; it is this love that allowed Jesus to go to the cross even if we did not love Him back. Agape can be translated into "charity" and describes exactly what God's love is, charity to all of us who do not deserve it.

Conditional love is how most humans love. We can easily love people until they disappoint us, anger us, or do not meet our expectations. This is normal human behavior; love can wax or wane depending on how the other person loves or treats us.

Jesus said in John 13:34, "A new commandment I give to you, that you love one another: just as I have loved you" (ESV).

God's love is long-suffering, meaning He is endlessly patient with us and slow to get angry with us. We can practice this with the people we love. The more patient we become, the more long-suffering we are becoming. Agape love is personal and intentional, it reaches people where they are, not where we expect them to be. Agape love is not jealous. We should find joy in other's blessings and accomplishments, not be jealous of what others are doing or getting.

Agape love is not self-centered — it is service-centered. We need to notice, serve, and fulfill other people's needs and wants, not only focus on our own needs and wants. Agape love is not conceited, it does not crave the feeling of promotion and validation, it lives quietly and meekly. Agape love is not easily angered; we need to strive to help others and not be irritated and angered by those we love. Agape love does not keep records of wrongdoing. Meaning, when we forgive, we let it go completely and do not bring it up in the future as fuel.

Agape love bears, believes, hopes, and endures. We need to bear some difficulties, we need to believe in the best in people, we need to hope people will rise to the potential, and we need to endure through some hardships. These are necessary traits in a strong godly marriage. A healthy kingdom marriage will naturally require compromise and agape love. You cannot have a thriving marriage without agape love; marriage requires a love born from being servant-hearted. Agape love

AGAPE LOVE VS. CONDITIONAL LOVE

forgives offenses, loves despite momentary feelings, and does the hard work of bridging gaps and using grace to cover inadequacies. Agape love is literally heavenly love; it is difficult and takes a lot of inner work to achieve.

Agape love is not a human intentional love; it is kingdom love. A love that God grants us, and it is a gift of salvation. We can learn and work toward loving like this; it takes hard inner work, great effort, and strong determination. The Bible tells us that agape love is greater than faith and hope. God is love, love is God's character, meaning if it is not love, then it is not of God. Since God loves us, and we are part of Him, we are enabled to love people like He does, instead of earthly culture's conditional love.

Agape love is not easy, and most people will not even deserve it. God's love means we can walk in love in every situation, even the difficult situations. Real love is deeper than romantic or true love. God's love is deeper and more unconditional than human love. Agape love is pure, forgiving, graceful, unconditional, and selfless. Sometimes agape love is quiet, patient, and waiting, and sometimes it will require us to be steadfast, strong, and courageous.

God's love is unconditional, meaning He loves us even if we fail, disappoint, or hurt Him. God does not stop loving us or love us less if we mess up. In fact, He loves us more to cover our shortcomings. What a glorious feeling to know that nothing we do or do not do can separate us from the love of God. It is so powerful and freeing to be loved so strongly, deeply, and truly. Imagine if you could give your spouse or children a type of deeper love that is truly unconditional. One that forgives, loves them in their faults, and is patient, kind, and selfless. I can tell you it is incredibly hard to love others like this; it takes a lot of dedication and work. Agape love is intentional, which means you must think about it and actively work towards a goal of agape love.

Agape love is a true challenge in our human nature. Agape love patiently waits and even loves its enemies. Our world is so cold and unfriendly sometimes, but agape love is kind to those who are unkind to us. Agape love is forgiving even when others are wrong and will not admit it or apologize. This kind of love is long-suffering, meaning we do not give up at the first sign of conflict or disagreement. God blesses us when we are persistent, and we keep pressing when the road is difficult. Especially with our spouses and children, agape love is important. It will elevate and bless our relationships. Agape love is sometimes unrequited, meaning it is not always given back to us the same way we give it. The same way that God loves those who do not accept Jesus as their savior, yet He still loved them enough to die for them.

Agape is sacrificial love; it does not mean necessarily dying for the other person. Sometimes it could be sacrificing your time to serve them, or your wants, needs, or desires. Agape love requires putting the other person ahead of yourself. It is not self-centered; it is servant-centered. It is sometimes giving generously and not expecting the same in return. It even could be buying your spouse a valentine's gift and not expecting one in return. Agape love is a true challenge; it is not easy, common, or popular. It is a challenge, but it is manageable. We must remember that if we are loving others as Christ loved us, then we are fulfilling a commandment and that means we will be blessed. Every commandment we keep equals blessings and grace from God.

Sisters, let us decide to love the assigned people in our lives with agape love. It will be hard but so worth it. This kind of love transforms life, marriages, and relationships. Learning to cultivate and give agape love revived MY marriage and has made OUR love deeper, stronger, and more steadfast. Remember, agape love is patient, kind. It does not envy, it does not boast, it is not proud. It does not dishonor others, it is not self-seeking, it is not easily angered, and it always protects, always trusts, always hopes, always perseveres. Love never fails. We were created to love the people assigned to our lives like this, and this kind of love will make our light shine brighter and be a powerful force for the kingdom of God.

AGAPE LOVE VS. CONDITIONAL LOVE

DAILY QUESTIONS:

1. Is there anyone that you need to begin loving with agape love?

_____

_____

_____

_____

2. What is the strongest part of agape love to you?

_____

_____

_____

_____

3. Have you ever considered the way God loves us needs to be passed on to those assigned to us?

_____

_____

_____

_____

DAILY PRAYER:

"God, thank You for loving me with pure agape love. Thank You for loving me with grace, redemption, and forgiveness. God, I thank You for seeing beyond my shortcomings and mistakes and still giving me grace and acceptance. God, I ask that You show me the people You have assigned to my life who I need to begin practicing agape love on. Lord, help me to see beyond the human way of thinking, Lord, open my mind to truly share Your agape love with those around me. God, it will take strength and determination, so please strengthen me to do this. I love You, Lord. In Jesus's name. Amen."

DAILY FOCUS:

1. Agape love is a true challenge in our human nature. Agape love patiently waits and even loves its enemies. Our world is so cold and unfriendly sometimes, but agape love is kind to those who are unkind to us. Agape love is forgiving even when others are wrong and will not admit it or apologize. This kind of love is long-suffering, meaning we do not give up at the first sign of conflict or disagreement.
2. Agape love is not a human intentional love; it is a love that God grants us, and it is a gift of salvation. We can learn and work toward loving like this; it takes effort and determination. The Bible tells us the agape love is greater than faith and hope. God is love, love is God's character, meaning if it is not love, then it is not of God.
3. Agape love bears, believes, hopes, and endures. We need to bear some difficulties, we need to believe in the best in people, we need to hope people will rise to the potential, and we need to endure through some hardships. These are necessary traits in a strong, godly marriage.

Day Sixteen

OLD-FASHIONED OR KEEP UP WITH THE TIMES?

Living kingdom down, not culture up.
COLOSSIANS 3:1-11

I HAVE BEEN CALLED OLD-FASHIONED so many times in my life, not for the way I dress or look, but because of my beliefs. We are constantly told, "Great that you are a Christian, but you need to keep up with the times."

Now, this is not saying that we need to wear dresses from the '60s and culottes. I am talking about core beliefs. This is speaking about our way of living, values, and standards. It could be, and probably will be seen by society as old-fashioned. Personally, I love dressing up, and I even had a career as a personal stylist at Nordstrom. I love fashion; makeup; hairstyles; accessories; and fun, feminine stuff just as much as the next girl. But this is not what I am talking about; our values need to be based in the Bible, not in what society deems is acceptable. This can include modesty, purity, and our entire value system.

Your family's value system needs to be set by you. If we allow our children to learn and form their own values, we are allowing the secular world to set the standard in what we believe and value. The Bible says, "Train up a child in the way they should go, and they will not depart from it" (Prov. 22:6). They may stray away as they get older, but those early values will always be embedded in their hearts. God promised that it would not return void.

Our family still believes in courting. Meaning, the pursuit of a relationship with the end goal being marriage versus the idea of just dating whoever strikes our fancy right now just for fun. We believe in biblical views about marriage and sex, that we are to hold ourselves pure, both girls and boys. We believe that our girls should carry ourselves as the princesses, whose father is the King of kings. We should dress accordingly. We are not cheap; we are priceless masterpieces that God has created. We protect ourselves as such. We believe that the values in the Bible were written for today just as much as in the "old times." The Bible is the Word of God; therefore, it is omnipresent and omnipotent, always for the time, and always being in the time. Modesty, purity, and accountability are not bad words to be hidden; they are a source of pride that we are not just like everyone else. We do not fit in with everyone else. We are unique, set apart, and called to a higher standard.

Modesty, meekness, purity, and virtue are not some ancient attributes made to be forgotten, hidden, mocked, or ashamed of. They are holy attributes of a godly woman. Modesty is not the covering up of beauty; it is about carrying ourselves as priceless, regal heirs to the kingdom. My daughter has said, "Modesty is walking, dressing, and carrying yourself like a princess. Expensive and classy." I love this explanation because we can still be fashionable and attractive, but it is the class with which we carry ourselves, and that we bring glory to the kingdom of God.

Meekness is not foolish weakness and not having an opinion, it is power under complete control. Purity is not just related to sexual purity; it is also the purity of our heart and intentions. Virtue is our reputation, not the gossip and our past, but the things we have done or are doing in our life that are the legacy we are leaving for the kingdom.

The most amazing thing is our God's grace. If you found Jesus later in life or just made some mistakes in your past regarding these things, you are a new creation in Jesus. You are only held accountable for the things you choose to do regarding this, now, once you know better. Biblically, you are completely forgiven for everything in your past, so we can let guilt, shame, and condemnation go.

With secular, public schools wanting to teach our children sex education and their very progressive value systems, we need to be on guard about the early foundation and belief system our children have. Whenever anybody attempts to speak into the culture about premarital sex, the baby mama trend, extended dating relationships, or broken families, they are quickly shunned and shamed into silence. We must be bold; the biblical way is the best. Let me explain why. The family unit is the basis of a healthy and successful society. Today our society is in chaos and dysfunction because as explained in a recent study, "Almost a quarter of U.S. children under the age of 18 live with one parent and no other adults (23%), more than three times the share of children around the world who do so (7%).... In comparison, 3% of children in China, 4% of children in Nigeria and 5% of children in India live in single-parent households."[4] An additional study found, "One of the largest shifts in family structure is this: 34% of children today are living with an unmarried parent — up from just 9% in 1960, and 19% in 1980."[5]

It has been said teaching children as young as elementary ages "safe sex" is better than teaching "abstinence" because abstinence is a "hard" or "nearly impossible" thing to do. This is ridiculous. We must teach children the highest biblical standard, tell them what the Word says, then keep loving them even if they go off track. But at least they know what the goal and standard and kingdom expectation is. We

---

[4]Stephanie Kramer, "U.S. Has World's Highest Rate of Children Living in Single-Parent Households," Pew Research Center, December 12, 2019, https://www.pewresearch.org/fact-tank/2019/12/12/u-s-children-more-likely-than-children-in-other-countries-to-live-with-just-one-parent/.
[5]Gretchen Livingston, "Fewer Than Half of U.S. Kids Today Live in a 'Traditional' Family," Pew Research Center, December 22, 2014, https://www.pewresearch.org/fact-tank/2014/12/22/less-than-half-of-u-s-kids-today-live-in-a-traditional-family/.

can't just allow children to aim low; let's teach them to have high standards and set expectations.

Society changes every day. What was acceptable yesterday is now considered offensive, and what was taboo yesterday is totally acceptable today. This new wave of political correctness is so unstable and ever changing that it brings with it stress, anxiety, anger, and hatred. No wonder half of society is exhausted, stressed out, and has depression or anxiety. That is a lot of stress and pressure to keep up with the culture. STOP.

Be encouraged. Our God was the same yesterday, today, and forever. He is steadfast and never changing. He is a strong anchor. He is a firm foundation that we can depend on to build our life for the long-term. If society is changing daily, and we base our life on that changing standard, our life will forever be in turmoil or unease, and we will always be struggling to keep up. Therefore, much of the secular population struggles with anxiety, depression, and insomnia. Their minds are always overanalyzing, working, worrying, and stressing to keep up to date on what is acceptable and what is not. They are always focused on the negative news of this world instead of the promises of hope in the Bible. God is not tired or defeated. He is still in control. The same God who put the planets in orbit is still holding the world.

When we build our life on God's words and ways that are steadfast, our life will be much steadier and more peaceful. He is our rock and a firm foundation to build our lives and values on. If the trends, beliefs, standards, and outlook of the earth are ever changing, that is why God's foundation was always created to be steadfast. The earth and the kingdom will always be opposites. The world has always been on a steady decline: morals, family values, and societal values have slowly been backing away from the way of the Lord, but this was forewarned in the Bible.

2 Timothy 3:1-5 warns us, "But mark this: There will be terrible times in the last days. People will be lovers of themselves, lovers of money, boastful, proud, abusive, disobedient to their parents, ungrateful, unholy, without love, unforgiving, slanderous, without self-control, brutal, not lovers of the good, treacherous, rash, conceited, lovers

of pleasure rather than lovers of God — having a form of godliness but denying its power. Have nothing to do with such people" (NIV).

This is a perfectly accurate and specific description of today's society. There are some hard truths that God opened my eyes to that I want to share with you. Not to condemn, just to shine light on.

Today, people will jump on any bandwagon quickly if it sounds politically correct or compassionate. We must discern the root issue of every social cause and weigh if it fits in with kingdom principles. Many people are chasing money, fame, popularity, and wealth as the biggest goals. The rich and famous are followed, even worshiped, as idols. We know more about celebrities' wants, likes, and everyday actions than those of the people living in our home with us, the people assigned to us. People are striving to find and have more followers and likes, as the goal of being "influential." Today many people want things handed to them without putting the work in, and that is making them ungrateful for the chance to forge their own path and make their own way.

People are conceited, believing in their own entitlement, and are chasing pleasure instead of wholeness because it is the "empowered, liberated, and free" thing to do. People want the rest of society to be responsible for their bad choices in life, and as compassionate as it sounds, this is not the Bible's way. Society's entire narrative today fits into 2 Timothy 3:15 perfectly. It has been a slow but steady decline into this current culture where loose morals are accepted, even celebrated. Again, God does not wish us to judge unbelieving people, or even other Christians, in their sin. He wishes us to know His truth and align our personal viewpoints and actions with His Word. More importantly, love people where they are and do not pass judgment. If you read this paragraph and the verse above, it would appear we really are in the "end times."

Sisters, this is hard to say in today's world, but the truth of the Bible is: You, as a believer, cannot bend the Word of God to fit into society's acceptable political correctness. Again, you do not have to preach at people or tell them how and why they are wrong. But you need to know what you believe personally and stand firm on biblical truth. The Bible cannot be twisted, edited, and redacted to fit into what society deems appropriate or politically correct.

Everything is not okay for you to follow. Once you know Jesus, God holds you to a higher standard than the unsaved. God is omnipotent and omnipresent; His stability is the exact opposite of the world's instability. He knew what the changes of the world's morality would be, and He wrote His Word in an unchanging way, so we would not bear the stress of continuing to learn the new beliefs, standards, and trends. You were created to be salt and light to the world not fit in with them!

Free yourself from mental slavery of trying to keep up to the times and the trends. We are called to live according to His Word, and in His Word is a peace that frees us from the culture, guilt, and inconsistent standards of this world. God's Word is the only standard you need to be concerned with. We do not have to offend, condemn, or judge. We must hold ourselves to our own individual moral standard and know the errors and misjudgments of the world, so we do not get trapped. There is freedom in that, there is peace in that, and there is joy in that. You are not like everyone else; you are a part of a royal legacy, for you are a child of the King. Remember, kingdom over culture.

DAILY QUESTIONS:

1. Have you been allowing society's culture to have more importance than heaven's culture? If so, how?

___

___

___

___

OLD-FASHIONED OR KEEP UP WITH THE TIMES?

2. Now that you understand modesty, what can you change?

_____

_____

_____

_____

3. What are the most important biblical values you want to establish in your life or family's life?

_____

_____

_____

_____

4. Do you see any of the culture's beliefs that are the opposite of kingdom beliefs? What should you think of these issues?

_____

_____

_____

_____

DAILY PRAYER:
"Lord, please help me set my value system by Your Word only. God, thank You for Your steadfast and stable and holy Word. Help me to

keep it, and only it, as the standard that I live my life by. Lord, thank You that the true peace is letting society's standards and beliefs go and to stop measuring my life by the standards in the world. Thank You for the grace that covers me every time I fall short. Thank You for freeing me from the mental slavery of the world and granting me peace that passes all understanding. Lord, help me to build my values based on the Word of God and to teach these to my family. Help me to discern when society's culture is pulling me away from biblical truth and help me to stand firm on Your Word. In Jesus's name. Amen."

DAILY FOCUS:
1. God was the same yesterday, today, and forever. He is steadfast and never changing, which is a strong anchor we can depend on to build our life for the long-term. If society is changing daily, and we base our life on that changing standard, our life will forever be in turmoil or unease. We will always be struggling to catch and keep up.
2. When we build our life on God's words and ways that are steadfast, our life will be much steadier and more peaceful. He is our rock and a firm foundation to build our lives and values on.
3. Free yourself from mental slavery. We are called to live according to His Word, and in His Word is a peace that frees us from the culture, guilt, and standards of this world.

Day Seventeen

OVERCOMMITTED AND STRESSED OUT

> "Just because we can do anything,
> doesn't mean we should do everything."
> LivingOurPriorities.com

IT IS GREAT TO set goals for every day. Personally, I am very forgetful, so for me a to-do list is the only way I can have a chance at remembering what I am supposed to even be doing. My kids have laughed at missed appointments saying, "It must not have been on Mom's planner."

But some people become slaves to their to-do list. They want to be a part of everything going on; they have FOMO. They strive to plan every hour of their life; they fill in every minute with frivolous activities and stringent plans. But then life happens, their plans get thwarted, and they are in disarray and anxiety.

It is a disservice to our families and our ministries when we overcommit ourselves. You may be able to comfortably dedicate yourself 100 percent to five or six things, but when you start having ten or fourteen priorities, something is going to fall through the cracks. It is said, "I would rather be really great at a few things than do a lot of mediocre things." Sis, there is true freedom in saying, "No." There are decisions you may be left out of, there may be plans and happenings you will not be involved with, but the peace of freedom of your time may be worth those things lost.

I struggled with this for years. I went through my life overcommitted, juggling 547 things, and only doing a great job on very few of them. I was stressed out, anxious, and even suffered from severe high blood pressure. My hardest things were not wanting to be "mean" in refusing. But I will tell you, there is a kind way to say everything. I have said, "I would love to help you with this, but I really can't take on anything else right now," or "I would love to help you, but I am handling so much, I can't dedicate the time you deserve."

I remember the first time I said "no" in one of these ways, I hung up the phone with the biggest smile on my face, not because I hate helping people, but because I was saying yes to the things in my life that I have set priority to. When you take on too much, your priorities get short-changed as you begin to try to make room. We all only have twenty-four hours in a day and seven days in a week, so the feeling of being overwhelmed is most likely a result of being overcommitted. Satan can use being overcommitted as a weapon to distract us from our kingdom assignments and callings.

We, as women, feel this ungodly need to do it all. Rest in the knowledge that we are not made to do it all. Jesus could have reached the whole world by Himself. Jesus was God incarnate, yet He recruited twelve disciples and many apostles to help Him carry out His mission. Jesus had a big mission, so He needed a team to accomplish His tasks.

If Jesus needed a team, I do not think He expects us to do it all perfectly by ourselves. We may not have a team, but we can marginalize and focus our mission to be dedicated to what is important to us. Your family, your spouse, and your children are a big part of your mission.

We all are called to ministry. Just because you do not preach, teach, or sing does not mean you do not have a ministry. Every person has a mission and a platform where they are placed. A wife is an important ministry to her husband and can often be his biggest prayer warrior. A mother is a major foundation-setting ministry to her children. A godly woman at work is a witness to God and minister of His goodness and grace to her associates. An entrepreneur is a ministry in how your business is set apart. Whatever spaces we occupy in life, we are a ministry of Jesus in the way we walk, talk, care, and minister. You can minister to the grocery store clerk through your kindness. There is something we are called to do every day to touch this world for Christ and His kingdom.

Do you really need to be the PTA president, a school volunteer, room mom, bake sale leader, and a greeter at church while still maintaining a healthy family life? NO. You need to set priorities. Maybe PTA is important, so say no to other things. Maybe church involvement is important, so say no to the other things. Maybe your career is important to your ministry, so say no to unnecessary things. We must determine the things that are our callings and give 100 percent of our effort and dedication to those things. Remember, it is better to do a few things very well than to do a lot of mediocre things. Choose and stand unapologetic in your priorities.

Do not sugar coat your reasons, and do not make excuses. State the truth kindly, and stand firm in your beliefs, and stand firm in your priorities. Do not expect others to understand, support, or agree with your priorities; they are your priorities, so their importance only matters to you and God. You cannot go through life trying to justify and campaign for others to understand you or your choices.

It seems a little funny, but plan on different ways to say "no" or "I can't." If you have a practiced way of saying no, when it comes time to say no, you will feel prepared and more at ease with a planned response. Pray about your decisions. Cultivate a willing and obedient heart to go where God is leading you. Start to ask Him for discernment to recognize His will and follow His lead. Pray for the courage and ability to say no if it is going to keep you from doing what God has designed you to do. Proverbs 16:3 advises us, "Commit your works to the Lord, and your plans will be established" (ESV).

We need to focus our limited energy on the most important things that God has assigned to us. When we begin to take on things not assigned to us is when anxiety and stress begins to add up. We need to weed out the necessities from the unnecessary stresses in our lives and restore balance and power to the order of our life and follow and soar in our callings.

DAILY QUESTIONS:

1. What are your planned responses for when you need to say "no"?

___

2. What are your top priorities?

___

3. What are the activities or commitments you need to let go of?

___

DAILY PRAYER:

"Lord, thank You for the freedom You give us to focus our effort on just a few things. Lord, help me to be directed to the priorities I am called to. Help me to learn to say "no." Please give me the wisdom of when to say "yes" and when to say "no." Lord, help me to stop overcommitting my time, so that I can focus on the blessings and tasks that You have set before me. Help me to set my priorities in a way that would please You. Thank You for Your grace, understanding, and love. In Jesus's name. Amen."

DAILY FOCUS:

1. You need to say "no." You have a limited amount of time and energy, so do not overcommit yourself and overwhelm yourself. Choose a few things and do them WELL.
2. Do not say "yes" to every request. Set your priorities and only make the time for things that fit into those priorities. Be kind but learn the power in your "no" and the power of your "yes."

Day Eighteen

DELILAH: WOMAN OF THE WORLD VS. WOMAN OF GOD

> "A woman of faith is protected by God, strengthened by God,
> and victorious in God, because she has favor.
> And that woman is YOU."
>
> UNKNOWN

I AM GOING TO GIVE you the modern-day version of the story of Samson and Delilah to refresh your mind. Before Samson was born, an angel told his mother she would have a child who would be a deliverer of the enslaved Israelites. She was instructed that he should never drink alcohol, eat anything unclean, or cut his hair. Samson was born as a vow between God and His people that God would use someone strong and deemed holy to deliver the Israelites. His mother had faith and was obedient to God. They were obedient to everything that the angel had asked of them.

As Samson grew, God blessed him, and his parents raised him in the obedience of God. Samson went into the land of the Philistines (the Israelites' oppressors) and saw a Philistine woman who he wanted to marry. His parents tried to dissuade him, but he disobeyed them and did not listen to their wise counsel. He married her, and during the wedding feast, he told the Philistines a riddle, which they were angry they could not answer. His wife pouted for all seven days of the feast until Samson told her, then she told her people, and Samson was angry and killed thirty men. They in turn threatened the wife's family, and her father gave his daughter to another man. Samson was even angrier and proceeded to kill one thousand men with a donkey jawbone.

Samson often ignored God and sought to please himself, and he feared no one because of his anointed strength. However, God did not give him his strength for himself and his personal battles, but for his anointed callings for the people of God. Samson was rebellious and repeatedly broke his vows to God. He was easily angered and foolish. His biggest mistake was the woman he later fell in love with, Delilah.

You see, she was beautiful and attractive, but she was sweet-talking and conniving and not trustworthy. Three times he told her a lie about his strength, and all three times she tried those things to drain his strength. She unquestionably failed the loyalty test. But, even with this knowledge of her deceit, he relented and foolishly told her the truth. She had his head shaved, and the Lord's strength left him. He trusted someone sent by the enemy to ensnare and capture him. He told the wrong person what secrets were in his heart.

Did God use this as part of his story to defeat the Philistines when his hair finally grew back? Yes. But he allowed a "Delilah" spirit to drain his anointing. Sometimes people in our lives will operate in a "Delilah spirit." They seek to get close to us, not to be a friend, but to gather information and expose our weaknesses. They want to exploit the weakness in our marriage, family, business, and knowledge, so that the enemy can destroy our anointing and blessings.

Delilah was the very definition of a cunning woman described in Proverbs 5:3-10 (NLT):

> For the lips of an immoral woman are as sweet as honey, and her mouth is smoother than oil. But in the end she is as bitter as poison, as dangerous as a double-edged sword. Her

DELILAH: WOMAN OF THE WORLD VS. WOMAN OF GOD

feet go down to death; her steps lead straight to the grave. For she cares nothing about the path to life. She staggers down a crooked trail and doesn't realize it. So now, my sons, listen to me. Never stray from what I am about to say: Stay away from her! Don't go near the door of her house! If you do, you will lose your honor and will lose to merciless people all you have achieved. Strangers will consume your wealth, and someone else will enjoy the fruit of your labor.

And in Proverbs 31, we hear the complete opposite description of a godly woman:

Who can find a wife of noble character? She is more precious than jewels. The heart of her husband trusts her. He will not lack anything good. She rewards him with good not evil. She draws on her strength and reveals that her arms are strong.... Her hands are busy planting her fields. She reaps her crops and sells them, and invests her profits.... Her hands reach to the needy and she has a prepared household. Strength and honor are her clothing, and she can laugh at difficult times to come. Her mouth speaks wisdom and loving instruction is her tongue.... Her children rise up and call her blessed and her husband praises her.... Charm is deceptive, and beauty is fading, but a woman who fears the Lord is to be praised. [My paraphrase.]

Those could not be two more different and polar descriptions. I believe sometimes we read the story of Samson and Delilah and blame just Samson. Yes, he made a vow to God, and he broke his vow, but he had some encouragement and persuasion from a cunning worldly woman. He allowed himself to be distracted and disengaged from his calling. Samson was at fault and responsible for his own shortcomings and bad choices, but Satan worked through a cunning woman to push him along that road faster. Imagine Samson had chosen a godly woman for his wife. Imagine he had married an Israelite who could have encouraged him to pursue God's purpose for his life, who could have uplifted him and kept his secret. How much more could he have done, with less suffering, to free the Israelites? Good company brings about good character; bad company corrupts good character.

Sisters, I long to be a Proverbs 31 woman. Looking at Proverbs 31, I long to have my husband stand proud of me, and I want to be: godly, modest, strong, meek, humble, and gracious. Proverbs 6 and 7 describe forbidden and worldly women as: cunning, brazen, loud, beautiful, bold, and sweet-talking, yet her life is unstable. It is funny how different these verses are. God has given us such strong descriptions of both sides that we have the freedom to choose. Remember, God makes recommendations and sets boundaries for us, but it is up to us to stay on the path and stay within His directives. We have been given free will to make our own choices.

The world will tell you Christian women are submissive (as a bad thing), a victim of a patriarchal religion, backwards, and foolish. Proverbs 31 is not a verse that talks of the weak submissiveness of a "good" wife — it talks of a godly wife in the Old Testament (over 3,000 years ago), who owns her own land, reaps her own crops, sells them, and invests her profits in her and her husband's household. Proverbs 31 was an early entrepreneur woman who worked along with her husband, had her own thing going, yet carried herself with the regal nature God gave her. She was not ordinary and cheap; she was priceless and a precious jewel. She brought pride to her husband while having her own healthy enterprises.

That does not match what the world says a godly woman is at all, does it? I have had many other women tell me I am missing out on life by not living a life of a modern "free," immoral woman. Please know, sisters — we are not missing out on anything being a Proverbs 31 woman. In fact, we skip a lot of the sinful and emotional pitfalls that other women get trapped in. We have promises God has made us that the world cannot give us.

In today's culture women are told to be bold and to say what we think, when we think it, without the consideration of anyone else's view, timing, and the appropriateness of the place. To be brazen, to be sexually experimental, and to satisfy every human physical desire outside of the "old-fashioned" confines of marriage. To be loud, to make sure we are heard and seen, and to demand other's attention and validation. To be cunning, to be smarter, to have underhanded ways to get ahead, to manipulate people and situations, and to use people to get ahead.

If you read any modern women's fashion magazine, they have entire articles of how to sweet talk your boss, boyfriend, or friend to manipulate them to do what you want. To be beautiful above all, to know all the tricks, to contour, have fake nails and eyelashes and lip injections, to be able to have a fake face if we desire. To be sweet-mouthed, to say the right things, to support the socially acceptable things and be politically correct by society's standards. Sisters, you are called to HIGHER things. This may all sound good to our human ears, but they should not sit well with our believer's kingdom heart. We aren't made to fit into the world!

Modesty does not mean wearing a paper bag to cover up everything. We can still be fashionable and attractive, but modesty speaks of the way you carry yourself while you are dressed up. I have explained to my daughters that modesty is "carrying yourself like royalty. Put together and pretty but regal and expensive. Not cheap and ordinary." We can choose to focus on our outward beauty, or we can focus and place the utmost importance on our inward or our heart's beauty.

Is it bad to look our best? No, but these verses are speaking on where our FOCUS is. As believers, we can be fashionable, stylish, and beautiful, but Proverbs 31 describes a well-rounded woman whose focus is on the things of God and her household, not herself first. We are not called to be self-centered, which is the way of the world. We are called to be Christ-centered, which is the way of the Lord.

Proverbs 31 tells us beauty is fading and charm is deceptive, but a woman who lives her life as God directs will be blessed and praised. She respects her husband, and he praises her; she is busy caring for her family and children, and they honor her. We are to pay our husbands with only good and not evil, and we allow our husbands to stand tall in their fields. Our mouths are used to only speak good and wise things, and we are to carry ourselves honorable and respectful.

Sometime in the last few decades, we lost this high standard of morality in the world. Sisters, anything the world tells you is a lie. God's Word is the only truth. Society may tell you being a Delilah is how you get ahead in life and that being a forbidden woman is independent and fulfilling, but you will have an emotional void that only God can fill. A blessed woman's way is directed by God, and He has anointed us and promised to provide all we need. The ways of God are always better than the ways of the world.

Whether you have recently found Jesus and had a complicated past or lived a Christian woman's life from childhood, remember, in Christ Jesus, there is no condemnation for your past shortcomings, sins, or mistakes. Christ only requires that we accept Him once. We change our ways, and we become accountable to Jesus after we choose Him as our Lord and Savior.

As women of God, we are not called to just turn heads. We are called to turn hearts toward our Heavenly Father. We are called to have deeper beauty than just our appearance, and we are called to have deeper character and foundation than the worldly woman. Sis, know who you are. You are a princess of heaven and a daughter of the King of kings. You are regal, anointed, poised, equipped, and redeemed. Walk in that truth today and begin to live as a Proverbs 31 woman of God. Let us aim to be independent yet respectful, strong yet submissive, regal yet humble, steadfast yet not brazen, blessed and priceless, women of God.

DAILY QUESTIONS:

1. What differences do you recognize between a worldly woman and a godly woman?

_____

_____

_____

_____

DELILAH: WOMAN OF THE WORLD VS. WOMAN OF GOD

2. What stood out to you most contrasting between the women in Proverbs 6 and 7 and Proverbs 31?

_____

_____

_____

_____

3. What can you change to realign yourself with the traits of a godly woman?

_____

_____

_____

_____

DAILY PRAYER:

"Lord, I long to be a Proverbs 31 woman. God, I pray that You build me to be a strong, resilient, gracious, kind, and meek woman of God. I pray that You help me to be the _____ that You desire me to be. God, please set in me the traits of a godly woman; help me to be light and salt to the world around me. God, I pray that You would take out all the self-centered and negative attributes that the world says we should be as women. Lord, help me to walk in modesty and purity and make my heart and mind pure before You. Lord, I pray that You work in me and change me into a godly woman who brings honor and glory to YOU. In Jesus's name. Amen."

DAILY FOCUS:

1. Sisters, you are not called to be a cunning, brazen, bold, beautiful woman of the world. You are called to be a loyal, pure-minded, humble, kind, and gracious woman of God. We cannot live as the world tells us anymore; now we are held to a higher standard.
2. As women of God, we are not called to just turn heads, we are called to turn hearts towards our Heavenly Father. We are called to have deeper beautification than just our appearance, and we are called to have deeper character and foundation than the worldly woman.
3. Sisters, anything the world tells you is a lie. God's Word is the only truth. Society may tell you being a Delilah is how you get ahead in life and that being a forbidden woman is independent and fulfilling, but you will have a void that only God can fill. A blessed woman's ways are directed by God, and He has anointed us and promised to provide all we need. The ways of God are always better than the ways of the world.

Day Nineteen

SOCIAL JUSTICE ACTIVIST OR WOMAN OF ACTION?

> "Our love should not be just words and talk; it must be
> true love, which shows itself in action."
> 1 JOHN 3:18 GNT

WE LIVE IN A world that is full of social justice warriors, influencers, and activists. It is a good thought to want everything in the world to be "right," but there is a sad reality: Since the Garden of Eden, when sin was introduced to the world, everything in the world was not perfect, and it never will be. There are some stark realities the Bible tells us about.

Proverbs 14:23 explains, "There is profit in all hard work, but endless talk leads only to poverty" (CSB). Matthew 25:35-36 tells us, "For I was hungry and you gave me food, I was thirsty and you gave me drink, I was a stranger and you welcomed me, I was naked, and you clothed me, I was sick and you visited me, I was in prison and you came to me" (ESV).

The first thing I saw in both these verses was action. They are not just talking about sharing a post on Facebook that makes you feel good or reposting, liking, or commenting on something that makes you feel better about an issue. These verses are based in real and tangible action. There is a huge difference between awareness and action. We live in a society that has a lot of people talking about issues to raise awareness, but then they are not changing or doing anything substantive to bring change. A post on social media does not help. If you are posting, lecturing, and not doing anything, then you are just jumping on the bandwagon of a cause to make yourself feel better about your indifference (harsh reality, sisters).

If you are passionate about a clean earth, start a cleanup group to pick up trash on your local roads or parks. If you are passionate about homelessness, start a drive to give them blankets, jackets, or other necessities or volunteer at homeless shelters or food kitchens. If you are passionate about youth in poverty, start a mentorship program. Begin to personally change their narrative and tell them the potential God put in them. If you are passionate about foster children, visit them, get involved, give them love and hope, and change their lives and mentality. Do something. Jesus had a word for those who only "talked the talk but didn't walk the walk." He called them "hypocrites," and He did it frequently with great conviction many times during His ministry.

If you genuinely care about these things, do it from the heart, and do it privately. Do not post about it on social media for attention or accolades, even if you are narrating it as "awareness." If you do it for the likes here on earth, then you will only have earthly rewards, but if you do it privately for only God to see, you will have heavenly rewards. Through the COVID pandemic I noticed many Christians choosing to wear or not wear masks and get or not get a vaccine. Believers were belittling others on how much more virtuous and moral they were because of said choice. Friends, this is EXACTLY what the Pharisees in Jesus's time did and Jesus condemned them time and time again. No Christian should make an individual decision here on earth then boast about their virtue and morality. This is virtue-signaling, and Jesus literally spoke against it saying:

SOCIAL JUSTICE ACTIVIST OR WOMAN OF ACTION?

> Beware of practicing your righteousness before other people in order to be seen by them, for then you will have no reward from your Father who is in heaven. Thus, when you give to the needy, sound no trumpet before you, as the hypocrites do in the synagogues and in the streets, that they may be praised by others. Truly, I say to you, they have received their reward. But when you give to the needy, do not let your left hand know what your right hand is doing, so that your giving may be in secret. And your Father who sees in secret will reward you. (Matthew 6:1-4 ESV)

Lately, social justice has become the move in society to make your social circle "aware" of an issue by just talking about it. This is an easy way for some people to feel as though they are making a difference without ever actually making a difference. Sisters, God calls us to be women of action. Activists (many of whom I refuse to even call that title) usually are the loudest in trying to tell others that the issues exist. Listen, we all know the issues are there. what are they doing about them? What are we all consistently doing to make a real, tangible difference? What you say doesn't matter as much as what you actually do.

A lot of people who preach about climate change as something they are passionate about, only drink water out of plastic bottles. A lot of people who post about women's rights are the ones who post about mocking or tearing down other women's appearances or insulting women whose viewpoints are different. A lot of the people who believe in race equality are the first ones to point out racism in every situation, adding to the anger, but they do not make any difference to inner city kids. A lot of the people who want help for the poor never donate any of their time or money. They never try to find a church that supports an orphanage, or take a mission trip, or even volunteer at inner city school to do free tutoring — yet they lecture the world about helping the poor.

This is not only hypocritical, but your inaction and counterproductive behaviors can turn off those who do want to make a difference. There are politicians who post all day about issues and injustice, yet when they have a chance to do something besides talk and can make a difference, they are nowhere to be seen. Stop talking about injustice; make a physical difference. Let us all aim to stop talking about issues and get up and put in the work to make it better.

It is good to have causes you are passionate about, it is good to care for the poor, to care for the fatherless, to care for those in less fortunate situations than you, but you need to get up and do something that makes a difference. Everything you do charity-wise needs to come from the heart, and it needs to be selfless without seeking validation or praise. It needs to be done between you and God. He sees everything, and He also sees your intent and motivation behind it. If your charity is done for the clout or for the "Gram," it will negate your blessings, and it will negate your kingdom impact. It does not have to change the whole world. We are called to reach people one person at a time. It is not supposed to be a global initiative; it is designed to be an individual initiative.

Before you share that post that looks good, before you lecture others about a social issue, take inventory of the actual action you are taking on that issue. Just like the great commission, Jesus said, "Go into all the world and preach the gospel" (Mark 16:15 NIV). If you believe in a cause and believe God wants you to fight for justice, as long as it lines up with the Word of God, then develop an action plan and do it. It is up to you to make a difference yourself. This will let your action and meek humility draw others into your cause with their genuine hearts. Your loud, self-righteous talk will only guilt them into joining you or "sharing" your cause. This is not the kingdom way.

We may have been assigned social issues that will allow us to make a difference in the world, but we need to weigh if these issues are only re-living, extending, or arguing about past issues or if they are really making an impact on the lives around us daily. We need to make sure we are not taking on additional pressure or the stress of ancient issues we are not able to solve or make a substantial difference in. We cannot just relive past trauma, whether it is cultural or social issues. We must heal and grow from everything from the past. You need to earnestly pray and ask God to help you know if a social issue is just adding unneeded stress, or if it is part of your assignment.

Sisters, please realize that we all know there were horrible atrocities in the world and all our pasts. Since the Garden of Eden, there was injustice and pain in the world. Just like Eve took a step of faith and planted her seeds, so must we. Nearly every religion and ethnic group has been enslaved, discriminated against, or treated wrongly at some time in history. Never get so caught up in the injustices and wrongs of the past that you do not look to your future. You cannot go forward in life looking backwards.

Sisters, there has been racial and social unbalance since the beginning of time. We are called to begin to sow seeds of faith around us and not just constantly talk about and highlight the negativity in the world. One piece of great advice my grandmother gave me was, "What you go out into the world looking for, you will surely find. So, choose to go out and find joy and look for the good people." Let us reset our perspective to find and highlight the good things in the world and work to actively sow seeds to change the areas that need our attention. If GOD has called you to try to bring about change in these areas, then act on it. We need more feet walking and more hands sharing than mouths just talking about these issues. The world does not need another social media post; we need another hand doing the work of the Lord.

Let us realign our priorities with the kingdom of heaven. Make sure the issues you are standing on bring honor to God. We cannot stand next to worldly issues that are plainly described as sin in the Bible and ask that our stance be blessed. Find your passionate causes, pray for guidance, develop a plan to go and take action to create a difference, and do not lecture others about it. Let your charity and causes be between you and God. If you are doing it out of a pure heart, others will be drawn to you to help you further your cause. Be a woman of action, not just a woman of talk. Remember, we must choose to have kingdom culture over worldly culture.

DAILY QUESTIONS:

1. How have you been guilty of being a woman of talk rather than a woman of action?

_____

_____

_____

_____

2. What are your causes or callings, and how can you make a REAL difference?

_____

_____

_____

_____

3. What do you need to change in your social media habits to become a humble woman of action, not a "social justice re-poster"?

_____

_____

_____

_____

SOCIAL JUSTICE ACTIVIST OR WOMAN OF ACTION?

DAILY PRAYER:
"Lord, thank You for the freedom You give us to be true women of action and not of idle talk. Lord, please show me the causes and injustices that You want me to stand for. Lord, show me a path to make an actual difference in these areas. Help me to weigh if these issues are kingdom issues and help me to stand on pure, biblical truth. God, please rid me of the need to publicize the charity I do. Show me a plan of how I can put my passions to action and be a woman after Your own heart. Lord, create in me a clean heart to take action to serve others as selflessly just as You did, Jesus. Lord, please help me to serve others while serving You. Please guide me so my causes line up with Your Word. In Jesus's name. Amen."

DAILY FOCUS:
1. Do not just repost things that sound good. Decide today to become a woman of action. Decide today to stop talking publicly about issues, but to act privately to make a difference in the world.
2. Do not just agree to causes that sound good; do your research and make sure the cause lines up with the Word of God and your moral beliefs. Make sure it is something where getting involved can bring glory to God. Steer clear of controversial things that go against God's Word.
3. Sisters, please realize that we all know there were horrible atrocities in the world and all our pasts. Since the Garden of Eden, there was injustice and pain in the world. Just like Eve took a step of faith and planted her seeds, so must we. Never get so caught up in the injustices and wrongs of the past that you do not look to your future. You cannot go forward in life looking backwards.
4. We are called to begin to sow seeds of faith around us and not just constantly talk about and highlight the negativity in the world. Yes, there is negativity in the world around us every day. One piece of great advice my grandmother gave me was, "What you go out into the world looking for, you will surely find. So, choose to go out and find joy and look for the good people." Let us reset our perspective to find and highlight the good things in the world and work to actively sow seeds to change the areas that need our attention.

Day Twenty
NEW AGE MENTALITY

> "Nothing seems to satisfy. Not politics, not education, not material goods. Some who refuse to turn their hearts toward God have created the New Age movement, with all of its aberrations. This is actually not new but only the latest attempt by man to place something other than Christ inside himself in a futile attempt to satisfy spiritual longings."
> — BILLY GRAHAM

NEW AGE BELIEFS ARE almost irresistible in their compassion and inclusiveness, but they are nearly impossible to define. New Age is an enormous set of various beliefs that mainly focuses on inner peace, God being in every object and animal, man is God, a person's experiences create their own truth, mother earth, and self-health centeredness.

This New Age belief system seems so innocent, compassionate, and well-meaning that a lot of Christian women are getting involved in it without realizing the effect it has on our faith. Celebrities are encouraging this belief system, like Oprah and other social influencers. As women of God, we must guard our hearts carefully. We need to know what we believe in and ground our beliefs completely in the Bible. Remember, the Bible clearly says, "Things are either from the world, or from God." We cannot have a little bit of both, because it is nicer and more inclusive; we cannot have one foot in the world and one foot in Christ.

Remember, when Satan tempted Eve, he tempted her with half-truths. He knew God said they could eat from every tree in the garden *except from one tree*. However, Satan twisted it to sound more innocent and the serpent asked her, "Didn't God tell you that you could eat of any tree in the garden?" He left out a miniscule part, and that one small detail made all of the difference and caused the first sin.

New Age seeks "higher consciousness" through meditation, activism, yoga, crystals, herbs, and spirit guides or gurus. New Age also teaches personal spirituality through "spiritual" religion, karma, reincarnation, and Earthism. No matter how New Age beliefs are presented, a lot of it stems from occult practices and Eastern religions such as Hinduism and Buddhism. It seems inclusive because many of its teachings say there are many ways to God, all religions are correct, or even simpler, we are God. It rids our needs of an omnipotent and omnipresent God whom we are accountable to, and this is very appealing for New Agers today. People can take any idea or group of ideas, call it "my individual spirituality," and then embrace those ideas as their truth.

Biblically, there is only one truth. "Jesus told him, 'I am the way, the truth, and the life. No one can come to the Father except through me'" (John 14:6, NLT). He was clear, concise, and definite in this statement; there is no room in it for what-ifs. We cannot substitute abstract wavering truth for steadfast biblical truth.

Colossians 2:8 tells us, "See to it that no one takes you captive through hollow and deceptive philosophy, which depends on human tradition and the elemental spiritual forces of this world rather than Christ" (NIV).

Colossians 2:8 is unquestionably clear. It warns that depending on new human traditions and spiritual forces or ideas of the world is dangerous, because it takes away from the only way and the truth, Jesus Christ. We need to guard our minds against anything that is contradictory to what the Bible says, as innocent as it may seem.

Let us take the "Mother Earth" belief. It seems innocent and environmentally friendly. Is the earth a valuable resource that needs to be cared for and maintained? Yes, however, the Bible tells us earth was created and is sustained by God Himself. He created all the systems in the earth, and He is the one who keeps it all working together age after age. We are to care for all the things that God created, but we are to worship God, not His creations. The earth is not a goddess to be worshiped; it is a resource that God has made that we need to care for. There is no such thing as Mother Earth or Earth Goddess in Christianity. Genesis 1:1 says, "In the beginning God created the heavens and the earth." We are to worship the Creator, not His creation. To worship His creation is to take away from the praise we give our great God.

Let us discuss the "God is in everything" idea. God is omnipresent and omnipotent. But to worship animals or items as a god is strictly forbidden in the Bible. Exodus 20:3-5 warns, "You must not have any other god but me. You must not make for yourself an idol of any kind or an image of anything in the heavens or on the earth or in the sea. You must not bow down to them or worship them, for I, the LORD your God, am a jealous God who will not tolerate your affection for any other gods" (NLT). And Deuteronomy 5:8 tells us, "Do not make for yourselves images of anything in heaven or on earth or in the water under the earth" (GNT).

God is God. He is the Beginning and the End, the Alpha and Omega. He reigns supreme. He did not shrink down to be placed in earth's objects, like the sea and the stars. He created those things, and He reigns above those things. God is not in them. God is everywhere, but there is only one God who reigns supreme over all things. He is not a thing, and He is not in everything. He is OVER everything.

The "one soul" or "reincarnation" belief is another trend I have noticed. We are individual souls, and we will be judged as individual souls for our actions and choices. We are not "one human soul." I am not responsible for your choices, and you are not responsible for mine. I will have to answer for me on judgment day, and you will answer for yourself. We have no ancestor or soul ties, and the Bible clearly says that after death, all souls rest in an eternal place. We do not have multiple lives, we have one life, and if we choose Jesus, we have eternity in heaven promised to our soul. We are not reborn; the

Bible says in Ecclesiastes 12:7, "And the dust returns to the earth as it was, and the spirit returns to God who gave it" (ESV).

My sisters, the Bible said we have one life, one death, and an eternity with Jesus promised for those who choose Him. Reincarnation is not a biblical principle. God is extremely specific that our body has one life, and it is mortal, but that our spirit will dwell in either heaven or hell. The Bible never speaks of second chances after death; it in fact highlights ONE CHANCE and the promise that every ear has heard the name "Jesus" to choose before death. Hebrews 9:27 tells us, "Just as it is appointed for man to die once, and after that comes judgment" (ESV).

The crystals, herbs, sage, horoscopes, meditation, and "spirituality" come from pieces of Eastern religions. They cannot be pieced together into your new "spirituality," as this is not the way of the Bible or the kingdom. Crystals do not hold some magical power to give you peace and strength; only God can grant you those things. Herbs like sage cannot cleanse the atmosphere around you; only the Holy Spirit can come in and remove any "evil spirits" that are around you, and the Holy Spirit alone can change the atmosphere.

Depending on sage or other herbs to cleanse the atmosphere around you is essentially placing your faith in a false god and, therefore, idolatry. Using these secular things can actually open the door for demonic or spiritual attacks that you may be unprepared for. Pictures or statues of elephants cannot bring you good luck. Horoscopes are plainly believing the stars have an impact on your future or personality. You are completely in control of who you choose to be. No horoscope or astrological sign can make you act in a specific way. The stars lining up do not give you luck or make you unlucky. God has complete control over everything that happens in our lives. Placing your faith in any crystal, horoscope, candle, herb, astrology, or practice that is not centered on the gospel of Christ is a form of idol worship and does not line up with kingdom principles. Meditation is not bad, but you must guard your heart to make sure any messages you are getting from it are biblically sound, not spiritual. The modern idea of "self-love" is another slippery slope for us as kingdom women. Yes, we should love, care for, and value ourselves, but it cannot become a conceited, self-sufficient, self-serving, self-fulfilling way.

We cannot really love ourselves and be confident with ourselves just the way we are now — without the redemptive power of Jesus. To leave Jesus out of it all, makes it completely superficial. We also cannot love every part of ourselves now because we are constantly progressing in our faith walk and constantly striving to be more Christ-like. To say we completely love ourselves is to negate repentance and the need to better anything in ourselves.

Self-empowerment is another dangerous trend. We need to realize we cannot empower ourselves or other women, as we are ultimately Holy Spirit-empowered. We can lift others up, offer support, encourage, and pray for them — but we ultimately cannot empower them. To say we can be completely self-sufficient ignores the need for Jesus to carry us through. We can only do "all things" through Christ who gives us strength, according to Philippians 4:13.

We cannot do and be everything, as we need Jesus for grace and strength. So many seemingly innocent ideas and earthly theories are truly anti-gospel and anti-biblical. Christianity is based on basic beliefs:

1. God created the heavens and the earth.
2. Jesus is the only begotten Son of God.
3. He came to earth and died for our sins.
4. He rose again then ascended to heaven.
5. He will come again for His Church.

We must be incredibly careful with even seemingly innocent ideas that are contradictory to what God's Word says. Remember, Satan does not come and get you to worship him outright and suddenly. He excels in the very small steps that turn your heart away from the things of God. God loves everyone, and Jesus came to die for everyone, but God gives everyone the free will to choose faith in Him and accept Him as their personal savior. Even if it seems harsh or non-inclusive, biblically, there is only one way to salvation, and that is belief in Jesus

Christ. Anything that tells us even a slight off-color truth about that fact is an outright lie.

We are to be salt and light to an unsaved world; we cannot bring light to them if we jump on their bandwagon beliefs. Sometimes it may make you stand out, but God tells us to stand out. He tells us we are different. We need to be comfortable standing firm in our beliefs, not judge people, and love them right where they are. We do not have to debate others or tell them they are wrong or condemn them for what they choose to believe. Remember, we are all free to choose. Our job is to love them and allow our lives and light to reach them.

Romans 12:2 warns us, "Don't copy the behavior and customs of this world, but let God transform you into a new person by changing the way you think. Then you will learn to know God's will for you, which is good and pleasing and perfect" (NLT).

We must guard our hearts and the hearts of our families from any distraction of the world and the lies of the enemy. The Bible says without any doubt, we cannot follow the ways of the world; we must stand in the ways of God firmly. We are to be 100 percent in for God, we must not be lukewarm and for both God and the world.

Revelation 3:15-16 says, "I know your deeds, that you are neither cold nor hot. I wish you were either one or the other. So, because you are lukewarm—neither hot nor cold — I am about to spit you out of my mouth" (NIV).

We must use discernment and reject any worldly ideals that contradict the Bible, as innocent as they may seem. We as kingdom women must look deeper and pray about anything that seems off to us. We cannot live with one foot in the kingdom and one foot in the world; we must be firmly grounded in one or the other. Kingdom over culture, sisters.

DAILY QUESTIONS:

1. Which New Age ideas or beliefs have you accepted that you need to reconsider?

_____

_____

_____

_____

2. How did this chapter change your views on New Age beliefs?

_____

_____

_____

3. What do you need to change in your social media or your belief system to realign with God's directives and commandments?

_____

_____

_____

_____

4. Are there any New Age rituals or idols you need to rid your home of today?

___

___

___

___

DAILY PRAYER:

"Lord, thank You for the Word of God, that even thousands of years later is still valid. God, I ask You that You open my eyes to anything that comes innocently but has a deeper or occult past. Lord, align my life and my beliefs to You and the Bible only. Please help me to have divine knowledge to know what Your will and commandment is and what is from the world. Lord, I do not want to be lukewarm to You; I want to be hot for You and cold to the world. Help me to reach the world for You and stand apart, and help me not to join them in their confusion and search for a "higher power." I know that all the power and all the glory and all the honor belongs to only You. In Jesus's name. Amen."

DAILY FOCUS:

1. Do not just repost things that sound good; our social media is a powerful platform, so make sure you are posting on true biblical truths. Spirituality is not Christianity. Christianity is the full belief in Jesus Christ as the Son of God, who died for us, was raised from the dead, and is our redeemer and intercessor. It is a black and white gospel; there is no room for compromise, progressive thought, or gray areas.
2. Stand firm in your belief, but remember, we do not have to judge other religions or tell them their religions do not have salvation. Our only job is to know what we believe and live our lives accord-

ingly. Our job is to love the lost, right where they are, and win them over with our kindness, love, and light.
3. I have never seen anyone shamed or nagged to Christ. If you show love, grace, joy, and peace, they will slowly begin to ask and seek for what you are modeling. Our job is to model Christ to the world.

Day Twenty-One

VICTIM MENTALITY

> "You can't expect to be a 'Victor' if you're living
> with a 'Victim' mentality."
> BILLY COX

IT SEEMS IN TODAY'S day and age everyone is an assumed victim of a sinister system. Women are the victim of a patriarchal system. Different races are victims of prejudices and racism. Religious groups are victims of types of bigotry. Political parties are victims of capitalism or other social groups.

Yes, there are real victims of crimes, bigotry, racism, and they need support and healing. I am not saying these prejudices and labels do not exist on earth; I am saying that God does not view us through these divides. I believe that, even when we experience these injustices in our life, God intends that we do not have to dwell in turmoil and defeat in this permanent status. God wants us to use these things to increase our determination, stamina, and strength and to build our testimony stronger for the kingdom. In fact, God tells us in the Old Testament, "For I know the plans I have for you, declares the Lord, plans for welfare, and not for evil, to give you a future and a hope" (Jer. 29:11 ESV).

God has a plan for good for all of us. There is nobody that He has no good intention for. If you live constantly in the thought of what has been done to you, or your circumstances, then you will never elevate above where you are or always have been. God designed life so that we are constantly growing and transforming. We are not supposed to just go on in the same way thinking the same old thoughts for the rest of our lives. If we believe we are someone's victim or a group of people's victims, we hand over our power and our destiny to them. We allow these people who are "oppressing" us to affect our potential and self-confidence.

We are to change our mindset. Do you realize that your mindset could be keeping you stuck in the past, unable to change your individual future? Do you have the mindset of a victim or a victor? The attention and emotional energy we give to these labels and divides are what keeps granting these labels power over the way we view the world. Our true power lies in the way we react to them or allow them to limit us. Remember, our God is a God of elevation and constant growth.

If our perspective matters, maybe we need to begin to take earthly labels out of it. I have lately shrugged off any label of a "minority woman" or an "orphan." I have rejected being introduced as "a minority business owner." Yes, I am a woman, and I am a business owner. I believe that the fewer labels and divides we live by, the freer we will be to reach our divine potential. Remember when we talked about how the trials in life are the times that our roots are digging deep so our tree can grow taller and blossom more? The earthly labels we segregate ourselves by are like placing our tree in a pot. We are limiting the depth and strength of our roots. Take yourself out of these labels, take your plant out of the pot, and plant yourself in the unbounded and unlimited soil by the River of Life.

I tell my daughters that they are daughters of the Most High King. That is their only label and that is their validation; anything else is secondary to that. Be careful of what you allow yourself to be labeled as. This does not mean we have to be awkward or rude, but you set the precedent for how you are perceived. If God created us all as equal souls, then choose kingdom over culture. Choose your labels carefully, and always know that Jesus has said you are not a victim of any label, trial, or circumstance in your life.

The hardships, trials, obstacles, or disadvantages in your past were just pressure placed upon you to turn your carbon into a diamond. Without pressure, carbon would never go through the chemical transition to become a diamond. Carbon requires an outside force to apply immense pressure on it to bring to the surface what potential was always deep inside. The pressure of its environment changes the carbon from ordinary and low-priced to unique, hardened, and priceless.

Yes, we still have our culture, we still have our cultural food, and we still have our culture's music and movies that we enjoy. But that is not the end all, be all of who we are; that is just a small beginning of who I am, and it is not my main focus. Constantly grouping and segregating yourself based on race, sex, or economic status is setting yourself to be only perceived as the world divides and labels people.

God created us all equal in His eyes. He does not see our race, gender, and economic status. Man looks upon the outside, but God sees our hearts, minds, and souls. He does not judge us or view us the way the world does. We need to set our eyes on the ways of God, not the earth around us. Anything else that takes our minds off the ways of God is a distraction. We need to see our hardships and discriminations in our past as God's pressure to refine and establish our strength and confidence. Nothing that happened to you was not in God's plan for you. Before you were formed in your mother's womb, God knew everything about you.

It has been said we often find what we are looking for, and if you look hard enough you will always see it, even if it is not there. I believe this is true. If you are looking for discrimination, you will find it. If you are looking for rude people, you will find them. If you are looking for hatred, you will find it. Change what you are looking for, start looking and focusing on the good, and you will find all the good and start noticing the negative less. People may be judging me based on my gender, people may be prejudiced against me because of my race, but I am not expecting, giving attention, or magnifying their actions enough to allow it to even steal a moment of joy from my day.

Now, that judgment they passed on me is on their soul, and they will have to stand before the throne of God and answer for it. I do not have that baggage. I went on with my day, kept my joy, and did not give that person any power over me and my emotions. Our power is in our reaction, and your power is yours. You can choose what you give your power to. If you want to judge me, do it, if you want to gossip about me, do it, but you must justify that to God later. I do not. Stop giving negative mindsets, prejudices, and people your power. God has called us to a deeper understanding of our lives and our purposes.

God equipped us to be more than conquerors. I believe when Satan can keep us in a victim mentality, he can keep us back from discovering the amazing plans God has for us to achieve. His playground is in our mind. If he can control our outlook and our perspective, he can control our future and limit our capability. Romans 8:37 says, "Now, in all these things we are more than conquerors through him who loved us" (NIV).

We all have circumstances that are trying and painful in life. I personally lost both my parents before I was sixteen years old, but honestly, now I can look back and look at the strength and resilience that this painful experience has created in me. God uses every setback and trial as a miraculous set-up for His glory to be manifested in our lives. Every pain brings strength, every trial brings resilience, every heartache brings wisdom, and in every loss there is a lesson. If we change our perspective and change our inner thoughts from "Why did this happen to me or my ancestors?" to "What can I learn from this, and how can I grow?", we will grow and learn so much more, and we will achieve so much more. Sometimes we miss today's joy by living in the angst of yesterday's trial.

Every limitation the world tried to put on me is deemed already conquered by the grace of Jesus. Sisters, I am NOT an orphan; I am a daughter of the King. I am priceless and strong and capable because the Holy Spirit is my victor, and, sis, so are you. Do not let this world and the enemy tell you any different. 2 Corinthians 4:8 assures us, "We are afflicted in every way, but not crushed; perplexed, but not driven to despair" (ESV).

The past world's history and injustices may have an impact on our families, beliefs, socioeconomic standing, or backgrounds, but that does not mean they place a boundary on your future. God has designed everyone's life to always become a consequence of your personal choices. You see this in athletes who come from "bad neighborhoods" but work tirelessly into the night to hone skills and make it into professional sports. You see this in students, who may not have had the best start, who study endlessly, gain scholarships, and soar to heights their peers never dreamed of. You see this in entrepreneurs, when they see certain struggles of limited income and take a step out in faith to earn and build more for themselves without limitations.

This is not luck; this is a plan by God to reward those who work hard and endure. We all have different obstacles and hurdles. How we overcome them is what will determine our success in the future. How we carry ourselves, educate ourselves, and the choices we make in our lives is what will either hold us back or propel us forward.

We all do have individual hardships. We all have different pains, different histories, and different life experiences. If we dwell on the limitations of the sordid history of our races, socioeconomic backgrounds, losses, despairs, let downs, and heartbreaks we will never have a clear vision to see the lessons God wanted us to learn from those things. He wants us to rise above and go further. As 2 Corinthians says, we can be tried but not crushed, we can be confused but not despair. We have hope. If we are breathing, God has victories in our future. You are not done. Your best days are not behind you; they are still ahead of you. Start focusing on that, and you will go further than you could have ever dreamed. Shed those worldly victim labels. Let go of any past discrimination. Know who you are and whose you are; do not let your mindset limit your dreams, anointing, and your potential.

DAILY QUESTIONS:

1. Have you ever accepted any victim statuses that you need to shed?

_____

_____

_____

_____

2. What is your victim status that you realize is a trap from Satan?

_____

_____

_____

_____

3. What do you need to change in your social media or your beliefs system to realign with God's directives and commandments?

_____

_____

_____

_____

DAILY PRAYER:

"Lord, thank You for the Word of God, that even thousands of years later is still so poignant. Lord, I thank You that I was created a conqueror and a victor. Lord, every battle that I walk through, You have already won for me. God, help me to realize that calling myself a victim of any worldly organization comes against what You say about me in Your Word. Lord, You have equipped me with everything I need for my race. Help me to shed the burdensome labels of this world and embrace what You have labeled me as. You have called me anointed, enough, redeemed, desired, special, and powerful — all these through You and Your Holy Spirit. Lord, I surrender my all to You. Change my mind to align with Your Word so that I can become everything You have called me to be. In Jesus's name. Amen."

DAILY FOCUS:

1. Do not label yourself as this world does. God has called you to a higher calling and to higher thinking. Do not limit yourself as the world limits you. You are everything the Word of God says you are and nothing that the world says you are. God has called you a victor, and God has won every battle for you.
2. Shed any label that does not align with what the Bible says you are. You are a child of the King of kings, the God who spins the world in orbit and formed you. You are not just your gender, your ethnicity, your socioeconomic background — you are who God says you are. The Word says that you are enough, able, a victor, Holy Spirit-powered, capable, knowledgeable, wise, anointed, called, and redeemed. Those are your new labels, sister, and those will live far past this earthly world, into eternity.

Day Twenty-Two

VALIDATION IS FOR PARKING STUBS NOT YOUR SELF-WORTH

> "Freedom on the inside comes when validation from the outside doesn't matter."
> RICHIE NORTON

I HAVE HEARD THE QUOTE, "If you live for the approval of others, you will die from the rejection of strangers." This is a true statement. Especially with the rise of social media, people are doing anything for the likes, followers, and attention. We want people to tell us we are beautiful, fit, skinny, smart, accomplished, and any other compliment that validates our worth. As Christian women, we must move past this worldly need for affirmation. We are constantly seeking for people to see all that we do, to tell us we are doing a good job, or we are measuring up to their standard of a "good" friend, wife, or daughter.

Why are we striving to please other flawed humans who may never understand our past or our future? People around us can only see our outward actions and words; God sees our intentions and our hearts. He knows what we think, when we do not say it; He knows our intentions, when we cannot even explain it. Society says, "I just need them to validate what happened," or "I just need them to validate my feelings".... why? What does that really change?

Colossians 3:23-24 advises, "Whatever you do, work heartily, as for the Lord and not for men, knowing that from the Lord you will receive the inheritance as your reward. You are serving the Lord Christ" (ESV).

We are instructed to do everything as if we are serving God. Meaning, if we volunteer at church and nobody notices, we did it for the Lord and He will validate and bless us. If we cook, clean, and take care of our families all day, and nobody says thank you, we did all of that for the Lord, and He sees it and blesses us. If we are constantly giving and pouring ourselves out in our time and our energy, but those around us are never grateful or thankful, we weren't ever doing it for them, we were doing it because God commanded us to. God sees every sacrifice, tear, effort, disappointment, and pain. God validates you, His daughter, in many powerful ways:

- He made you in His image and delights in you (Gen. 1:27).
- He loves you even when you are unlovable (John 3:16).
- God is for you not against you (Rom. 8:31).
- His plans for you are good (Jer. 29:11).
- He has given you unique gifts, talents, callings, and strengths (Rom. 12:6).
- You are the apple of His eye (Ps. 17:8).

When Jesus died for you on the cross, He validated His love for you. When He chose to come to earth, leaving heaven and becoming a lowly human, He was validating you. Sometimes other people, even if it is your parents, siblings, spouses, friends, or children, do not have the understanding and ability to see your efforts and give you the praise you need. But if we are constantly expecting praise from other people and then living in sorrow and disappointment when we do not receive it, we are living in a constant roller coaster of emotions. God desires that we live emotionally stable lives, full of peace and hope. When you release your spouse, parents, kids, boss, or friends from the pressures of constantly validating you, it will extend them grace. You will seek to serve, rather than be served; it will change your heart posture, and you will be more confident and sure of who and whose you are.

The peace of knowing God sees all and God will reward all will release you from the pressure of pleasing people. God has promised to reward us in heaven for every good thing. Why seek the reward on earth? Because it is human nature. We must move past human nature and grow in heavenly nature. You are called to live deeper, think deeper, and give deeper.

If we do things only for other people to praise us or appreciate us, we will tire of doing good for ungrateful people. This is exactly why God thought of having us do good for Him, instead of other people. God knew that if we did all our good deeds for Him, we would never become tired of giving other human beings grace. You need to reset your intentions in doing good things and remember you aren't doing your good deeds, giving your grace, or forgiving others for wronging you for others — you are honoring God by doing this. God will thank you one day. God will tell you, "Well done," one day. Do all your good in the world only hoping for this heavenly response.

There is freedom in becoming totally in control of our reactions and emotions and realizing nobody on earth can take away or add to your self-value that was originally assigned to you by your Creator and Heavenly Father. No person on earth should have the power to minimize or distract you from your goals, value, callings, self-worth, or potential. Just as nobody on earth can empower you, you are empowered by the Holy Spirit only.

Start to speak this affirmation over your life and to strengthen you in case people are trying to insult or put you down: "I am proud to be unoffendable and unaffected. Nobody can offend, upset, or distract me, because my self-worth, peace, joy, and value were assigned to me from MY Creator in heaven and nobody on earth can corrupt this. I, alone, am in complete control of my behavior, attitude, outlook, potential, perspective, and opinions. No other person can add or take value away from me. I am unique, equipped, anointed, and have no desire to 'fit in.' I do not want to act, think, behave, or believe just like everyone else in a lost society today. You and your disbelief, non-support, hate, confusion, or personal dislike have no effect on me, my goals, my callings, my self-worth, or my potential. You are powerless over my destiny. Keep walking your journey, and I will keep learning and leveling up in MY journey. If our destination is not the same, we do not need to travel together. I can still love you from over here."

Sister, Jesus is the well that will never run dry. Every time you begin to doubt yourself, instead of looking for humans to validate you and pick you up and make you feel better, open your Bible, or open this book, and read what God says about you. Humans can not satisfy your soul; only Jesus can do that. The Word says that you are enough, able, a victor, Holy Spirit-powered, capable, knowledgeable, wise, anointed, called, and redeemed. Sisters, you are empowered to run the race that He assigned you, and you can do all things through Christ.

DAILY QUESTIONS:

1. How have you expected other people to validate you or allowed that to determine your self-worth?

_____

_____

_____

_____

VALIDATION IS FOR PARKING STUBS NOT YOUR SELF-WORTH

2. Is there anything about validation that you realize is a trap from Satan?

___

___

___

___

3. What do you need to change or reconsider since God validated you on the cross?

___

___

___

___

DAILY PRAYER:
"Lord, thank You for the amazing love and dedication that You showed when You validated my life and purpose on the cross. God, I am so grateful to be loved and desired by a God like You, who would sacrifice Himself on a cross to show me what I am worth. God, please remove the human desire to be validated by people, and help me to remember my worth is truly what You say it is — and I am Your everything. God, help me to begin releasing my spouse, kids, boss, friends, and everyone else from having to validate me. God, I want all my praise and self-worth to come only from You. You are my all in all, not people. I love You, Lord. In Jesus's name. Amen."

DAILY FOCUS:

1. As your faith grows, so will your emotional strength and self-worth. Sister, you do not need any human to tell you you are special, pretty, or enough. Jesus did that on the cross. He said you were all these things and more. There is such peace in releasing the mere humans around you from validating you.

2. Jesus is the well that will never run dry. Every time you begin to doubt yourself, instead of looking for humans to validate you and pick you up, open your Bible, or open this book, and read what God says about you. Humans cannot satisfy your soul; only Jesus can do that. The Word says that you are enough, able, a victor, Holy Spirit-powered, capable, knowledgeable, wise, anointed, called, and redeemed. Sisters, you are empowered to run the race that He assigned you, and you can do all things through Christ.

3. Start to speak this affirmation over your life and to strengthen you in case people are trying to insult or put you down: "I am proud to be unoffendable and unaffected. Nobody can offend, upset, or distract me, because my self-worth, peace, joy, and value were assigned to me from MY Creator in heaven and nobody on earth can corrupt this. I, alone, am in complete control of my behavior, attitude, outlook, potential, perspective, and opinions. No other person can add or take value away from me. I am unique, equipped, anointed, and have no desire to 'fit in.' I do not want to act, think, behave, or believe just like everyone else in a lost society today."

4. When people begin to be adversarial to you, remember they and their disbelief, non-support, hate, confusion, or personal dislike has no effect on you, your goals, your callings, your self-worth, or your potential. They are powerless over your destiny. Let them keep walking their journey, and you will keep learning and leveling up in YOUR individual journey. If your destination is not the same, you do not need to travel together. You can still love them from your next level.

Day Twenty-Three

WORRY IS A WASTE OF TIME!

"Worry will paralyze your mind so that you cannot formulate a better idea to solve your problem. Be anxious for nothing and rely on God's solution."
JOHN HAGEE

OUR ENTIRE WORLD SEEMS to revolve around worry and anxiety. I remember the "old me," so riddled and overrun with panic, worry, and anxiety that I felt as though I could not catch my breath. I felt stifled and isolated in my stressed mind. I am so thankful for the biblical knowledge and experience that allowed me to escape that repetitive mental torture, and I cannot wait to share it with you.

The world tumbles from one panic to the other. In the first four months of 2020, it went from World War III worries to flu worries to political divisiveness to economic panic to election integrity to COVID-19 panic. If you follow the world's views, there is always something new to panic about and focus on. Are some of these panics real? Yes. But, are they all worth our mental health? No, sisters.

When the COVID-19 saga began, I was flabbergasted at the amount of worry, anxiety, fear, and despair I saw in the world. I was not attempting to be judgmental, but I just did not feel the worry; deep down inside, I was not worrying. I am not saying that I didn't care or take any precautions. I am saying, even when the world around me was inundated with panic, fear, worry, and anxiety, I had practiced spiritual peace for so long, I couldn't even feel anxiety. It was no longer my normal triggered response.

I cannot help but think of when Peter took that legendary step out of the boat. His personal faith was so powerful and intense, and it so pleased Jesus, but can you imagine what an unbeliever looking at him must have thought? Then he gave into the doubt, and instantly began to sink, which made Jesus laugh and say, "Ye of little faith, why did you begin to doubt?" (Matt. 14:31).

During the COVID-19 panic, there was twenty-four/seven panic news and social media coverage. The press had "experts" predicting deaths when in reality, you cannot predict deaths because there are so many deciding unknown factors, including the body's immunity strength, placebo effects, personal health history, etc. The press was panicking and fearful, and it seemed everywhere I went people were fearful, which made them anxious and downright angry. It was amazing for me to experience it, as I had been on the journey of writing this book and living in what seemed an "alternate" calm and peaceful reality.

But I could tell the believers through this pandemic. I met so many people that were at peace and joyful (crazy people like me), and we shared our testimonies, and we strengthened each other in faith. I had strangers reminding me that God is always in control and Christians cannot win souls panicking like the rest of the world. The church must be steadfast; when the world is flailing, a fearful world needs a fearless church for hope.

I am not supernatural, I am not different from you, I am not more privileged, I am not self-righteous — that is not my stance, intention, or my heart. I am a regular woman like you, my sisters. God can change your reality, and you can join me in my "step out of the boat" mentality.

I have heard it said before that "fear not" appears 365 times in the bible. I have not counted personally. That would be one "fear not" command for every day in a year; nothing is a coincidence. Just off the top of my head, there are more than thirty verses I found about worrying.

Philippians 4:6-7 is my favorite: "DO not be anxious about anything, but in everything, by prayer and petition, with thanksgiving, present your requests to God. And the peace of God, which transcends all understanding, will guard your hearts and minds in Christ Jesus" (NIV).

During the COVID-19 pandemic, do you know what my "fear not" mentality looked like? It looked uneducated, it looked careless, and it looked "unwoke." It made my own family mock me and friends think I was insane. Remember, there is a difference between using wisdom and caution instead of dwelling in mindless anxiety and worry. It was to the point where even my children picked up on it, and I was lost about how to explain my outlook, until I read 1 Corinthians 3:18-19: "Do not deceive yourselves. If any of you think you are wise by the standards of this age, then you should become 'fools' so that you can become wise. For the wisdom of this world is foolishness in God's sight" (NIV). And verses 21-23: "So then, no more boasting about human leaders...or the world or life or death or present or the future—all are yours, and you are of Christ, and Christ is of God" (NIV).

These are some loaded verses. These verses literally describe that those who look foolish to the world are truly wise to God and His way. Those who think they are smart in today's technology and "wokeness" look foolish to God, because He alone knows the past, present, and future.

My ten-year-old said something that shook me to my core. He said, "If God knows the future, and He is already in the future, why do we need to worry about the future? He is already there, so He has already solved it all. We just need to live to get from the present to the future." Yes, my son babbles, but there is so much wisdom in his statement. If God has designed the future, why are we wasting our lives worrying about the present or the past?

Sisters, if our mind is Satan's goal and the Bible says he comes to kill, steal, and destroy, why is it he would not steal our joy of today by destroying our peace and killing our hope of tomorrow? This is a life-changing and outlook-altering realization for me and hopefully for you too.

Worry is how Satan keeps our minds feeling busy, while we are unable to accomplish anything. It is a trap, set by the enemy to entrap us and keep us from advancing the directive God has given us. When we refuse to worry, we are defeating SATAN; when we CHOOSE peace over panic, we are fighting a spiritual battle. Sisters, we are not women of faith, who are just meek, quiet, simple minded. We are empowered, warrior women of God who battle Satan and spiritual warfare daily. Every choice we make is a battle, and every decision and word we say is advancing our warfare with the enemy.

Christianity is not just a religion; it is a way of everyday life. It is a relationship with Jesus, a new mindset, and a fresh perspective. When we move past "religion" into mindset and perspective, that is when our spiritual eyes will be opened. We can see the world's society as foolish and biblical truth and predictions as wise. Sisters, we often lament about the signs of the times and the decline of values, but they were predicted. Just like Jesus's death was predicted, both through Scripture and His own warnings from the mouth of Jesus, and yet His disciples, His best friends, could not understand.

We, as women of God, must pray for spiritual eyes, to see that all these things were written. Pray, read Revelations, and ask that God open your spiritual eyes to see that everything going on in the world all points to the truth that Jesus is coming soon. Through the pandemic in 2020, revival has broken out all over the world, and this is definitely a great awakening of the faith. This is resulting in Facebook shares and Instagram posts, even by those who aren't believers. The name of Jesus is being spread viral like never before. Sisters, we are living in powerful times. It is a great time to be alive and to be a believer.

Sisters, do not surrender your mind to Satan and his demons of worry. Claim your mind back for it is your most powerful weapon. God created us with a sound mind, and we must take back everything that the enemy stole from us. It is our commandment. You were made to live and stay in peace; you were made to be steadfast in an ever-wavering world. Sister, you have the power over the enemy of worry. Claim it, decide it, and live it. This peace passes human understanding, but it is an all-consuming peace: "Peace be with you."

DAILY QUESTIONS:

1. Have you ever accepted any worry as a normal part of life, like during the COVID-19 panic?

___

2. Is there any "worry" trending that you realize is a trap from Satan?

___

3. What do you need to change or rethink in your beliefs system to realign with God's peace?

___

DAILY PRAYER:

"Lord, thank You for the peace that You have promised that is SO advanced the world thinks it is foolish. Lord, I would rather be foolish to the world and wise to You. Father, please make peace my state of mind so that the trap of Satan in worrying has no presence in my life. God, I want to be so full of You and Your supernatural peace that fear, anxiety, and worry cannot even fit. Father, I thank You for Your love, redemption, and peace that passes understanding. I love You. In Jesus's name. Amen."

DAILY FOCUS:

1. As your faith grows, so will your peace. When your peace looks foolish to the world, rest assured it looks righteous to God. You are called to be different from the world; the world needs steadfast, strong, stable women of God, not wavering, scared, panicked women. We must stand apart for we are Holy Women of God. Our minds are not on earthly panic but on heavenly peace.
2. Worry is how Satan keeps our minds feeling busy, while we are unable to accomplish anything. It is a trap, set by the enemy to entrap us and keep us from advancing the directive God has given us. When we refuse to worry, we are defeating Satan. When we choose peace over panic, we are fighting and winning a spiritual battle.

Day Twenty-Four

HAPPY WIFE, HAPPY LIFE?

> "Marriage is an ongoing, vivid illustration of what it costs
> to love an imperfect person unconditionally.
> The same way Christ has loved us."
> — UNKNOWN

SISTERS, IF ANYTHING IN *this section in any way convicts you or makes you feel out of place, please remember God knows where you are, and He will fulfill all your needs. Remember, nothing in this study is meant to condemn or ridicule, only to encourage us women back to the way the Bible tells us we should align our thinking. This section is for the wives and single women wondering if marriage is still desired and how it was originally designed by God. Please know, wherever you are in your life (whether you are a single mother, divorced, or anything else), it is a part of God's plan for your life, and you are exactly where you are supposed to be.*

According to the National Survey of Family Growth representatives, PolitiFact.com estimated in 2012 that the lifelong probability of a marriage ending in divorce is 40-50 percent.[6] That is a scary fact. Could divorce be necessary in cases of adultery, abuse, or other extreme circumstances? Of course, but I honestly believe a great number of these divorces may stem from a societal distance from core biblical beliefs in a marriage.

Approximately 40 percent of American children are now born to single mothers. The poverty rate for women-headed families with children was 36.5 percent and 7.5 percent for families headed by a married couple. Those are some hard hitting numbers and statistics by themselves. In 2012, an MIT study found that "fatherless boys are less ambitious, less hopeful and more likely to get into trouble at school than fatherless girls."[7] These are secular studies that show a nuclear family is beneficial and needed by the children of society, no matter what the modern world tries to tell us differently.

I have been married for seventeen years. Now, that is not the most, and some women reading this book may have been married even longer, or never married, or are in a single season. This day is for all women, no matter their marital status. Here's a disclaimer: My husband is a wonderful man and truly my absolute best friend, but every marriage has those couple of things we wish we could change about our spouse. For the first ten years, I prayed earnestly for my husband to change a few things, and alas, I became angry and saw no change. About five years ago, I realized maybe I needed to change. There were shortcomings I had that only I could truly change in myself. I stopped focusing on his shortcomings and focused on mine and changed what I could. My focuses were the way I spoke, my own joy, my outlook, respectfulness, and to tame my tongue.

Within one year of working on myself (staying quiet, becoming meek, being kind, thoughtful, showing agape love, and being respectful, even if I was not receiving those things from my husband), he slowly became what I was treating him like. I learned you must move

---

[6] Erin O'Neill, "Steve Sweeny Claims Two-Thirds of Marriages End in Divorce," PolitiFact, February 20, 2012, https://www.politifact.com/factchecks/2012/feb/20/stephen-sweeney/steve-sweeney-claims-more-two-thirds-marriages-end/.
[7] Mona Charen, "Feminism Has Destabilized the American Family," New York Post, July 7, 2018, https://nypost.com/2018/07/07/feminism-has-destabilized-the-american-family/.

beyond treating others as they are right now, love them as you imagine their best version to be, and they will become that higher version of themselves. It's almost as if you are loving them to the next level! As I did this, my husband grew into the version of himself that I was treating and respecting him as. This has been life-changing for me, I have realized that the life I am living now is what I prayed for then. It took me changing myself for my husband to progress into this version of himself.

Remember, God is a God of opposites. He tells us to bless those who curse us, and love those who hate us. I felt led and began to treat my husband as if he already were exactly what I felt he needed to be, and slowly he became all of that and more. It amazed me that the ways of God are truly the opposite of the world and society. If you want obedience, allow your spouse more freedom, and he will begin to ask for your opinion on decisions. If you want respect, give more respect, and it will draw him closer to you and build a stronger respect for you. If you want more romance, be more romantic, and it will teach him your wants and needs. If you want a loyal husband, be less domineering and critical, allow him to lead and be the man he was created to be, and he will become faithfully loyal to your family as he grows into a strong and loving leader.

Over my seventeen years of marriage, one big lesson I learned was do not degrade him in public. Do not ever speak an ill word against him, even if he is wrong. He will realize the respect you have for him, and he will attempt to match it. If you want a happy home, you can make it a happy home. Make it a place of laughter and joy and grace; no negativity or critical thoughts or being critical. My husband has told me our home feels like the most peaceful place ever, because we, as women, can set the tone for our homes, sisters. Now, I am not the neatest or most organized wife; sometimes with four little ones the house looks like a tornado. It isn't always the appearance that matters as much as the atmosphere.

You may be reading this and scoff, "Not my husband." Remember, if God can turn Saul, who murdered Christians, into Paul, who was one of the greatest apostles ever, what more can He do for you or your spouse? Remember, my husband and I are Indian — one of the most patriarchal societies. Let me tell you, when you sow into God, He can change any heart. Only God can soften hard hearts and right every wrong. This is not manipulation; this is following the way God has instructed us to live, and He will bless our long-suffering and faithfulness.

You must start to change yourself first and look for your shortcomings, and as you work on those, God will mold and mend your partner's shortcomings to become a power couple for the kingdom.

Let me say this, Satan always attacks the things we care for and are invested in the most. For many women that is our marriages, relationships, and children. Now, remember from Day 1, even though Satan will bruise our heels, we are still able to crush the enemy. We, as kingdom women, are given complete power over all of Satan's attacks. We must be able to discern his attacks on our marriages, children, and our family structures.

In current culture, there is an all-out war on women, traditional family values, and traditional parenting. We must realize the biblical way is always better than the trending earthly way. As a wife, you are at war for your husband's spiritual health. As a mother, you are at war for the faith and health of your children's souls. You have an important job, sisters. You cannot take this battle lightly — it has eternal consequences.

In modern society, we have forgotten how to forgive, communicate, endure long-suffering, give grace, be selfless, be kind, give support, and compromise. Society has told women to be belligerent, assertively brazen, independent, and domineering. Society has told men to be weaker, manipulated, and less manly. Society's culture has also told us that marriage is not a necessity in the modern world and being a single mother is a strong, independent, and brave way to raise children. We have demonized men who are strong and manly leaders of their families, and we have scoffed at women who are supportive, kind, meek, and godly. Many marriages on television and movies are portrayed as miserable. They show weak and scared husbands and their domineering, aggressive, nagging, moody, and possessive wives. Sis, we were not created to have dead and dull marriages. Marriages are supposed to thrive and grow in love and joy, not just survive.

It should not be anti-feminist to realize that men and women need each other. In Genesis, we learn that God created women as a helpmate to the man, because it was not good for men to be alone. Women were created with some amazing and unequivocal strengths that are so important to a marriage. We are sensitive, caring, nurturing, yet strong, capable, and determined. A lot of Christian women and men are not taught and, therefore, not living the way the Bible says we should live and run our family unit.

Women are wonderfully designed by God to be nurturing and supportive. Nurturing could be caring for kids, or supportive could mean the wife has a professional career and is the breadwinner of the family. We are not talking about income earning versus stay-at-home wives and mothers. I may make more than my husband sometimes, since we own two separate businesses, but that does not mean I suddenly become the "man" in the relationship. That is a very incorrect way to think.

No matter what, men are hardwired by God to be silent providers; they are hardwired with stresses and worries they usually deal with silently, that we women do not have or even perceive sometimes. Adam was hardwired by God to care for the land and animals and toil and work hard. Women are hardwired by God to be helpmates and raise the next generation (whether through our own children, adoption, ministry, teaching, or mentorship). We also were designed to want to talk and comfort and be social and analyze issues. There are vast differences between men and women, but when we as spouses begin to cover our spouse's shortcomings and weaknesses, this is when we tap into the true joy and strength of a godly marriage. We are created so different, but those differences, when understood, can be a powerful tool for the kingdom.

Today women are told to wait for a "prince charming" and a man who "completes" them. Nobody can complete you; there is nobody who is "your other half." You must be a full person to have a healthy marriage. It is not 50/50; it is 100/100. You must get your worth, validation, and encouragement from Jesus and your Heavenly Father. Society has said marriage is for our spouse to serve our needs, and therefore, a great number of marriages are failing. We, as believers, must reset our mindset to know that we were placed into this marriage to serve our spouse and then serve God together. As a wife, if your job is to serve your husband, and your husband's job is to serve you, and you two are to serve God. This completes the design God created. Is it easy? No. Does it work? Yes. Is it worth it? Yes.

"Most important of all, continue to show deep love for each other, for love covers a multitude of sins" (1 Pet. 4:8 NLT).

In marriage, we need to cover our spouse's shortcomings; this means we do not publicize every way he falls short. We do not post on social media to make others feel sorry for us, and we do not need to let everyone know all the ways he has failed. Sisters, we must cover our partners because God covers our sins in forgiveness and grace, and we need to try to do the same for others. If your husband forgets an anniversary, do not publicize it; simply say it was a great day and keep going. Believe me, that grace that you show him will be repaid to you in a much greater way.

If your husband disrespects you, consider forgiving without him asking, moving on, and leaving that disrespect with God. This does not mean we sweep things under the rug and never address them. Rather, we must learn to let go after it is addressed. Even if he never admits his wrongdoing, that is his sin now with God, for when he sins against you, he sins against God.

We cannot vindicate every wrong. Remember, God is your vindicator. We must realize half the time a word or reaction upsets us, the other person never realizes it even was an issue, and sometimes it was never the intention. If the disrespect needs to be addressed, do it in private in a calm and respectful way. Set your boundaries and explain your feelings and your perception, and allow room for explanation and reconciliation. There is a high probability he will apologize and mean it 100 percent more than if you gave him the silent treatment, bash him with your friends, and treat him just as bad as he treated you. Proverbs 14:1 says, "Every wise woman builds her house, but a foolish one tears it down with her own hands" (CSB).

Build your house with a strong foundation of faith, and do not tear it down with the failing ways of the world. Build your home with love, respect, grace, forgiveness, kindness, and joy and keep it running on these principles. Marriage is still meant to be a God-ordained joining of two individual people's lives together to grow together and fulfill their callings and further the kingdom of God.

We need to realize how God hardwired men and not expect them to not react or act like men, and we need to realize how God made us as women and embrace and grow in how we were created. We cannot spend our entire life fighting the qualities we were created with; we will never achieve our purposes and callings. Embrace the way you and your spouse were created different, embrace the differences, and work at becoming a helpmate.

We are called to be world changers with our spouses; we are not called to have a mediocre marriage in this world. Every marriage God brings into existence is a power couple. You are a power couple. Not a "celebrity power couple" of this world with money and fame, but an even greater power couple for the kingdom of God. You are called to live above the way the lost around you live. Our marriages are to be lights in the darkness.

Our marriages are blessed by God, and we are called to have a holy marriage, not a typical sitcom marriage. We are not ordinary women, struggling and fighting to find our identity and strength. We know that our identity is a daughter of the King of kings, and our strength is in Christ Jesus. We have the answers, and we are extraordinary women of Christ. We are called to a higher way of living. We are called to a different way of thinking and behaving, even if the world around us thinks we are crazy.

DAILY QUESTIONS:

1. Have you ever noticed the negative view the world has of marriage and the nuclear family?

2. What are any godly marriage views you have learned?

3. What do you need to change in your marriage to become a power couple for the kingdom?

4. What do you need to reevaluate about biblical family structure?

_____

_____

_____

_____

DAILY PRAYER:

"Lord, thank You for the creation of a godly marriage and partnership. God, please help me and my (spouse/future spouse) become a true power couple for the kingdom. Lord, help me to unsubscribe to the worldly view of marriage and help me to become the helpmate and friend that my spouse needs. Lord, help me to identify and change what I can change in myself, and help me to work and dedicate true change in my shortcomings. Lord, please make me the wife that I need to be for _____. Help me to be strong where he is weak, and help him to be strong where I am weak. Lord, teach me how to compromise and how to be selfless and gracious. Teach me how to cover his shortcomings so that he can grow into the man of God and leader of our marriage and family the way You designed him to be. Lord, I praise You that we will be a power couple to be light to others around us. In Jesus's name. Amen."

DAILY FOCUS:

1. If you want obedience, allow your spouse more freedom, and he will begin to ask for your opinion on decisions. If you want respect, give more respect, and it will draw him closer to you and build a stronger respect for you. If you want more romance, be more romantic, and it will teach him your wants and needs. If you want a loyal husband, be less domineering and critical, allow him to lead and be the man he was created to be, and he will become faithfully loyal to your family as he grows into a strong, loving leader. If you

want more respect, be more respectful, do not degrade him in public, and do not ever speak an ill word against him, even if he is wrong. He will realize the respect you have for him, and he will match it.

2. Marriage is still meant to be a God-ordained joining of two individual people's lives together to grow together and fulfill their callings and further the kingdom of God. We are called to be world changers with our spouses; we are not called to have a mediocre marriage in this world. Every marriage God places together is a power couple. You are a power couple, not a "celebrity power couple" of this world with money and fame, but an even greater power couple for the kingdom of God.

3. We are not ordinary women, struggling and fighting to find our identity and strength. We know that our identity is a daughter of the King of kings, and our strength is in Christ Jesus. We have the answers, and we are extraordinary women of Christ. We are called to a higher way of living. We are called to a different way of thinking and behaving, even if the world around us thinks we are crazy.

Day Twenty-Five

CLAP BACK AND CANCEL CULTURE: WHERE'S THE GRACE?

> "A Jesus girl who rises up and unexpectedly gives grace when she surely could have done otherwise reveals the power and mystery of Christ at work in her life and in the world."
> — Unknown

IT SEEMS LIKE TODAY'S society is stuck on "clap backs" or impulsively jumping to defend oneself by pointing out others' inadequacies or telling others off if they "need to be checked." This is an actual culture on social media, with certain celebrities or influencers ready to "clap back" on any comment they deem inappropriate or not politically correct. There are women whose entire career and fame is based on being the "clap back queen" and often answer people's opinions and judgments by demeaning and pointing out others' shortcomings, and sometimes mocking others as part of their defense. Yet, they are extremely sensitive to any criticism about them personally, and nobody stands a chance of being "right" with them.

Now, it is not wrong to stand up for ourselves, but we are not ordinary or worldly women seeking validation from others. We are part of a royal priesthood, a holy nation, and heirs to the kingdom of God, so we must walk and talk and act differently. Sisters, it does not matter what the world says about you, only what God says about you.

While clap backs are thought to be witty and woke, they are often pointed and disparaging comments aimed at anyone who disagrees or has a different viewpoint or opinion from you. It can almost be slightly childish in its impulsiveness and defensiveness. It is a new culture of needing to right every wrong, correct every different viewpoint, teach anyone who we believe does not understand, and put down or demean anyone who dares to say anything slightly wrong or misconstrued against you. Clap backs are a huge phenomenon of this generation and today's society, but what could the Bible possibly say about it?

1 Peter 3:9 tells us, "Do not repay evil for evil or reviling for reviling, but on the contrary, bless, for to this you were called, that you may obtain a blessing" (ESV).

We are not called to tell everyone off in a hasty and impulsive manner, no matter how witty and humorous we are. However, this does not mean we are to be punching bags and scapegoats for others' mocking or demeaning. Remember, meekness is not my weakness; meekness is your power through God under complete self-control. We need to be straightforward, respectful, and lay out our boundaries without being impulsive, disrespectful, demeaning, or accusatory.

We are not called to be rude or loud and brazen. We are called to be humble, speak with integrity, and carry ourselves with grace. We do not need to stoop down to other's ground level standards; we need to stay upright on our level and address them as respectful and educated and Holy Spirit-led women. No acting crazy and no cursing; this is not of God. When we take time to pray, God will lead us in how to answer, when to ignore and walk away, when to assert ourselves, and when to speak up to set our boundaries. Stay away from impulsive and instant responses. We need to have God and the Holy Spirit guide us in every situation.

"As for a person who stirs up division, after warning him once and then twice, have nothing more to do with him" (Titus 3:10 ESV).

CLAP BACK AND CANCEL CULTURE: WHERE'S THE GRACE?

The Bible is pretty straight forward about this practice. If someone "checks" or insults you, warn him once, then twice. If his heart isn't open and receptive enough to hear your message, have nothing more to do with them. Now, warning them does not have to be public; it needs to be private. We are not to live like the world, publicly admonishing, shaming, mocking on social media, and I think we have forgotten this. Praising and honor should be public, but correction and admonishing should always be done privately. Public shaming always leads to hardened hearts and hurt feelings. We can build others up in public and strengthen those bonds by correcting them behind closed doors.

I have started to directly communicate with those who offend or judge me. We need to stop allowing small things to fester and become bigger issues or drama. We need to aim to be polite, educated, respectful, and well spoken. We can say something like, "Hi _____. Hope all is well with you. I am trying to be more honest with my feelings, so I wanted to reach out to you. I saw you commented _____. You are of course welcome and entitled to your opinion, but I found your comment (hurtful, accusatory, judgmental). I value you and your opinion, and please next time communicate this type of thing directly to me one-on-one, so we can discuss it in private, not in a public forum where others can judge or misconstrue."

Simple. Concise. Mature. Respectful. Straightforward. Nothing hurtful, nothing shameful, nothing accusatory, just your honest feelings laid out with a clean heart. If that is not respected and the situation, insult, or judgment happens again, then this person is not going to respect your boundaries, and you need to have nothing to do with them further.

Many times we have grown beyond another person's level of understanding. Some people cannot grow to the new levels God is taking you to. We need to stop trying to drag "old friends" with us to new destinations. Sometimes we may be going to our promised land, and they have not earned the blessing of being with us in our promised land.

I really cannot comprehend wasting our emotional energy on a stranger on social media; this is just taking on extra drama and anxiety and stress that is not even assigned to us. Let's see if the Bible has a verse that agrees with this perspective of staying away from unnecessary arguments. 2 Timothy 2:23 warns us, "Stay away from stupid and senseless arguments. These only lead to trouble" (CEV).

Again, the Bible has an answer for every modern question. It is black and white.

Sisters, we all feel this natural innate need to educate or teach those who we think are judging or not understanding us. You cannot teach someone something who is not willing to learn. You cannot force information into someone and force them to see your perspective. You can only truly teach or reach those who come to you humbly with an open heart and mind willing to hear and listen and learn. Sometimes, I think we waste our time trying to get someone to understand why we did or said something instead of inspecting and analyzing first if they are trying to learn or just trying to condemn us. You cannot water someone who does not even have the desire to grow.

Can you imagine how many Pharisees and high priests Jesus could have "clapped back" at in His day? But He kept silent, and He kept walking, and He only reached and taught those who had open hearts and minds to hear. Sisters, stop trying to teach unteachable people. Those who are assigned to learn from you and your testimony will be brought to you, they will seek you out, and they will ask you. God has those who you are supposed to teach. He has your ordained testimony to reach them. You need to stop yelling into the wind, as you are wasting your powerful message on deaf ears. Let God bring your audience to you. Find a quiet, private place, and love them where they are, while your testimony reaches and teaches.

We all have a story, a long story, that begins in our childhood and continues to where we are now. Every chapter, every injustice, every pain, every triumph, every heartbreak, every trial has contributed to the person we are now. Sometimes, especially with social media, people only see the chapter you are on now. They don't see the beginning of the story, and they don't know the whole plot, but they judge you on one sentence of one chapter of your story.

You cannot win against people like this, you cannot require that these kinds of people validate or understand your experiences, and we must stop expecting that people are reading our stories in context. Only God knows your entire story. He knows every word in your story, and that is why only God can validate you. We have to free mere humans from this. We must have grace, forgiveness, and understanding that not everyone is on the same level as us.

Sisters, do not be led by your instant reactions and emotions; instead be mindful that self-control and grace are fruits of the Spirit, and you will be known only by the fruit you show. Sisters, do not lower yourself to the levels of this impulsive world. Remember, your straightforwardness and polite, calm honesty will catch people off guard; it may even offend them. Today's world is not used to eloquent, collected, and respectful dialogue. They are ready to curse and argue and yell, but your calm and classy responses will surprise them. Expect that and do not give into their desperate pull to bring you to their level. God placed you on your higher level, and you need to stay there. Nobody should be able to make you come down to their level. You have been there and moved past it, so do not go back. We are moving forward, never backwards. We are moving forward, and our destination is to become more kingdom-minded. Let's not be distracted by earthly things.

I also wanted to mention another worldly culture that is growing in today's world — cancel culture. This is the "canceling" or ostracizing and destroying of someone's career, business, or reputation based on a decision they make or an issue from their past. We must remember God gives us grace that covers our mistakes. We should be so thankful God does not "cancel" our destiny and blessings because of mistakes in our past. Christianity requires constant growth and progression, not perfection. God's grace is always sufficient to cover our faults, mistakes, and shortcomings.

We must extend this same grace to others. It is not our job to jump on the bandwagon of shaming and destroying others because of their past or present mistakes. Mistakes are part of the process of growth. Be firm in grace, even if you stand alone, and reject this worldly notion of cancel culture. As God's women, we cannot cancel people because of their past or current mistakes.

Everyone is constantly growing and progressing; canceling them would be saying they have no future potential to grow. We need to remember when we come to Jesus, He uses the messy parts of our past to create our powerful message of redemption. Our stains and mistakes are the very things He uses to show His power of forgiveness. Our past is exactly what qualifies us to share our testimonies. Jesus is not looking to punish you for your past. He erases it and forgives it and redeems you with grace. We need to be the models of this kingdom principle on earth.

You are a daughter of the King of kings; you are part of a royal priesthood; you are called, anointed, equipped, empowered, Spirit-led, and redeemed. Sisters, we need to walk differently from the world, talk differently from the world, and think differently from the world. You are called to a higher standard, and we must keep reaching for our Father's way, not for the ways of the world. Remember, choose kingdom culture over worldly culture. Clap back culture and cancel culture have no place in kingdom culture.

DAILY QUESTIONS:

1. What have you noticed about the negative "clap back" culture?

_____

_____

_____

_____

CLAP BACK AND CANCEL CULTURE: WHERE'S THE GRACE?

2. What godly "clap back" views have you learned?

_____

_____

_____

_____

3. What do you need to change in your mindset about reacting to people?

_____

_____

_____

_____

4. Have you fallen prey to cancel culture? How can you have a different stance now?

_____

_____

_____

_____

DAILY PRAYER:
"Lord, thank You for the guidance of the Bible on how to react to insulting or judgmental people. I pray You give the self-control, meekness, and guidance on how to carry myself and either brush off

or react calmly. Lord, help me to remember I am not told to live by the impulsiveness of the world, but I am called to a higher standard of self-control and grace. Please lead me, Lord, and help me to carry myself like a daughter of the King. Help me to hold myself and my reactions and emotions to a higher godly standard. Please help my speech, actions, and emotions to mirror Your love and grace. In Jesus's name. Amen."

DAILY FOCUS:

1. Consider letting their injustice, judgment, or insults go. If it is serious enough to address, do so in a respectful, gracious, and well-spoken way. Always keep in mind, you are a representative of your Heavenly Father, so we must act like it even if it is hard and we are being "tried."
2. Now, it is not wrong to stand up for ourselves, but we are not ordinary or worldly women seeking validation from others. We are part of a royal priesthood, a holy nation, and heirs to the kingdom of God, so we walk and talk and act a little different than the regular woman.
3. We need to be straightforward, respectful, and lay out our boundaries without being impulsive, disrespectful, demeaning, or accusatory. We are not called to be rude or loud and brazen; we are called to be humble, speak with integrity, and carry ourselves with grace. We do not need to lower ourselves to stoop down to other's lower standards; we need to stay upright on our level and address them as respectful and educated and Holy Spirit-led women.
4. We need to jump off the cancel culture bandwagon. If our destiny is not canceled because of our past, we have no right to not extend that same grace to others. This does not mean you become a doormat or allow someone to take advantage of you. You can walk away and pray for them from a distance, but you must not sully or seek to destroy their reputations, career, or life. You must walk away from people with a pure heart and no vindication. This is grace.

Day Twenty-Six

IS YOUR SQUAD S.Q.U.A.D.?

(Sanctified*Queenlike* Uplifting*Anointed*Divine)

> "A good friend shouldn't just be someone to hang out with,
> but someone who encourages and challenges us to
> be more like Jesus in our daily lives."
> — UNKNOWN

I GREW UP BEING TOLD "bad company corrupts good character" and "choose your friends wisely," and I thought this was important for your adolescent friends so you could stay on the right path during a tough and confusing season. But this is still so relevant and important, maybe even more important as adults and believers. Sometimes as adults we desire to be so inclusive and compassionate that we do not properly vet or measure our friendships.

Sometimes we allow people into our inner circle, ignoring their negative traits and tendencies, even seeing it as an opportunity to minister to them. The problem is sometimes you can be holding on to bad company and having people take up space in your life and not have the capacity to accommodate the anointed people God has ordained to take you to the next level of your calling. We cannot be dedicating our time and energy into "seasonal" people who were not even assigned to be lifetime friends. What if this meant the actual lifetime, God-ordained people would not even fit into our lives, because we never made room for them? If people do not understand you, that means they were not intended for this part of your journey. No chasing, no pleading, no hard feelings — just keep moving, God has others in store to take you to the next level.

As believers and women, we need to surround ourselves with people who edify our values and push us into our God-given destiny. We need to let go of naysayers, blessing blockers, and pessimistic people. If people are not building you up and depositing into your destiny, then they are withdrawing and pulling you down to a lower level. Remember when we talked about change and how something that is not growing is slowly dying? It is the same with un-ordained friendships. I am not saying you cannot be friends with someone of a different faith — of course you can — but it is not healthy for them to be the main person you are turning to with problems and advice. The believers' outlook and perspective are not the same as the world's, and your closest confidante needs to know what your value system and goals truly are in the kingdom's standard, not the world's standard. We need people who can speak into our potential, destiny, and push us forward towards our anointings.

God is always propelling us forward and onto new levels; He is a God of constant growth not stagnant comfort. God desires constant progression from us, not perfection! The people God has assigned for your life are supposed to be people who can edify, propel, encourage, and cover you. God has not assigned people who use, drain, deceive, or treat you as less than. God has designed your squad to be powerful for the kingdom not the world. You do not need an entire group of girlfriends to be your squad — you just need a good one or few, you need to focus on quality over quantity.

Sis, you are not ordinary, so your friends cannot be ordinary. If you are focused on the things of heaven, your friends also need to be focused on those things. It does not mean every time you get together it needs to be a religious gathering. You can still have fun and relax, but when you are a believer, your values and goals will be blessed and heavenly, not worldly. It is more about your outlook, perspective, and values than the things you are actually doing together.

"Walk with the wise and become wise, for a companion of fools suffers harm" (Prov. 13:20 NIV).

This verse is a straightforward reminder that we are a product of the people we surround ourselves with. We all want to grow personally, spiritually, and emotionally, and we need to form and nurture friendships with those who have similar goals and values. The sadder part is, however, that also means we must prayerfully and carefully end friendships that hold us back. You may have to walk away from unreliable friends, broken friendships, and people who do not have the same values, beliefs, or outlooks as we do.

Ecclesiastes 4:9-12 says, "Two people are better off than one, for they can help each other succeed. If one person falls, the other can reach out and help. But someone who falls alone is in real trouble. Likewise, two people lying close together can keep each other warm. But how can one be warm alone? A person standing alone can be attacked and defeated, but two can stand back-to-back and conquer. Three are even better, for a triple-braided cord is not easily broken" (NLT).

This passage shows that friends aren't supposed to just be social company, hang out partners, or time-fillers; they were designed to be the people who could stand back-to-back with you to cover you and fight with you and for you as you cover and fight for them. This is a powerful picture. When you stand back-to-back with someone, you can fight what is behind their back and they fight what is behind your back. It is a practical picture of what godly friendship was designed to be. The last part of the passage states, "a triple-braided cord is not easily broken," and refers to a third person in your friendships, who should be God. He has promised when, "two or three are gathered in my name, I will be there" (Matt. 18:20). Therefore, a friend who can pray for and with you will guarantee God will be listening and advancing both friends' growth.

Today's society has re-invented friendships to be my circle, clique, and squad with many friendships seeped in fights, deceit, drama, and gossip. "Girlfriends" today frequently gossip, backstab, hurt, manipulate, and lie to others to further their own personal agenda. This is not the godly purpose of friendships; God made friendships like the one David and Jonathan had in the Old Testament: protective, faithful, loyal, and true.

Today, many friends overshare personal pasts, gossip, and betray each other repeatedly, and this is apparent in all of today's sitcom narratives. We are not called to live in society's standard; we are called to live higher and purer. We are not made to live in gossip, drama, anger, and stress. If your "friends" make you feel any of these negative ways, then they are not assigned to you by God.

Are your friends interceding on your behalf? Are they calling out the seeds of greatness inside of you? Are they pushing you to fulfill your destiny and filling your mind with the things of the kingdom? If not, they are not kingdom friends. They are not the people God ordained to push you into the next level of your destiny. Are your friends pushing you to become a better woman, wife, mother, or worker? If not, then they may be distracting spirits sent by the enemy to hinder your growth and limit your potential.

People who are influential in your life need to feed you spiritually; they need to be part of your journey to your destiny. We need people who see where we have been, see our value, and see where God is leading us in our future. We do not need people who only connect with our past version of ourselves; we need people who see our potential without being jealous or envious. Just like seasons have an expiration date, some friendships also have an expiration date.

We are typically good at attracting people into our lives who want what we have, but we need to begin to attract people who love like the 1 Corinthians love. We need to take ourselves off clearance and put ourselves back behind the glass case where the priceless items go. Sisters, we must remember who we are and whose we are. We must square our shoulders and view ourselves as our Heavenly Father sees us — redeemed, priceless, and anointed. We need to value those who value us not for our bank accounts, job titles, or social standings, but value us for our testimony, anointings, and callings. We need to feed those who feed us; we need to sow into our friends and support, pray, and cover them in their anointing and callings as well.

We are not bandwagon women; we are part of a royal priesthood, a Holy Nation, and heirs to the kingdom of heaven. We were not created to have "frenemies," who are self-focused or lead us into temptation. We are to have friendships that point us towards God, telling us hard truths, with those who are loyal, faithful, and servant-hearted. We were created to stand apart and above and to keep advancing the kingdom culture. Sometimes we need to let go of toxic friendships of the past, not because we are better than them, but because we are called to a higher standard and destiny.

2 Corinthians 6:14 asks, "Don't team up with unbelievers. How can righteousness be a partner with wickedness? How can light live with darkness?" (NLT).

Sis, you are not called to be ordinary; you were designed to be extraordinary. There is an old saying, "Show me your friends, and I will tell you who you are." What story is your company telling? Now, God never calls us to be messy, dramatic, or severe, but you can begin by becoming less available while you filter out what God's direction is for your life and new levels. Slowly become less available as God changes your mindset, and He will draw those who are unhealthy away from you. Do not be hurt or wounded. See every drift away as a shifting in your direction for the kingdom. Celebrate the places God has destined for you. You will conquer NEW territory for the kingdom with your blessed and ordained S.Q.U.A.D. — women who are: Sanctified, Queenlike, Uplifting, Anointed, Divine.

DAILY QUESTIONS:

1. What do you think about the company you are investing in?

_____

_____

_____

_____

2. What godly friendship values should you consider?

_____

_____

_____

_____

3. What do you need to change in your current friendships?

_____

_____

_____

_____

DAILY PRAYER:

"Lord, thank You for the guidance that You give us in the Word on friendships. God, I pray that You will bring into my life those who will edify me and are ordained by You to be part of my journey. God, please cleanse my life and take away anyone who has ill intentions or is toxic for where You are taking me. Lord, help me to not be hurt or hardened against anyone who You remove from my journey. God, please send me companions who share my love and values in Your kingdom. Lord, please make my friendships honorable in Your eyes. Please cleanse my mind, heart, and life. In Jesus's name. Amen."

DAILY FOCUS:

1. We cannot be dedicating our time and energy into "seasonal" people who were not even assigned to be lifetime friends. What if this meant the actual God-ordained people would not even fit into our lives, because we never made room for them?
2. We are not called to live in society's standard; we are called to live higher and purer. We are not made to live in gossip, drama, anger, and stress. If your "friends" make you feel any of these negative ways, then they are not assigned to you by God.
3. We were not created to have "frenemies," who are self-focused or lead us into temptation. We are to have friendships that point us towards God and tell us hard truths, with those who are loyal, faithful, and servant-hearted. We were created to stand apart and above and to keep advancing the kingdom culture.

Day Twenty-Seven

"WHY FIT IN WHEN YOU WERE BORN TO STAND OUT?"

(-Dr. Seuss)

> "She doesn't follow the crowd and she doesn't fit the mold because being like the world is not really her goal. Her trust is in the Lord, and she longs for much more than anything this world could ever have in store."
>
> UNKNOWN

IF YOU PICK UP any magazine or read any blog, you can find article after article of how to fit in with different groups and cliques. All children, and especially teenagers, hate being isolated and mourn standing out at all. I was the same. Looking back now, I am glad I was taught that I was important and loved by Jesus as a child, because that held a lot of my self-worth together through those difficult years. I now, as a mother, aim to teach my children that we were all created by God to stand out. We must be able to teach our children that standing apart from the crowd is something to be proud of.

God has designed us as unique, and He has set us apart from the rest of the world. Our validation does not come from friends, being popular, or being accepted by society or the world. Our validation was established when Jesus deemed us important enough to die on the cross for us. In fact, many of the girls I envied in school for being popular, looking at their lives now, I would not want to trade paths with them. What seemed "acceptable" or "cool" in school led to a lot of bad life choices and a difficult life as an adult.

"If you belonged to the world, its people would love you. But you don't belong to the world. I have chosen you to leave the world behind, and this is why its people hate you" (John 15:19 CEV).

I love when the Bible addresses a subject in a straightforward and blunt way. There is no guessing — the Bible tells us that if we were like the rest of the world, the world would accept us and love us. But, if we are living for God, they will not understand or accept us, and they may even hate us. They hated Jesus because He was unconventional and living in a higher mental and spiritual realm. Sis, you are not ordinary, and you were not created to be ordinary. That is a blessing, even if it feels isolated or lonely sometimes. We need to evolve to a mindset of not even wanting to fit into society anymore, where we have no desire to "be like everyone else" because we know we are called and destined for greater things. When we sacrifice a biblical directive or commandment to try to fit in or we take a step we know is not of God just to have others accept us, we are giving up some of God's guidance and blessings. We are called to stand firm, not to waver with society. You cannot be an earthly follower and a kingdom leader at the same time.

God tells us we are required to do things and live a life different from the world. Remember, we are called salt and light. We are commanded to not conform to the ways of the world, but peer pressure and fitting in are difficult forces to resist. Nobody wants to feel like we are on the sidelines not having fun, but, sis, living God's way, you will never lose out. The peace, joy, and fulfillment that comes from choosing God's way will always trump any "fun" or "acceptance" the world and society has to offer. Living our lives in God's way instead of the world's way will become less of a chore once we realize this.

The world goes looking for one validation to another, one high to another, one loving feeling to another. God is steadfast and continual. We do not have to search for "inner peace;" we are given it at salvation. We do not have to seek validation, find ourselves, and look for love; we are given all of this and more by our Heavenly Father. Even if the world's way looks carefree or fun, the world is living in darkness, and we are children of the light. Even if the world looks free-spirited and enjoyable, that worldly road always leads to destruction, depression, unfulfillment, and despair.

We must be different from the world, or how will we reach them? How can we be lights in the darkness to the world if we are living just like them? If we give into worry and anxiety every time the world does, how is our faith on display? If we get upset and angry at every mishap, how are we modeling grace and love?

Paul tells us in 1 Thessalonians that we are "Citizens of Heaven, living on earth." In plain language, we are to live in the world but not act like the world. Remember, if you are salt and light, you cannot dilute salt, or it will lose its saltiness, and darkness cannot overcome the light. We cannot continue to shrink ourselves, our values, and our destinies for the world to understand and accept us.

Kingdom living will result in us being above the world's thinking and understanding. The ways of the Lord are always higher than the ways of the earth, as heaven is above earth. We must find our peace about being different. We need to practice this, until standing out from the world makes us more confident. I rejoice when people say I am different; I am happy that I do not "fit in" with the "normal" women cliques of women my age. Honestly, we do not have values, beliefs, or goals in common, because I am chasing something different. If our destination is not the same, then our journey will not fit together. There are kingdom principles that the people living in the worldly mentality cannot even see, let alone comprehend. Remember, it does not require animosity and hate to level up; it requires kind distance and loving, slow separation.

The Bible tells us truth, while, since the beginning of Genesis, the enemy tells us lies. The society of the world today tells us a lot of lies that contradict the truths in God's Word. Now for some hard truths:

(1) God called us to lead moral lives — while society tells you that

sexual promiscuity is feminine freedom and empowering. God calls us to be pure of body, mind, and heart. God tells us sex is sacred to marriage. No matter what society twists and changes, the Bible is steadfast and everlasting. Is that a necessity or does premarital sex cancel your salvation if you found Jesus later in life? No — we can be pure of mind and body from salvation forward; God forgives the past. Living life in a biblical, moral way will be "weird" to the world. Today's culture is full of women degrading themselves, oversexualized celebrities, and proud promiscuity. These are not biblical; therefore, we cannot agree with, promote, or follow these trends. I have been shamed for only being with one man. I have heard I am "naive, inexperienced, and don't know what I am missing." It was not my job to defend, answer, or shame this person, I simply smiled and walked away. Is it unique and different? YES. But is it naive? NO. I am priceless, and you must be invested in me through marriage to gain access to me, because I am set aside as part of a royal priesthood. I am not easily attainable (there's a mindset shift for you). I don't care what the world says; this is also the way I am raising my daughters. If this is not your story, that's okay, sis. Just like the story of Rahab and the Samaritan Woman, Jesus's love and grace is always enough to cover anything in our past. He wipes our slate clean, but you must NOW live a life that shows how much Jesus has changed you.

(2) God calls us to be faithful, humble, kind, and convicted — while society tells you to be self-centered, empowered, brazen, and politically correct. The Bible is one of the most straightforward religious texts there is; there are no gray areas. The Bible tells us to love everyone and not judge them, for judgment is the Lord's, but it says we will be judged. Therefore, we must know what we believe because we will be judged for our sins. Do you know what you believe? More than that, do you live what you believe? Society changes every day. What is acceptable now was not acceptable ten years ago. In the '50s or '60s premarital sex was not "normal" or "acceptable." Now being a virgin is shunned and even mocked. Society pushes us to be more free-minded, wealthy, influential, and woke, but it never explains the crab barrel mentality that people use to gain these things. People today will climb and step on everyone who is disposable on their way

up. This is not the way of the Bible. The Word tells us to be humble, servant-hearted, and kind. Stand firm and convicted in your beliefs, do not mock or judge others, and simply live your truth.

(3) God calls us to opposites. Love those who hurt you, bless those who curse you, forgive those who condemn you. We all know society's thoughts — if someone insults you, clap back. If someone hurts you, hurt them more. If someone curses you, curse louder and stronger. These are not the ways of God, and our entire belief system is based on being opposite of the world. Sis, if Jesus could forgive those who were killing Him while He was hanging on the cross, if He could pray and intercede for them in that moment, is anything too much for us to do? If on the Thursday of the last supper, knowing fully the betrayal and pain that lay ahead, Jesus still gave thanks, can't you give thanks in this moment you are standing in? We must strive for more. The world says to always hit back, or better yet, hit first, but this is not the way Jesus taught us. We must live above the world, we must think above the world, and we must focus above the world. We cannot be like the world — we were commanded to be the opposite of the world.

I will be honest and transparent with you; I have no desire to fit into the regular world anymore. I have shed the desire to be like everyone else. I no longer want to shrink myself to fit into society's preconceived boxes. I have accepted that my Heavenly Father has called me to higher standards and better peace. Does it feel lonely sometimes? Yes. Is it frustrating that others do not understand my perspective? Yes. But we need to realize the unbelievers around us cannot comprehend our way of life, callings, and convictions. Until they find Jesus for themselves and feel His calling to a higher standard, they cannot even begin to understand your reasoning or actions. Do not waste your time, energy, or testimony defending yourself or condemning them. Instead know and live your truth and let your love win them over.

I use this analogy of eagles and chickens often with my children (I grew up on a chicken farm). Think of the eagles. Their DNA predestined them to soar at an altitude that the chickens on the ground of the earth cannot even fathom. All chickens really do is peck at the dirt and peck needlessly at each other. Watch chickens for a few hours: they literally fight constantly, peck at the dirt, eat, poop, and run in circles. Imagine if an eagle were to lower their mental level and begin to peck at dirt and stay on the ground level of the chicken. First, they would look ridiculous, but more importantly, they would never soar to the heights that God designed them to live in. God designed us as eagles. There are heights that we can discern and soar to that those on the ground level or "earthly" level cannot even see, let alone begin to understand. As eagles, we cannot hate the chickens, but we must keep our eyes laser focused on our level so that we can become all God created us to be. We were created to soar like the eagles, not peck like the chickens.

I want you to join me here, because this place is stress-free, peaceful, joyful, and steadfast. There is no anxiety, no worry, no pressure. I no longer must stress myself out with keeping up with the Joneses, keeping up to date with political correctness, or aligning my thinking to the ever changing things the world and society tell me are important. You cannot jump on any bandwagon, support every cause, and agree to every lifestyle. You are called to stand firm on the strong foundation of the Word of God, love others, and allow your love to attract them to the kingdom. You are an eagle not a chicken.

I have the Word of God as my only standard, and it addresses any question I have. I am validated by Jesus Christ only. I am accountable to God only, and I know what my focus and goals are. I am just passing through this earth on my way to my heavenly home; this earth is not my home or my goal. I love being "strange," I love my peace that passes understanding, I love my joy the world cannot comprehend, and I love standing out.

Will you join me? Will you leave the ever-shaking, wavering world behind, and join me on the steadfast foundation rock of God? He was the same yesterday, today, and forevermore. Girl, do not shrink yourself to fit into other people's boxes. We are eagles, so let's soar together, sisters!

"WHY FIT IN WHEN YOU WERE BORN TO STAND OUT?"

DAILY QUESTIONS:

1. When have you felt the pressure to fit in?

___

2. How does knowing you were created to NOT fit in help release some pressure on you?

___

3. What do you need to change in your current mindset or perspective?

___

4. What do you now understand about kingdom versus worldly mentality or eagle versus chicken mentality?

___

___

___

___

DAILY PRAYER:
"Lord, thank You for seeing so far in advance that the Bible would cover subjects like peer pressure and societal pressure and fitting in. God, thank You for creating me unique and set apart. God, it does take a lot of strength and resilience to be comfortable not fitting in and being "normal." God, I want a life that is set apart for You. I want to be everything You have called me to be and nothing that You have not assigned me to be. God, give me the strength and determination to be comfortable with what I believe, and send me my squad that will bring me into alignment with heaven's goals for my life. Help me to keep being salt to this unsavory world and light to the darkness around me. In Jesus's name. Amen."

DAILY FOCUS:
1. God has designed us unique, and He has set us apart from the rest of the world. Our validation does not come from friends, being popular, being accepted by society or the world; our validation was established when Jesus deemed us important enough to die on the cross for.
2. You are not ordinary, and you were not created to be ordinary. That is a blessing, even if it feels isolated or lonely sometimes. We need to evolve to a mindset of not even wanting to fit into society anymore, where we have no desire to be like everyone else because we know we are called and destined for greater things.

3. The ways of the Lord are always higher than the ways of the earth, as heaven is above earth. We have to find our peace about being different. We need to practice this, until standing out from the world actually makes us more confident.

Day Twenty-Eight
WHAT KIND OF MOTHER ARE YOU?

> "Motherhood is not a competition to see who has the smartest kids, the cleanest house, the healthiest dinners, the nicest clothes....Motherhood is YOUR journey with YOUR children."
> — HOT MOMS CLUB

IN TODAY'S ULTRA-PUBLIC AND competitive society, modern motherhood has become some twisted competition. Just like we all have different personal stories, experiences, and perspectives, nobody's marriage or parenting can be the same. Even if you are not a mother yet, this day is still for you. We all play "mothering" roles even if we are not mothers, sometimes to friends or the young women we can influence for the kingdom.

We need to get back to the basics of motherhood and take all the guilt, shame, insecurities, and pressure out of it. Being a mother is stressful enough. We need to stop trying to live up to the other "perfect" mothers' images on social media or in mom groups. We need to stop caring who is judging or shaming or even silently giving us the side-eye. If we raise our children God's way and impart God's Word and give them an example, we are pleasing God.

You did not just get "these" kids by accident. God assigned your children to you because only you can guide and parent them. The Bible first tells us about the first mother — Eve, who was a true, equal partner to Adam. Although she had her faults and made some mistakes, she took care of her spouse and dedicated her life to the Lord's will and purpose. There is an abundance of Bible stories and verses about mothers to prove that godly women are strong, resilient, kind, loving, and filled with faith. Let us explore a couple verses about mothers in the Bible. Proverbs 31:28-29 says, "Her children rise up and call her blessed; her husband also, and he praises her: 'Many women have done excellently, but you surpass them all'" (ESV). Proverbs 31:26 tells us, "She opens her mouth with wisdom, and the teaching of kindness is on her tongue" (ESV).

The Bible describes mothers as calm, faithful, wise, and kind. It is their assigned mission from God to pass down these qualities to their children and everyone in their circle, and we are to honor and praise them for doing so (and listen to them). Obeying and honoring your mothers and fathers is the only commandment that comes with an attached promise: "So your life will be long." It is the only thing God commanded us to do, where He bluntly promises us it will benefit us in the long run here on earth. One of my favorite verses in the Bible is Proverbs 22:6: "Start children off on the way they should go, and even when they are old they will not turn from it" (NIV).

Mothers, be assured. If you teach your children the love and Word of God from the beginning of their lives, they will be faithful to God as they grow up. Then, they will pass down their love for the Lord on to future generations. This will be your powerful legacy as a mother. Sometimes we get so tied up in not seeing the results of our tiring labor now in the present, and we get discouraged and depressed if we are not seeing the results. We must remember when you plant a seed, you must water it and tend to it, long before the roots begin to grow, and you see a tiny sprout. I believe the faith of our children is the same as that little seed; it will bloom in its assigned time. On those hard days when the kids won't obey, get along, or try your patience, remember every seed takes time to grow. Just because your children aren't displaying the things of God you have taught them right now, it doesn't mean those seeds you planted are not taking root and will not blossom later.

Momma, those kids they are taking in everything you are sowing into them, and they will blossom in God's time — not ours. Keep sowing, keep planting, keep watering, because your children are good soil, and those lessons will blossom into more than you could ever dream or imagine.

Listen, now let's be real. Do us mommas lose it sometime, give everyone cereal for dinner, and show them off to bed so we can just breathe after a stressful day? Yes. There are some really hard, tiring days. Moms can have off days and lose their patience. We are human. Even Mary lost Jesus when He was twelve years old. But we need to know that God always forgives our shortcomings, and He is our strength when we are weak. We need to let go of guilt of not being good enough, because we all fall short of the glory of God at some time or another. If you have a hard day with your kids, embrace that, admit it, and pray over them as they sleep. Even tell them, "We had a hard day today, but we will try harder tomorrow." There are days we all want to run away, but hold on momma, there is always sunshine after the rain. The fact that you did not run away is something to be celebrated, too.

The next thing godly mothers need to do is stop looking at other moms. It is not healthy. One of the fastest ways of discouraging yourself and getting trapped by the sin of envy is by comparing yourself to others. Social media has set this trap for us as moms, and it can be so painful if we fall for it. God has a specific plan for you, and you will not accomplish that plan by looking at others.

2 Corinthians 10:12 assures us, "Of course, we would not dare classify ourselves or compare ourselves with those who rate themselves so highly. How stupid they are! They make up their own standards to measure themselves by, and they judge themselves by their own standards!" (GNT).

That is very straightforward. We must stop comparing ourselves to other moms or wives, immediately. Most mothers who present themselves as put together and perfect are usually crumbling underneath. We cannot make up our own standards to measure if we are succeeding or not. The biblical standard is the only one that really matters.

Everyone has multi-faceted lives, yet with the rise of social media we get to see only the chosen, edited, photoshopped, and best parts of everyone. But we often compare all the facets of our lives to the best parts of their lives, not seeing their downs and messy parts. We know our messy parts. We know our laundry pile, unwashed dishes, sibling fights, and we take those into consideration when we compare ourselves to the best part of Insta-moms and Pinterest-moms. That is not healthy or encouraging.

I have a good friend who I follow on Instagram. I know her and her children, and I see and love their messy parts at times. But online she looks like she is Martha Stewart and Joanna Gaines all in one super momma. I would be jealous and envious if I did not know the messy parts. I know the messy parts, and it makes me relate to her and love her more. We need to stay in our lanes, walk our own path, and focus on our own assignments. When you start looking beside and behind you, you will slow down. What you see online, in magazines, and in parenting books are opinions, not necessities. Stop overanalyzing, stop comparing, stop contrasting, and stop putting yourself down, because your kids are not their kids. You are on your own individual journey with your children, and they were assigned to you from God Himself. Let go of that pressure.

The next part is letting go of mom guilt. A lot of this guilt can come from comparing, so if we can fight that attack from the enemy, it will help. But stop being guilty of things you did or didn't do. Think about what your main goal is as a mother. That is your own personal goal, and now this and only this is your focus.

We are human. These unique kids are born, and they do not come with an instructional manual. We must recognize from the time we are born that Satan has his eye on conquering our beliefs, minds, and ultimately our souls. Every stress and pressure on you as a mother and every pressure on your child is an attack from the enemy and every choice is a battle won for either the enemy or God. If you focus every stress and disagreement as a spiritual attack and know that Jesus has given you victory over the enemy, then my sister, you can defend yourself and children against every attack of the devil.

Whether it is disobedience, lying, dishonesty, bad company, peer pressure, or addiction, it is all spiritual attacks to get you and your children away from God. Stand against it. You are empowered through the Holy Spirit to overcome any attack from Satan. Condemn and speak against all the evil things and speak to the seeds of holiness and goodness in your children — God has called you to call out the greatness in them.

You are a victorious, blessed, Holy Spirit-powered, anointed, equipped, strong, redeemed mother. You are not a worldly mother, wandering around social media for compliments, likes, and validation. Momma, know who you are and whose you are and stand firm that these children were assigned to you by God because only you have what it takes to raise them. You have no condemnation, no guilt, no comparison, no depression, no anxiety in Jesus's name. You are more than a conqueror. Momma, go in the grace of God, go in the strength of Jesus, and go in the peace of the Holy Spirit. Go and be the momma God has called you to be; ignore every judgment, comparison, and negative comment, and focus on your goal for your children. Forgive yourself for the tough days and let God be your strength when you are weak.

DAILY QUESTIONS:

1. When have you felt "mom guilt"? Do you now realize it is an attack of the devil?

_____

_____

_____

_____

2. How do you feel knowing God has assigned your children to you?

3. What do you need to change in your current mindset or perspective on mothering?

DAILY PRAYER:
"Lord, thank You for these children You gave me. Thank You for equipping me for this journey with my children. God, please take away the need I have to compare myself to every other mom and what they are able to do. God, help me to realize that I am not them; I am exactly who You called me to be. Help me to solely focus on my life and my destiny; help me to block everyone else's negativity, judgments, or comments out, because I want only to please You. Lord, help me to plant seeds of godliness in my children, and help them to take root and bloom and blossom and flourish in Your perfect time. Help me to work hard to sow and have the patience to see them grow, even if it is not in my timing. Lord, make me a mother of Proverbs and help me to follow the path of Your Word. Help me to stay my course, focus on

You, and chain myself to the steadfast Word of God. In Jesus's name. Amen."

DAILY FOCUS:

1. You did not just get these kids by accident. God assigned your children to you because only you can guide and parent them. Even when it gets tiring and disappointing, dig in deeper to how equipped you are to mother these children.
2. These unique kids are born, and they do not come with an instructional manual. We must recognize from the time we are born; Satan has his eye on conquering our beliefs, minds, and ultimately our souls. Every stress and pressure on you as a mother and every pressure on your child is an attack from the enemy, and every choice is a battle won for either the enemy or God.
3. You are a victorious, blessed, Holy Spirit-powered, anointed, equipped, strong, redeemed mother. You are not a worldly mother, wandering around social media for compliments, likes, and validation. Momma, know who you are and whose you are and stand firm that these children were assigned to you by God because only you have what it takes to raise them. You have no condemnation, no guilt, no comparison, no depression, and no anxiety in Jesus's name.

Day Twenty-Nine

RUTH: LOYALTY AND FAITH LEAD TO ABUNDANCE

> "Be a Ruth, loyal in all your relationships, walk the extra mile,
> and don't quit when things get tough. Someday you'll see
> why it was all worth the effort."
> — THE BEAUTY BARN

THERE ARE ONLY TWO books of the Bible named after women, Esther and Ruth, and there are only five women important and influential enough to be mentioned in the genealogy of Jesus Christ, and one important one is Ruth.

Let us review the summary of the story of Ruth. She married and lived in Moab with her husband, his brother, and her in-laws. We are told that her father-in-law, brother-in-law, and husband all died. Her sister-in-law, after a little persuasion, decided to go back to the country of her family, from which she came. Naomi, her mother-in-law, decided she would also go back to the land of her family, and she instructed Ruth to leave and go back to her parents' home. Ruth was adamant that she would not leave her mother-in-law to fend for herself. She literally argues and follows Naomi to a foreign land that she has never been to. They travel and settle into Naomi's homeland, and remember, Ruth does not know anyone in this foreign land. She begins to glean grain from the vineyards of a rich man, who happened to be Naomi's distant relative.

Long story short, Ruth went from gleaning the leftover wheat of Boaz, the wealthy landowner, to him noticing her loyalty and beauty and him marrying her. She was a widow, and in that day getting married again and having children again was a far-stretched dream. She was one of the five women mentioned in the genealogy of Jesus, and her son Obed was the grandfather of King David. From her loyalty, love, and kindness to Naomi, she became part of a long legacy of royalty that produced the Messiah. There is a "faith through hard times" element in Ruth's story. It would have been easy for her to accept her future as a widow and gone back to her parents' home defeated and probably looked down upon, but she didn't.

Naomi, Ruth, and Orpah were all widows. Some parts of the world still are not kind to widows today and being a widow was even more difficult back then. In fact, Naomi encourages both girls to go back to their parents and find new husbands who can take care of them. Ruth refuses, and she does not choose this easy option; even in her heartbreaking pain of losing her husband, she chooses to take care of, follow, and obey her mother-in-law. She chooses to go to a country that she knew nothing of, leaving all she knew behind her. She walked into an uncertain situation full of faith and loyalty.

God rewards those of us who are faith-filled, and He will reward our difficult steps of faith. Ruth went from gleaning fields after the wheat was cut, like the poor widows do, to owning the very field she once begged from. Our God is a God of sudden promotion. He will force doors to open and put us in positions we sometimes don't expect or deserve. He will suddenly shift dimensions in our life, and if we are faithful, our circumstances can change in an instant.

Another lesson from Ruth is the fact that there is always hope even in our most hopeless and devastating times. It is difficult to lose a child or husband or parent, but it is these times that our hope and faith in God, who promises restoration, is most important. Our God

RUTH: LOYALTY AND FAITH LEAD TO ABUNDANCE

is not a God who takes away and does not give back; He is a God of double portions of complete restoration. Remember the story of Job. Even though he was tested, he kept a strong and unshakable faith in God, and though his own wife told him to "curse God and die," he decided to stay the course. God also restored Job's wealth, his family, and his health, not back to the way it was before, but two times better than before.

Ruth lost her husband, and she mourned him. The power of her story is that she kept her focus on the things she could control, she kept the faith, and her faith was rewarded with new love and new blessings. Sometimes we tend to have faith until something bad happens, and then we lose our faith because of a trial or hard time. This is the natural human response, but our God requires we keep our faith through the hard times. We all will have our faith tested in different ways. Ruth didn't choose to live in her loss and allow herself to dwell in depression. She sought joy and healing and taught us what matters is how you walk in faith during the hardest trials.

A great saying is: Your faith level determines your blessing level. We see this time and time again in the Bible. When Jesus healed, He often said, "Your faith has made you well." It isn't always about the miracle being performed, and then we have faith. It is about having the faith that produces the miracle as a result. We must realign our way of thinking like this: I will have faith for the unseen miracle, and my faith will produce the miracle.

Sometimes we could shed anxiety or worry if we just held tightly to faith. Whatever you are facing, remember this, God has already worked it out in your favor in the spirit realm. Meaning, God has your solution already set in place; you just need to have the faith to walk it out in the earthly realm. Faith is taking the first step out of the boat, knowing you have never been able to walk on the water before, knowing science says there is no way humanly possible, but still stepping out of the boat.

This immense faith takes practice. It is just like building a muscle, so for it to become stronger and stronger, you must constantly work on it until it becomes a habit. Faith is not something you store up for a rainy day; it is a muscle that needs to be used and strengthened every day to keep it activated and healthy.

The third amazing thing about Ruth was her obedience to Naomi. As grown women, it is hard to be obedient to those in authority or older than us. Of course, there is always the exception for distracting people or toxic family members. In the story, Ruth constantly went to Naomi for advice and guidance, but then she did what her mother-in-law advised her to do. We must be able to discern if those in authority are advising us in a biblical way, and if they are, we must be able to take good advice. Remember, if someone is confirming something that is biblical, it may be that God has sent them as guiding confirmation. Let us remember Ruth did not know the customs in this land she was unfamiliar with, so she allowed herself to be advisable. Ruth did as Naomi instructed her to, and it placed her in the right places at the right time, and with a respectful demeanor, that drew Boaz to her spirit.

Start viewing the hard times or the troubling trials as an opportunity to strengthen our faith and work it out, not a time to give up to anxiety, worry, and defeat and let it weaken us. Only through perseverance do we truly discover our real strength. Start viewing the trials as opportunities to show Jesus you have faith that He has already given you victory over the circumstances. Jesus has said you are a victor, you are anointed, and He has you in the palm of His hands no matter what you are facing. You are not alone, He is carrying you through, and you are not limited by earthly possibilities. The one who owns it all is holding you.

Sisters, embrace this. Be loyal in your faithfulness to others, trust God even in the hard times, and remember God will replace everything the enemy took from you. Allow yourself to be advisable by godly counsel and always keep a teachable spirit. Choose to be a Ruth, and you will be blessed beyond measure and your legacy will produce greatness. You will look back and see that your greatest setbacks were actually setups for God's greatest blessings.

DAILY QUESTIONS:

1. Now that you know that every setback is a divine setup. Are there any past setbacks you can make peace with or see God's hand at work?

_____

_____

_____

_____

2. What are you struggling with now where there can be a release of pressure knowing God has already made provision in the spiritual realm?

_____

_____

_____

_____

3. What do you need to change in your current mindset or perspective on faith?

_____

_____

_____

_____

DAILY PRAYER:

"Lord, thank You for revealing the power in the story of Ruth to me. Help me to practice my faith daily, not to just accept defeat or anxiety about my circumstances. God, please help me to zoom out and see the bigger picture and have the faith that it will all connect in the future. God, I ask that You give me loyalty like Ruth to follow the ordained path set before me, so I can reach every destination that You have laid out for me. God, help me to seek out divine appointments You have ready for me to walk into in the heavenly realm. Lord, I ask that You give me the immense faith of Ruth to step into the unknown, knowing You are holding me up, and my feet will not hit a stone. God, strengthen my faith through the hard times, believing You have gone before me to make crooked ways straight. In Jesus's name. Amen."

DAILY FOCUS:

1. It is in the most difficult times that our hope and faith in God who promises restoration is most important. Our God is not a God who takes away and does not give back. He is a God of double portions of complete restoration.
2. Whatever you are facing, remember this, God has already worked it out in your favor in the spirit realm. Meaning, God has your solution already set in place; you just need to have the faith to walk it out in the earthly realm. Faith is taking the first step out of the boat, knowing you have never been able to walk on the water before, knowing science says there is no way humanly possible, but still stepping out of the boat. This immense faith takes practice. It is just like building a muscle, so it becomes stronger and stronger.
3. Our God is a God of sudden promotion. He will force doors to open and put us in positions we sometimes don't expect or deserve. He will suddenly shift dimensions in our life, and if we are faithful, our circumstances can change in an instant.

Day Thirty

GOD WILL TAKE YOU DOWN TO LIFT YOU UP

YOUR PLAN:

GOD'S PLAN:

SOMETIMES LIFE JUST IS unfair. Things fall apart, our hearts get broken, and we struggle to go on. If you are in that season, I see you, and I know it hurts. I have been there and still go there sometimes. When you don't get the promotion you want, people lie or gossip about you, you get fired, a friend walks away, or a relationship falls apart. Those things hurt, but I want to offer you a perspective shift.

We are going to summarize the story of Joseph in the Bible — you know, the guy with the colorful coat. We think the Bible is filled with boring old stories, but sometimes the Bible is better than a soap opera. Follow this dramatic story: Joseph was his father's favorite son (and his father made it known). His father gifted him a very colorful handmade coat of many colors, which made his brothers jealous. Then, one day, God gave Joseph a dream. In the dream, he saw a metaphor for him being king, with his brothers all bowing before him. He told his brothers the dream, and this obviously did not go over well with his brothers.

He went to visit his brothers in the fields one day, and they were overcome by jealousy. They ripped his coat off and threw him in a pit. Then a few hours later, they took him out of the pit and sold him into slavery. They lied and told his father he was dead. He was taken as a slave into Egypt, where he was a servant in the house of Potiphar, the pharaoh's right-hand man. He did so well there that Potiphar made Joseph the chief of the house, and he oversaw all of Potiphar's business. Things went well there, and he had favor, and God was with him.

Joseph was a handsome man and Potiphar's wife set her eyes upon him, demanding he sleep with her. When he refused, she lied and said he raped her though he did not touch her. Potiphar had him thrown into prison. But the Lord was with him. In the prison he served so well, the warden put him in charge of all the prisoners, and he had favor. He was known to have the ability to prophesy and to decode dreams, and when other inmates get released, he begged them to remember him when they were in society. They let him down.

Later, Pharaoh was tormented by nightmares. The warden remembered Joseph, and he was brought up to tell Pharaoh the meaning of his dream. Famine was coming, but Pharaoh was being warned by God so he could prepare. Pharaoh saw the favor on Joseph, and he was placed as the most powerful man in Egypt next to Pharaoh. Then his brothers came because the land they were in dried up, and they were presented to none other than Joseph. They didn't recognize him, and he sent them back for their father, and he fed, clothed, and cared for them in the palace.

See? Soap opera storyline, right? And people say the Bible is boring.

I am going to show you that God has designed every pitfall in your life as a launching pad. He has created every heartbreak to mold your mind and teach and develop you. It is our perspective that disqualifies or discourages us from moving forward.

The first point of this story is that Joseph shared his dream. Sometimes God calls us, gives us a word, a dream, or a prophecy, and we are so excited we begin to share that word. We tell everyone what we are working on, we explain to everyone in detail what God said. Is it bad to have a calling and be excited? No. But sometimes we need to do like Mary did, and "hide these things in our hearts." That passage from Matthew literally means she took the information personally, believed it, and kept it quiet in her heart and mind.

Sometimes I think we can make others jealous by telling our dreams. Now we don't have to be incognito, but I think there is power in a word given to you by God and you quietly work to manifest it without needing the validation, encouragement, or praise from others. We need to be about our business and building our anointing and conquering new territory without blabbering to everyone around us. There is wisdom and strength in quiet humility.

As for the second point, Joseph knew God said he would be powerful. God gave you a word, He told you a calling, but when you look around this does not look anything like the word you got. Sometimes we set in our mind what our destination is supposed to look like, and we get so upset and heartbroken when we aren't where we thought we'd be by now. There is anxiety and stress and letdown in this thinking. When we become believers, the hardest thing is to accept that God has a plan and posture our hearts and wills to walk in the way He is guiding us.

You need to serve well where you are today. Joseph knew he would be in a position of power, but he became a slave. I can imagine him thinking "God, you said I would be powerful, but I am a slave, sold into slavery by my own brothers." How easy would it have been for him to develop a bad, ungrateful attitude? What if Joseph did not "serve" well in those positions? When he went to Potiphar's house, he quickly was recognized for serving well, and he was favored and promoted. What if he decided he was a victim, and this was unfair and had a bad attitude and did not serve well? His destination would have been altered. In every pitfall Joseph faced, he has one thing that always remained: he was favored by God. Listen, if you are a child of God, you have favor everywhere. You do, and you need to serve like it. You can be at a job you don't like, or you could be in a situation you don't deserve that seems like a mishap, but you need to serve well where you are today.

We are not in these places by accident; if it came to you, it is part of God's plan. You can choose your heart's posture and be the best version of you, regardless of the environment or circumstances. Joseph served well in Potiphar's house and in the prison, and those bad places were his steppingstone to his destiny. Attitude and outlook matter the most. Stop viewing your situation as unfair or yourself as a victim. You are where you are, you came from that side of town, you had that dysfunctional family, because God needed you to walk through those situations to form that part of you that needed to be recognized and strengthened through those adversities. Where we disqualify ourselves is seeing these things as our downfall or disadvantages; then we get discouraged and we camp out and choose to live in turmoil in the place we were just made to walk through. Stop living there; pack your stuff up. You must keep moving, you must serve where you are well and grow from it. This is a rest stop, not your destination.

God's plans don't look like our plans. Joseph probably had a neat little plan book written of how he would become powerful. That plan probably did not include being put into a pit, sold into slavery, put into prison when things were just getting better, and then being lied about and gossiped about. What if God had Joseph's brothers sell him into slavery because he would have never left his father's loving house otherwise? If he never went to Egypt, his whole family would have died in the famine. Only through him going to Egypt and having his ups and downs was he finally placed in a position where he could rescue his family and care for his father and brothers during a time of death and disease. Even when things do not work out the way we want them to, we have to remember, it is part of God's plan.

Joseph's life was as up and down as you can get. It was unstable and rocky, but God put him in a position he was not guaranteed by birthright. He was not even Egyptian to have been eligible for such a high position. But through the bad treatment of his own brothers, God propelled him to his destiny in the palace. When someone walks away from you, when you get furloughed or laid off, when you do not get the business deal, free yourself from anxiety, and embrace it as God's plan. Keep your attitude positive and your eyes focused on Jesus. That is the only way that you will keep moving towards your destiny.

People Joseph loved condemned, betrayed, gossiped, accused, imprisoned, stabbed him in the back, and let him down all through this story. Yet, he still had favor, he was still promoted, and he still lived in the palace and fulfilled his destiny. Sis, it doesn't matter who revolts against you and what they do. When the favor of the Lord is upon you, the adversity will not prosper in the long run. We need to stop magnifying the negative naysayers and those who do us wrong. We need to magnify the destiny we know God has called us to. Whatever the enemy brings to you, he cannot thwart God's plans for you. God will use every situation in your life and flip it around for your promotion and His glory. We need to stop writhing in these misdeeds people do to us. If God took them out of your life, view it as a blessing; He is removing bad company. Your strength is in your resilience.

God is a God of opposites; He will take you way down to push you way up. He wants to see your heart's posture in the downtimes though. Will you praise Him even in the pain? Will you surrender to Him even in the confusion? Will you serve with a clean heart to the best of your ability even if this season is not what you thought it would be? Will you keep that word you got hidden in your heart even if this does not look like what He said? God wants to see your faithfulness; He wants to see if you have intense faith, to step out of the boat and take that first step. Sis, you have a calling on your life. No matter where you came from, what you did, what others did to you, and what you are walking through, your destination is still ahead of you. Your best days are ahead of you, and you have not missed anything. Surrender to what God's plan is for your life and stop interjecting your ideas and your plans. The beautiful thing about God's plan is He knows the future and all the adjoining details, and He is always working to knit them together. God is right there down with you in that place. His favor is still upon you. Keep your heart posture humble and serving. Even if the place you are in is not deserved, God will bless your faithfulness, and He will propel you forward suddenly.

DAILY QUESTIONS:

1. In Joseph's story, have you ever considered the lows God took him to, only to raise him to a position of great power later? How does this correspond to our stories?

_____

_____

_____

_____

2. What do you now realize about the journey of the plans God has for you?

_____

_____

_____

_____

3. What can you take comfort in during the low parts of your story?

___

___

___

___

DAILY PRAYER:

"Dear God, thank You so much for giving us the promise of the story of Joseph. Help me to take comfort; for every low in life, You have a blessing in store for me. Lord, help me to serve well and walk confidently through all the low parts of life, so that I can receive everything You have for me. God, help my heart not to harden during the tough times in life, help me to keep my eyes focused on You, and keep my faith strong. Please help me to remember and take comfort in the fact that You will finish every good thing You have started in me. I stand ready to serve well in every season You bring me into. In Jesus's name. Amen."

DAILY FOCUS:

1. Sometimes God calls us, gives us a word, a dream, or a prophecy, and we are so excited we begin to share that word. We tell everyone what we are working on; we explain to everyone in detail what God said. Is it bad to have a calling and be excited? No. But sometimes we need to do like Mary did and "hide these things in our hearts." That passage from Matthew literally means she took the information personally, believed it, and kept it quiet in her heart and mind.
2. We are not in these places by accident. if it came to you, it is part of God's plan. You can choose your heart's posture and be the best version of you, regardless of the environment or circumstances. Joseph served well in Potiphar's house and in the prison, and those

bad places were his steppingstone to his destiny. Attitude and outlook matter. Stop viewing your situation as unfair or yourself as a victim.

3. God is a God of opposites; He will take you way down to push you way up. He wants to see your heart's posture in the down times though. Will you praise Him even in the pain? Will you surrender to Him even in the confusion? Will you serve with a clean heart to the best of your ability even if this season is not what you thought it would be? Will you keep that word you got hidden in your heart even if this does not look like what He said? God wants to see your faithfulness; He wants to see if you have intense faith to step out of the boat and take that first step.

Day Thirty-One

RAHAB: FROM PROSTITUTE TO HERO

> "Jacob was a liar. Moses was a stutterer. Gideon was a coward. David was an adulterer. Rahab was a prostitute. Esther was an orphan. Balaam's donkey was...well, a donkey. Yet God used each one to impact His Kingdom."
>
> UNKNOWN

RAHAB WAS IN THE land of Jericho before the Israelites occupied the land. She and her family operated a tavern on the city wall (the outer wall was where the poorer population lived), and she was known as a "lady of the night" in a city that was full of idolatry and lawlessness. However, there is more to the Bible story of Rahab — so much more. Rahab recognized the God of Israel as the one true God, not the idols her country worshiped. She trusted and feared the God of Israel. She told the two spies sent into Jericho that:

> I know that the Lord has given you the land, and that the fear of you has fallen upon us, and that all the inhabitants of the land melt away before you. For we have heard how the Lord

dried up the water of the Red Sea before you when you came out of Egypt, and what you did to the two kings of the Amorites who were beyond the Jordan, to Sihon and Og, whom you devoted to destruction. And as soon as we heard it, our hearts melted, and there was no spirit left in any man because of you, for the Lord your God, he is God in the heavens above and on the earth beneath. (Josh. 2:9-11 ESV)

Rahab recognized that the God of the Israelites was the only true God. God always prepares a way before we even get there. The people in Jericho knew about the God of the Israelites before the Israelites even got to the city and they were fearful. They were not fearful of the people of Israel, but the God of Israel. Rahab's heart was attracted to the power of God, because in worshiping idols, she never saw them actually do anything for the people. *God will open doors, soften hearts, and prepare a way, even before you get to where he is sending you.* Rahab was planted in a place where she was instrumental for the purpose of God, before she even knew what her purpose was.

Rahab's faith is an example to all of us that *God can use all of us, no matter what our history is.* Sometimes, we allow our complicated history to disqualify us from what God is calling us to. When God calls us, we tell Him excuses: We are not strong enough, we don't have enough resources, we don't have the right degrees, we don't come from the right side of town, we are not the right ethnicity, we aren't married, we aren't financially ready. We tell God all the reasons why we are not qualified to pursue our purpose.

Let me present a fact to you — God does His best work in the areas where we are weak. If you were fully qualified for the things God called you to, then you would do your calling by your own strength; God wants you to bring the glory to Him through His strength. Think about almost every story in the Bible. God does amazing miracles, and He does extraordinary things through the most ordinary and unqualified people. Nothing in your history can hold you back from what God has called you to. I have heard it said, "God doesn't call the qualified; He qualifies the called." If He has called you to it, do not let the enemy

RAHAB: FROM PROSTITUTE TO HERO

tell you all the ways you are not qualified. Those same weaknesses are what God will use to propel you towards your destiny.

Remember, Satan's battleground is our mind. The number one way he can hold us back from being our full potential for the kingdom is in convincing us that we are not good enough to fulfill our callings. He tells us lies like, "You are not good enough," "You have messed up too much in the past," "You are not qualified," and "You are not strong enough." Today, you need to rebuke those lies — and anything that tries to disqualify you from the callings that God is directing you toward. We need to stand firm against every lie and attack from the enemy. Do not let him have any power over your mind and your self-belief and abilities. We need to be protective over the thoughts in our minds. God has not brought you this far to leave you.

Rahab was a well-known poor prostitute, living on the wrong side of town. She came from a family who ran a tavern, a den of sin, and she was living the moral-less life she was raised in. Yet, none of that prevented God from using her for His purpose and fulfilling her potential as a believer. Because she believed in God and remained planted in her faith, she was on the right side of God, she and her entire family were spared and welcomed into community with the Israelites. The gratitude one of the spies, Salmon, felt for Rahab grew into love, and God's grace erased her former life of shame, and he made her his wife. It is mentioned in the Bible that he was one of the princes of one of the tribes in Israel. Sis, God took Rahab from being a shameful, poor prostitute to being a princess of one of the most prominent tribes of Israel: Mother to Boaz, great grandmother to King David, and mentioned in the lineage of Jesus! There is no limit to where God can propel you if you choose to stand in faith and abandon your past.

Another thing that is learned from the story of Rahab is the fact that she was a natural caretaker of others. When she knew Jericho was going to be stormed, she begged not only for her life, but that the lives of her parents, brothers, and sisters be spared by the Israelites, as well. The spies told her to hang a scarlet cord out of the windows, so they would know which houses to spare. Scarlet was the color of shame, and it was the same color that ended up saving their lives. It is funny how God can use the exact things that represent our sordid and shameful past to propel us into the glorious new future He has set apart for us. Remember, our tests will become our testimony and our messes will become our message.

It does not tell us in the Bible that Rahab's whole family were believers, yet, for her sake, God spared her entire family. Sis, it only takes one person, one woman, to bring about the salvation of entire families. It only takes one woman to set a new legacy for generations to come. Out of Rahab's faith, her entire family was welcomed into one of the most prestigious Israelite families. I am sure that they saw accepting love and salvation for themselves, but what if Rahab had never taken that leap of faith, of hiding the spies and helping them sneak out of the city? What if she was too scared? Her entire family would not have been saved. Are you standing in the gap for anyone in your family's salvation? If you are, stand firm. It only takes one faithful and strong woman to change all the lives connected to her.

Sometimes, as women, we minimize the effect that "one woman" can have. Not only did Rahab save her *entire* family from the invasion of the Israelites, but she also took a risk to hide and save the Israelite spies. Rahab, for all her faults, was a brave and courageous woman. She stood for what she believed in and took a brave risk even when it was not easy. Rahab decided not to continue to be a victim of her poor circumstances and prior bad choices. She decided to change her mindset and take a stand, and it changed and redeemed the rest of her life. Every day we can choose to change the world by the way we interact with the people around us, whether it be our family or the strangers we encounter.

It is a little scandalous and eyebrow-raising that a woman like Rahab is named in Jesus's family tree. Rahab may have chosen her questionable profession from a place of deep childhood trauma or abuse that left her self-worth determined by pain or shame. Maybe Rahab had been abandoned and made a desperate choice just to survive and eat. Night after night may have become a negative life pattern she probably never intended to choose. What lying thoughts did Rahab hear from the enemy? Condemnation, fear, shame, worthlessness? Was it too many mistakes, too much regret, and way too late for her to try to change?

RAHAB: FROM PROSTITUTE TO HERO

The good news of Jesus is that no bad choice we've ever made — no past is too shameful, no substance too abused, no evil words spoken over us, or amount of abuse — can keep us from the saving grace and forgiveness of Jesus Christ. We are anointed, enough, called, redeemed, forgiven, equipped, empowered, and called through the salvation of Jesus. All of our prior scars do not disqualify us from our purpose; each day is the chance for a new beginning.

I think it is telling that Matthew went out of his way to list Rahab and four other women in Jesus's genealogy, just to show us we all play an important role in God's plans. I believe Matthew saw firsthand how Jesus valued women and chose to include them in His ground-breaking ministry. I believe, as kingdom women, we all can fulfill every calling of God in our life no matter what we have done or been through in our past. In fact, God will use your story for His glory. Walk in that truth today.

DAILY QUESTIONS:

1. Have you ever considered how important Rahab was to the Israelites' victory over Jericho?

_____

_____

_____

_____

2. Have you realized before how sordid her past was, yet how she was

placed in a place of honor, redeemed, cherished, and remembered? How does this give you hope?

_____

_____

_____

_____

3. What can you do now, not allowing your history to limit you?

_____

_____

_____

_____

4. Are there any negative life patterns you want to change? How can you begin today to change them?

_____

_____

_____

_____

DAILY PRAYER:
"Dear Lord, I ask that You remind me daily that I am a new creation in You. Lord, no matter what the _____ (sin,

shame, regret, etc.) in my past has been, I am forgiven, redeemed, and pure in Your eyes. God, thank You for Your redeeming and cleansing love. I ask that You use everything in my past to teach me and help to allow letting go of _____. God, I ask that You help me to break the limits in my mind that my past dictates my future. Thank You for allowing anyone to further the kingdom, no matter where we have been in our pasts. I love You, Lord. In Jesus's name. Amen."

DAILY FOCUS:

1. Rahab's faith is an example to all of us that God can use all of us, no matter what our history is. Sometimes, we allow our complicated history to unqualify us from what God is calling us to. When God calls us, we tell Him, we are not strong enough, we don't have enough resources, we don't have the right degrees, we don't come from the right side of town, we are not the right ethnicity, we aren't married, or we aren't financially ready. We tell God all the reasons why we are not qualified. Let me present a fact to you — God does His best work in the areas we are weak.

2. Sometimes, as women, we minimize the effect that "one woman" can have. Not only did Rahab save her entire family from the invasion of the Israelites, but she also took a risk to hide and save the Israelite spies. Rahab, for all her faults, was a brave and courageous woman; she stood for what she believed in and took a brave risk even when it was not easy. Rahab decided not to continue to be a victim of her poor circumstances and bad choices. She decided to change her mindset and take a stand, and it changed and redeemed the rest of her life.

3. Sis, it only takes one person, one woman, to bring about the salvation of entire families. Are you standing in the gap for anyone in your family's salvation? If you are, stand firm. It only takes one faithful and strong woman to change all the lives connected to her.

Day Thirty-Two

RACISM AND OUR BIBLICAL RESPONSE TO IT: PART 1

> "The closer the people of all races get to Christ and His cross, the closer they will get to one another."
> BILLY GRAHAM

> "At the heart of racism is the religious assertion that God made a creative mistake when He brought some people into being."
> FRIEDRICH OTTO HERTZ

THIS IS GOING TO be a real day, a transparent, God-convict-our-hearts kind of day, because it matters, on earth and in the kingdom. Let me first state — I am not on a specific side. Many authors write about this topic being on one side or another side; I am strictly on the biblical side. There are no hidden agendas, and there are no biases from where I stand; I am aiming at an unadulterated, biblical perspective. I am half white, half "colored." My ethnicity is from a "very colonized" former British colony. I understand all sides.

But above all of what I claim to be, I am a Christian, and that comes first. Kingdom over culture at all times.

Yes, there are many cultures who have been disenfranchised, discriminated against, and left behind, some much more than others. Yes, they may still be struggling, angry, hurt, and feel victimized. My heart hurts for them; every oppression and every single loss of life is grieved by God and myself. But Jesus always brought all people to the table, He interacted with all people, and He was the great equalizer. He approached every person as relatable and worthy, and this is the aim I take in my life daily. I aim to love them where they are and pull them up out of their pain, and I will say there is hope and there is a better way, and His name is Jesus.

We cannot make progress if we keep reliving the atrocities of the past. We must keep healing, moving, and improving. We must keep creating change around us, one person at a time. Jesus is the hope to the hopeless and the conqueror to the imprisoned. He is the rock on which we can all build from. I know there is a past hurt for some races. I empathize — my grandparents were impoverished indentured servants of the British brought to the Caribbean from India, as one step above a slave. I get it. But I do not hurt from it. I have healed and want to reconcile all races together with God as our third cord.

For one of the first times during this study, I will tell a part of my story. I believe when you are disenfranchised, it can build silent strength. I was born in an inner city and my grandparents decided they wanted to move south to the countryside. So, I ended up being raised in the rural country on nearly three acres of farmland. As a light brown (as I called myself) five-year-old, I began in a school that was all white children. My parents never told me I was different, so I never knew I was different.

I began school and was quickly introduced to literal KKK children. I didn't assume this — their parents were literally KKK leaders in our area. They wore it on their clothes, bumper stickers on their trucks, and it was posted on their properties. It was not hidden. Over the years, our front porch and lawn were lit on fire, our mailbox was smashed in over six times, and our car windshields were shattered. Our car trunks were hammered with crowbars. I was even kicked, slapped, and spat on. I was even forced off the road while driving, and they called the cops on us every now and then "just to check" if we were illegal (I was born in the States). I lived in this country town for eighteen years of my life (until I got married), and I was treated like this for all twelve years of school. It did not change, but I did. My heart got hard. I mean, they hated me, so I began to hate them, too. Fair is fair. Listen, it was hard, it was not fair, and I didn't deserve the way they treated me. My life went about as normal. I did not think I was racist or prejudiced. I was just reacting to the way I was treated and predetermined to guard myself from being hated again.

Then one day, as He always does, God convicted me, and I went on a long journey to discover what I am going to share with you. It was painful, I cried, I mourned, and I grew. But sisters, this change of heart, has to begin with the CHURCH. Jesus told us we had to go into all the world and preach the gospel. How can we win them for Jesus if we are not even talking to the lost? This is a complex issue, so over the next two days, I will be making some specific points that have allowed me to heal and grow from my past hurt and resentment.

POINT ONE - KINGDOM CULTURE COMES FIRST. EARTHLY CULTURE COMES LAST.

"When anyone is in Christ, it is a whole new world. The old things are gone; suddenly, everything is new!" (2 Cor. 5:17 ERV).

Sisters, when we accept Christ, we are told this verse. This means when we get saved, we leave the worldly things, thoughts, mindsets, perspectives, and feelings behind. It is like they have died; they are to be forever gone. But these are replaced with heavenly things, so we must develop heavenly thoughts, mindsets, perspectives, feelings, and visions.

That alone was my strongest conviction. Our theme in life, in every situation, must be "kingdom over culture." We cannot truly be a new creation if we do not let go of our past prejudices, hurts, notions, and ideas. I shared my story because the way I was treated was not fair and I had every earthly right to be upset. However, Jesus redeemed me, and I am now a new creation in Him. If my old life is dead and I hold onto this hate, then I am truly not a new creation. My old hurts, prejudices, and beliefs were not of God; therefore, I had to let them go. Remember, if it is not of God, it is of the world. There is no gray area. Jesus said time and time again that we cannot live kingdom-minded with one foot in the world and one foot in our faith.

"Set your mind on things above, not on things on the earth" (Col. 3:2 NKJV).

Jesus did not come just for the Jews — He came for all the world. Even His disciples did not understand His ministry's aim to all people. They thought the Messiah would overthrow just the Roman emperor and free the Jewish people, but His aim was to redeem all people to Himself. We need to align ourselves with this idea. We need to begin to care about all the people around us daily.

Our personal culture is neat and fun; we love our food, music, and language. We do not have to completely lose these unique qualities to be kingdom-cultured. It means these things add to the uniqueness of our kingdom's culture. My skin color cannot go away. I will always be brown, and you will always be your skin color, but I can choose my first culture to be Christian. I can cook and eat our food and listen to our culture's music, but my views and actions must align with the kingdom. If God looks at the hearts of men, I must begin to judge people of their characters and their hearts, not their skin color. I have taught my children I do not care about what your friends are. I care about where they are going and who they put their faith in. You can truly become "colorblind" if you are living kingdom-cultured.

POINT TWO - HEAVEN WILL NOT BE SEGREGATED.

Every Christian's goal is heaven. When we get to heaven, we will have glorified bodies. We are going to be one multitude of saints, all praising God together in unity, the way God originally designed humanity to be, before the first sin.

Revelation 7:9 tells us, "After this I looked, and behold, a great multitude that no one could number, <u>from every nation, from all tribes and peoples and languages</u>, standing before the throne and before the Lamb, clothed in white robes, with palm branches in their hands, praising God" (ESV, underline mine).

This imagery paints a picture of a crown of unified saints, not a crowd of White people over here, and Indian people over there, and Black people over there, and Jewish people over there — WE WILL BE ALL TOGETHER IN ONE ACCORD or purpose. Our job is to be the ambassadors of heaven here on earth, to be examples of Christ's character here on earth. If Jesus served all, saved all, and showed grace to all, how should we be treating all people? God designed us to all live in unity as humankind before the fall of man. He designed us to live in heaven on earth, but sinful nature intercepted this. With Him sending Jesus to redeem us back to our sinless and faultless nature through His blood, we have the ability to live like it is heaven on earth. The church cannot be divided by race, ethnicity, or skin color; if it is, then it is falling for the spirit of division from Satan himself. Jesus went to every city, and He stepped out of the social norms for a Jew in His day. He was perfectly Jewish and perfectly kingdom. If the kingdom needed Him to step out of His earthly culture to help further the kingdom, He was Spirit led and did so. He modeled on earth how heaven was designed; He came to redeem all people.

Even in the Lord's Prayer Jesus prayed, "Our Father who art in heaven, Hallowed be thy name, Thy Kingdom come, thy will be done on earth as it is in heaven." As God's anointed women, we are to be the light to the world, not to just the White world, not to just the Black world, not to just the Hispanic world, not to just the Asian world, but to the whole world. No matter what race you are, you were created to make a difference. God created you; He did not make a mistake. He designed your skin color, hair texture, and eye color, and you are exactly what He intended you to be.

DAILY QUESTIONS:

1. Have you ever allowed the spirit of division to prevent you from loving all people?

_____

_____

_____

_____

2. Now that you understand anything that seeks to divide people is an attack from Satan, what can you do about it?

_____

_____

_____

_____

3. What do you understand about how God designed us to live with one another?

_____

_____

_____

_____

RACISM AND OUR BIBLICAL RESPONSE TO IT: PART 1

4. Do you have any prejudices you need to acknowledge and grow from?

_____

_____

_____

_____

DAILY PRAYER:

"Lord, thank You for creating us all as beautiful, different, and unique human beings. God, I ask that You help me to begin to live here on earth, as in heaven. Help me to see all people as you see them. Help me judge based on only people's character, not earthly attributes and labels. God, I ask that You open my spiritual eyes to love all people how You love them. Help me to broaden who I reach out to daily based on grace not race. Lord, please help me to be light and love in this dark and hateful world. Help me to stand out as an equal opportunity friend, no matter who I come into contact with. Please help me to see the world through kingdom focuses, not earthly labels. Thank You. In Jesus's name. Amen."

DAILY FOCUS:

1. There are many cultures who have been disenfranchised, discriminated against, and left behind, some much more than others. Yes, they are struggling, angry, hurt, and feel victimized. My heart hurts for them; every oppression and loss of life is grieved by God and myself. But Jesus always brought all people to the table. He interacted with all people, and He was the great equalizer. He approached every person as relatable and worthy, and this is the aim I take in my life daily.
2. We cannot make progress if we keep reliving the atrocities of the past. We must keep healing, moving, and improving. We must

keep creating change around us, one person at a time. Jesus is the hope to the hopeless and the conqueror to the imprisoned; He is the rock on which we can all build from.

3. We will all be together in one accord in heaven. Our job is to be the ambassadors of heaven here on earth, to be examples of Christ's character here on earth. If Jesus served all, saved all, and showed grace to all, what should we be doing to all people? God designed us to all live in unity as humankind before the fall of man. He designed us to live in heaven on earth, but sinful nature intercepted this. With Him sending Jesus to redeem us back to our sinless and faultless nature through His blood, we have the ability to live like it is heaven on earth.

Day Thirty-Three
RACISM AND OUR BIBLICAL RESPONSE TO IT: PART 2

> "God created our skin tones with beautiful variety, but all of our souls are the same color."
> DAVEWILLIS.ORG

I KNOW THIS IS A tough subject, and it can be uncomfortable and convicting, but I think it is one of the areas of this study where instead of changing just our personal perspective we can begin to change the world around us. We can make a difference if we work through the uncomfortable convictions and stand firm on the Word of God. In today's devotion time, we will be looking at two more points, so let's jump back into this difficult subject so we can start to change the world around us.

POINT THREE - YOU BRIDGE THE GAP. YES, Y-O-U.

It is uncomfortable being uncertain. It is hard to step out of our comfort zones and interact on different levels. But it is necessary and important. WE must be the change, not because of our race, but based on God's grace. If racism or prejudices still exist in your surroundings, that means it is an opportunity for you to be light and salt, like we have talked about before. We are to be in the world, but not of the world; therefore, we must take a firm stand and engage others.

Sounds like a big and complicated job, right? Let me tell you a secret I learned while managing commission retail sales: the best opening line is a compliment. I have engaged others by saying, "Your earrings are so cute," or "Your hair is stunning." Almost every time the person is so caught off guard that they stumble in finding a response back. If they do, I will say, "I know, people don't compliment each other these days, but I just wanted to tell you how cute your _____ is." If it is uncomfortable, you can compliment their car, shirt, child, dog, cat, anything; you must find a way to break the ice. And for the other one percent that ignore me, give me an attitude, or a dirty look, do you know what I do? I smile, and as I walk away, I pray for them, for God to heal their hearts and soften their minds so the next time a saint approaches them, they will be open. I played a part, and I do not take it personally or give up because a few people do not react the way I want. Some people have had such a tough life; it will take the teamwork of a few saints' positive interactions to open their hearts to dialogue.

Do not target one race or type of person to interact with. I believe this will result in you missing some people you may overlook in trying to find the person. Instead, interact with everyone put in your path. The cashier, the cart guy, the crossing guards, children, stressed out moms, teachers, coworkers, janitors, police, CEOs, neighbors. You need to pay attention to the people placed in your path every day. Our God is a God of divine appointments. Begin to imagine each person you meet as a test or opportunity God gave you to leave a positive impression. It can be a compliment, conversation, or a quick genuine smile and a "have a blessed day." We can start deciding every day, in small ways, to begin to interact with people outside of our "social norms."

If it comes to you, it is your battle. Whether you are Black, White, Hispanic, Asian, Indian, European, Middle Eastern — whoever you are

— you, as a believer, are assigned this. Do not wait for someone else to do it because you are "owed" it. You do it because God overlooked your sin and gave you grace, so you must pass it forward. Christianity is an individual belief, meaning that every soul is individual and will be judged as an individual. Christians cannot continue to segregate and have a group think mentality. We must hold ourselves accountable for the actions we take as individuals. Once you are comfortable with the people placed in your path daily, we can start being intentional, which is the next point. The world's politicians and elite will keep any division alive because as long as there's division, people will be distracted and easier to control. Be aware you do not fall into this trap of division from the enemy.

POINT FOUR- STOP POSTING AND START GOING.

A lot of times we talk about race, racism, prejudices, wrongs that need to be fixed, and gaps that need to be bridged, but how do we start? What do we do? We need to stop talking and start going. Remember, we are not called to be social activists; we are called to be godly women of action. Do not just post the moving picture or emotional video with a famous quote. Get up, girl, and go.

In the story we studied of the woman at the well, Jesus went to Samaria intentionally, found His divine appointment, approached her, spoke to her, interacted with her, and then reached her soul with love and no judgment. This opened a door for Him to minister to an entire city that would have been overlooked by typical Jews in that day. Our Jesus, He came for the bad side of town, and He came for the good side of town because He came for every side of town. He crossed the railroad tracks and talked to "those" people, and He bridged an over five-hundred-year cultural feud between Jews and Samaritans in one day. He used Jews and Samaritans in parables to prove this to us too. Jesus waited at the well and sent the disciples for food because He had a divine appointment with this woman. Not only a Samaritan woman, but a woman whom the Samaritans did not even respect; she was the most undesirable citizen of an undesirable city. She was the worst of the sinners, yet He respected her. He reached her where she was, empathized with her, and He pulled her up to His level with the love of Christ. What a powerful example of what we should be doing!

Here are a few things you can investigate doing to make a real difference. Find a ministry you can support; maybe do a homeless feeding or volunteer at a shelter on "that" side of town. Do some mentoring talks at a mentoring center, or volunteer to tutor at a public school. Get into the community so you can show them Christ's love. It takes one positive interaction with someone different, and it can change a person's perspective for a lifetime. Be that person. Do not sit on social media, complaining and demanding change if you are not willing to personally take a brave step in faith and do something tangible to make a difference. Peter could have thought about how cool it is to walk on water like Jesus, but he did not just talk or think about it. He had such an intense, courageous faith level, that he took that scary first step out of the boat, and God rewarded his step of faith with provision.

We can change the world one person at a time, one interaction at a time. Think it would not make a big difference? Let us say ten women decide to interact with just ten different people in a month — that is one hundred people a month impacted. If ten women from ten churches do it, that is one thousand souls touched and perspectives and mindsets changed. A powerful movement can start with a single flutter of wind, sisters. Let us start a tornado of gap bridging and life touching! Find five kingdom women and make a pact to witness, encourage, and love on five strangers a month! We are anointed, equipped, called, and able to start loving all of God's people. Let us stop talking and start reaching today.

Sisters, racism is real. Prejudices are real. Pain is real. But that is not the end because healing is real. God is real. Grace, hope, and love are real too. We cannot be silent and go with the past norms. Jesus was unconventional, He stepped out of the "social norms" of His day, and He changed history and eternity. We also cannot continue to speak about and relive past atrocities and disenfranchisement with no action. Social media has allowed some to "support" a cause without ever putting in the actual work or time to make a difference. We are called to be salt and light. Light isn't made to be hidden; we must

RACISM AND OUR BIBLICAL RESPONSE TO IT: PART 2

stand tall and be different. We were not created to blend in; we were created to stand out and be unique.

We must break these patterns of distrust and prejudice and begin taking real steps to change hearts, mindsets, outlooks, and perspectives. If you are a part of the group that has been victimized or shortchanged in history, you must not keep carrying the hatred of others who were not even alive then. You must also forgive and begin building mutual respect and godly, loving relationships. It will take everyone to forgive, progress, heal, and build a new outlook and love of all humans. If you are a part of an earthly labeled "oppressor" group, free yourself from any guilt or the need to "repent" for the atrocities our ancestors may or may not have done, but you can decide to realign your heart and begin treating others with mutual respect today.

Also, please do not just jump on the bandwagon of any cause that seems like good sounding "social justice." Research and pray that you can discern and understand if the underlying principles align with biblical principles. Many believers have been sidetracked and supported earthly causes that had underlying anti-Christian and anti-biblical theories. We must weigh everything against the Bible before supporting or furthering earthly causes. Much of "social justice" or "modern theories" are sweet sounding, meaning they sound innocent and great, but they have an underlying demonic agenda. Pray and use discernment in all things.

Sis, you are a daughter of the King. You are anointed, equipped, and strong enough to do all that is assigned to you. Decide today to let go of past injustices, pain, prejudices, anger, resentment, and begin to live in heavenly culture over your earthly culture. Decide to step across the bridge, reach out your hand, and sow into the lives around you daily. You want to change the world as a woman? This is how we can leave a legacy of grace and love and unity for generations to come, and our rewards will be eternal. We are called to be God's hands and feet on this earth. I love you, sister. Join me today and let us all pledge to do God's work of racial reconciliation together. Remember, Jesus already reconciled all people to Himself on the cross; you just need to point all people to that redeeming cross!

DAILY QUESTIONS:

1. How can you begin building bridges today?

___

2. Have you ever been guilty of social media activism without real action?

___

3. What should be your kingdom mindset regarding races and prejudices?

___

4. Are there any earthly causes you need to reconsider?

DAILY PRAYER:
"Lord, thank You for allowing me to make a difference in all the lives I interact with each day. I pray You guide me as I try to begin making a difference each day. Lord, help me to be brave enough to start living comfortably uncomfortable. Help me to begin bridging gaps and not waiting for others to make the first step. Show me every way my love can have action; show me the ways I can sow seeds of love where they are needed the most. God, please help me to remember You created us all equal, and in Your sight, we are all the same. Lord, please help me to see the world through grace not race and a kingdom mindset. In Jesus's name. Amen."

DAILY FOCUS:
1. It is uncomfortable being uncertain; it is hard to step out of our comfort zones and interact on different levels. But it is necessary and important. We must be the change, not because of our race, but based on God's grace. If racism or prejudices still exist in your surroundings, that means it is an opportunity for you to be light and salt, like we have talked about before.
2. A lot of times we talk about race, racism, prejudices, wrongs that need to be fixed, and gaps that need to be bridged, but how do we start? What do we do? We go. Remember, we are not called to be social activists; we are called to be godly women of action. Do not just post the moving picture or emotional video with a famous quote. Get up, girl, and go.

3. Sisters, racism is real. Prejudices are real. Pain is real. But that is not the end because healing is real. God is real. Grace, hope, and love are real too. We cannot be silent and go with the past norms. Jesus was unconventional. He stepped out of the social norms of His day, and He changed history and eternity. We also cannot continue to speak about and relive past atrocities and disenfranchisement with no action.

Day Thirty-Four

I HAVE NO SUPPORT FOR THE THINGS GOD CALLED ME TO

> "Whenever God calls us to a task, He will equip us
> and enable us to complete that task."
> UNKNOWN

SOMETIMES AS BELIEVERS, GOD leads or calls us to things out of the realm of our normal life. It may be to write music, lead worship, lead a Bible study, volunteer at a school, mentor at-risk children, or even write a book. When we feel His tugging at our hearts, many of us begin to look around us to see who we know that will further our calling or support us in completing it. We need to realize that if God has truly called you to something, He has already prepared the way to it.

There are many instances of heroes in the faith doubting God in the Bible, but He never gives up on them and finds someone else. Moses's excuse was "he was slow of speech" (Exod. 3:11). God even allowed his brother Aaron to speak for him. Gideon asked God if He knew "he was from the smallest tribe, and in that tribe, he was the least worthy" (Judg. 6:15). After God told him that He would still use him, Gideon took it a step further and asked God to prove it was really Him, and God performed the Test to assure Gideon (Judg. 6:37). God also made him send most of his army home, so that when the small group of ill-armed men defeated the enemy, they would know it was God's power not their own.

Sometimes we turn to our friends and family and become disappointed and discouraged if they do not get excited or immediately begin to support us. Sisters, we must realize this is a trick from the enemy. The enemy sets people in our path to dissuade us from our callings. We must be purpose-focused, then take a step of faith. We must trust that He has made provision for us. When God calls us, He is testing us to see if we will take the first step in blind faith. When you take that first step, He will equip you with everyone and everything you will need along the way. God has promised to supply all your needs, not with what you have earthly available, but with all the riches in heaven.

I was asked a good question one day while mentoring: "How do I know if something is of God or not?" It made me really think.

I described it to them like this: Remember when Jesus called Peter to walk on the water in the storm? Peter asked, "Lord, if it is really you, command that I come to you." He wanted to discern Jesus's voice, because he spent time with Jesus; he knew His voice. If you have regular prayer and reflection time with God, you will also learn to discern His voice. The more time you spend with Him, the more identifiable His voice will become. After Jesus commanded Peter to "come," Peter took that famous first step out of the boat on pure, intense faith, and he walked on water. The provision to walk on water was already there, but he only realized it when he stepped out of the boat.

God often calls us to uncomfortable places. He often requires that we stretch higher and further than we think is possible. Our God is not a God of comfort; He is a God of growth. Remember, He is always pushing us to learn, grow, and advance. We must pass the small tests, even when we feel insecure or ill-equipped. I have heard it said, "God doesn't call the qualified. He qualifies the called." This means if He calls you, He and He alone will equip you to fulfill your destiny. Stay

I HAVE NO SUPPORT FOR THE THINGS GOD CALLED ME TO

in peace. God is not going to call you to an area if He made no provision for you there.

After you know to discern His voice, the second part will come with ease. When God calls you to something you are not equipped for by yourself, learning the new skill will be surprisingly seamless. God will have divine appointments; He will bring people into your life for the exact purpose of furthering that calling. They will already have a seed planted; it will not take much convincing or begging. It will be something miraculous. You will run into the right people at the right times, you will say the words that spark something inside of them, and you will draw out their calling to join yours. Things that are of God usually flow naturally. I've had people tell me in my business meetings, "I usually don't trust people, but there was just something about you!" Sis, that "something" is Jesus's favor!

We must not listen to the lies of the enemy. If he tells us we are not enough, we do not know the right people or we do not possess the correct connections, he is wrong. You may not know the people, have the knowledge, or have connections, but your Father in heaven does. He knows exactly what you need before you can even ask. The Bible tells us Jehovah Jireh, "our Provider," and that "He is sufficient." We need to cling to that promise. God will not call you to something then leave you lacking in that place.

"For we are God's handiwork, created in Christ Jesus to do good works, which God prepared in advance for us to do" (Eph. 2:10 NIV).

We cannot let others, our families, friends, even mentors dissuade us from something we know we are called to by God. We must break out of needing support, encouragement, and validation. It is a normal need, but in the kingdom, we must be willing to have intense faith and mental strength to follow God, wherever He leads us. Some people will never understand our faith, never understand our passion, and never believe we are capable of our callings, and that is okay. You must grow above those twinges of resentment or hurt. There will be people in your life who you expect to support you or understand you, and you need to release them from that responsibility. We should celebrate and love the ones who do, but don't let the ones who don't celebrate you or who try to hold you back, make you harden your heart.

If they do not understand or support you, then consider that God has not destined them for this part of your story. Keep growing and keep going.

When Peter was walking on water, he was doing great, but then he looked at the scary wind and waves that surrounded him. Peter only began to sink when he took his eyes off Jesus and looked at his circumstances. When you are walking on faith, it is imperative you do not begin to look at the hardships and impossibilities around you, or you will begin to sink. When you have the faith to take the first step off the boat, allow that faith to carry you through without beginning to doubt or worry about your surroundings. Don't allow pessimism and negativity even a foothold in your mind.

It does not matter if nobody supports your calling, anointing, or talents. If God is calling you to something, He will equip you to go through it. God alone is your strength and your provision. We also must remember many people in our families or social circles are not on the same faith level we are. They may not be able to comprehend, perceive, or understand our callings. Do your best in all seasons. Give your callings your full energy and stop wasting energy on who you think should support you. The right people will come in the divine, ordained timing.

Sisters, please remember in whatever you do, you are doing it for the Lord first. We are validated, called, equipped, anointed, and led by the Lord God, not by other people. Remember, you have been validated completely when Jesus died on the cross, not by those people around you now. We must grow past the need to be celebrated, supported, or praised by the people around us.

What is God calling you to that you have been apprehensive about? Is there something you feel led to do, but not qualified to do? We must still fulfill our calling, even if nobody on earth supports or celebrates us. These callings are not about the earthly praise; they are about piling up your treasure in heaven. So, take that first step today.

I HAVE NO SUPPORT FOR THE THINGS GOD CALLED ME TO

DAILY QUESTIONS:

1. What is a calling in your life that you need the courage to take the first step toward?

___

2. How do you feel now that you know God has already made provision in that area?

___

3. What are three actions you can take to move forward on your calling?

___

4. Who must you forgive for not supporting you?

DAILY PRAYER:

"Lord, thank You for every calling You have placed in my heart. Lord, I ask You to reveal the callings You have placed upon my life. I ask that You make Your voice be distinct to my heart and that I would know what is from You and what is not of You. Help me to build the strength and courage needed to take the first step out of the boat. After I step, God, help me not to take my eyes of You, help me not to look at the wind and the waves, so I will not sink, in Jesus's name. God, please help me to trust Your timing, even if it is late or different than my expectations. God, help me to remember if You called me, You would equip and make provisions for me. God, please help me to forgive and let go of any resentment for anyone who has not supported me in the way I have wanted. Please give me peace that if they were meant to be a part of Your plan, then they would be. Help me not to harden my heart or harbor resentment. In Jesus's name. Amen."

DAILY FOCUS:

1. Sometimes we turn to our friends and family and become disappointed and discouraged if they do not get excited or immediately begin to support us. Sisters, we must realize this is a trick from the enemy. The enemy sets people in our path to dissuade us from our callings, and we must be able to discern if it is really of God. Then take a step of faith, trusting He has made provision for us.
2. God often calls us to uncomfortable places; He often requires that we stretch higher and further than we think is possible. Our God is

not a God of comfort. Remember, He is always pushing us to learn, grow, and advance. We must pass the small tests, even when we feel insecure or ill-equipped. I have heard it said, "God doesn't call the qualified. He qualifies the called."

3. We must not listen to the lies of the enemy who tells us we are not enough, we do not know the right people, or we do not possess the correct connections. You may not know the people, have the knowledge, or have connections, but your Father in heaven does. He knows exactly what you need before you can even ask.

Day Thirty-Five

SARAH: GOD IS FAITHFUL EVEN IN OUR DISBELIEF AND IMPATIENCE

> "Happy is the one who learns to wait as he prays and never loses his patience, for God's time is the best time."
> UNKNOWN

THE STORY OF ABRAHAM and Sarah is well known in the Bible. God promised Abraham early in his life that he would be father to numerous descendants, yet, into his incredibly old age, his wife, Sarah, produced no children. I want us to focus on a few aspects of their story that I think we never noticed.

The first lesson we can learn in Sarah's story is God's faithfulness even in our unbelief. Sarah first laughed when it prophesied to her that she would have a child. She laughed out loud the first time she heard that promise and then lied to the angel that she had laughed at the promise. That is refreshing, because I can imagine her laugh escaping at the insanity of the prophecy and the panic at being called out. Yet, God still blessed her, even though she didn't believe.

It is so hard to hold onto our faith when we cannot see a human, physical way. However, God is not bound to what is possible by earthly standards. He is the creator of the Universe. He can make the impossible possible. When we struggle to believe and begin to doubt, God stays faithful and looks past our disbelief and still brings our miracles to life. Sarah went year after year not having a child, and in her frustration, she tried to force the promise of God in her own strength. She sent her husband Abraham to sleep with her maid, Hagar, and Abraham fathered an illegitimate child and illegitimate promise. Abraham was eighty-six years old when Ishmael was born. Even though she doubted God's promise, God was still faithful to her. Fourteen years after she tried to force God's hand, Sarah delivered Isaac, and God fulfilled His promise.

Sarah didn't just have silent doubt; she had such strong disbelief that she went totally out of God's plan and tried to do it in her own power. I can imagine the look on Abraham's face when she came up with her plan. He must have been in total shock. In our earthly thinking, since she disobeyed God and did not fully trust him, God should withhold His blessings. But He did not because we are told in the Word, "being confident of this very thing, that he who began a good work in you will perfect it until the day of Jesus Christ" (Phil. 1:6 ASV).

This verse tells us to be confident, to be steadfast and sure that if God begins something in us, He will make it perfect up until the time Jesus comes back. Sisters, we must be confident, not unsure of God's promises. We cannot blame Sarah. She was probably so excited when she was told she would have a child, but fourteen years is a long time to wait. I can understand her pain, hurt, frustration, and resentment. These feelings are natural as humans, but we can learn to be either discouraged or strengthened by them. We must learn to trust God's timing, because He is never going to fail us. Even if it takes longer than we want, or it seems improbable, we must remember that He will begin everything He starts. He is faithful.

The enemy loves to convince us that God is lacking or absent in His promises. We must stand firm against these doubts. Anything God

SARAH: GOD IS FAITHFUL EVEN IN OUR DISBELIEF AND IMPATIENCE

promises and calls us to He will divinely deliver with perfect completion. We cannot fall for the tricks of the enemy like discouragement and doubt. We must stand firm.

We learn from Sarah's story, that even after jealousy, bitterness, and bad choices, God's grace will still forgive and redeem us. Imagine how Sarah pushed Abraham into having an affair and fathering a child with Hagar, and later, the presence of Ishmael and Hagar got under her skin so much that she turned bitter. She tried to turn on Abraham first and blame him for the situation, but he was quick to remind her it was her idea, and she could deal with them how she wished. Sarah could not stand to see the result of her hasty, impulsive decision and banished Hagar and her son for some time.

Have you ever considered that the turmoil we see in the Middle East up to this day is a result of these two half-brothers' ongoing hatred? Ishmael's descendants settled in the land that is now known as the Middle East, and he is considered the start of the modern religion of Islam. Isaac's descendants are, of course, the Jewish people in Israel. Sisters, our impulsive and ungodly decisions do not only have consequences for our lifetimes, but they can also carry on for generations, and even thousands of years. We must know there is grace for our short-sightedness, but we must use our wisdom to try to make the best choices.

We must learn from Sarah that every decision carries a consequence, but in repentance, every bad past decision does not cancel the grace God has for us. No mistake or bad decision we make can cancel the blessings God has for us. God loves us with agape love. That is love that is not conditional or limited. He will always finish every good thing He begins in our lives. No mistake is too big for Him to cover with grace; no past is too messy for Him to clean up and restore. No matter what bad decision you have made in your past, you will still receive every promise over your life. Just wait on God's timing. It is not our timing, and it is hard and confusing, but stand firm. He will finish every good thing He has begun in you.

Fourteen years after she tried to force God's hand, Sarah delivered Isaac, and God fulfilled His promise. Can you imagine the pain, frustration, and confusion Sarah felt for those fourteen years? Can you imagine how many friends, family, and even strangers told her to give up? It is estimated Sarah was ninety years old when Isaac was born.

I have often thought about why God would have waited that long to bring His promise to fruition. I think I know why: If Sarah had gotten pregnant at thirty, forty, fifty, or even sixty, it could have been explained by human ability. But at the impossible age of ninety, there was only one explanation: a miracle done by God. I believe God wanted it to be so supernatural that there was only one way that Sarah had Isaac — God's power. God wanted everyone around Sarah and Abraham to know the miracle was brought to life only by God's favor and power.

Sometimes, there is an easier way that we think God should do things, but we need to surrender to the fact that His timing is better than ours could ever be and trust that there is a reason in every season of waiting. Sarah's waiting period was only to bring glory to God when the promise finally came true. We need to seek out the lessons in the waiting, because God's best lessons and strengths are built in the waiting. Sis, be strong, courageous, and patient, even in the long periods of waiting on God to bring His promises to life.

DAILY QUESTIONS:

1. Have you ever considered that the reason God takes so long bringing the miracle is because He wants you to know it is only being done through His power?

_____

_____

_____

_____

SARAH: GOD IS FAITHFUL EVEN IN OUR DISBELIEF AND IMPATIENCE

2. After hearing Sarah's story, how do you feel about God's timing?

_____

_____

_____

_____

3. What lessons can you learn from the waiting?

_____

_____

_____

_____

DAILY PRAYER:
"Lord, thank You for the ability and responsibility You give us of trusting Your timing. Lord, I ask that You keep performing miracles in Your timing and help me not to move out of Your will in the waiting. Lord, please teach me all the lessons in the waiting time. Help me not to be anxious or worried while I wait for my miracle. Lord, for all the times when I went around Your will to try to make it happen myself, please forgive me and help me to still reach my promise. Lord, I trust You with my life, and I trust You alone to finish every good work You have started in me. In Jesus's name. Amen."

DAILY FOCUS:
1. The enemy loves to convince us that God is lacking or absent in His promises. We have to stand firm against these doubts; anything God promises and calls us to, He finishes perfect to completion.

We cannot fall for the tricks of the enemy like discouragement and doubt. We must stand firm.

2. We must learn from Sarah that every decision carries a consequence, but in repentance, every bad past decision does not cancel the grace God has for us. No mistake or bad decision we make can cancel the blessings God has for us. God loves us with agape love. That is love that is not conditional or limited. He will always finish every good thing He begins in our lives. No mistake is too big for Him to cover with grace; no past is too messy for Him to clean up and restore.

3. Sometimes, there is an easier way that we think God should do things, but we need to surrender to the fact that His timing is better than ours could ever be, and trust that there is a reason in every season of waiting. We need to seek out the lessons in the waiting, because God's best lessons and strength is built in the waiting.

Day Thirty-Six

KEEP GROWING, EVEN WHEN IT HURTS

> "God has placed you where you're at in this very moment for a reason; remember that and trust He is working everything out!"
> — UNKNOWN

IF THERE IS ONE thing we can be sure of in life, it is that there will be hardships, obstacles, despair, hurt, betrayal, and pain. Whether it be the untimely death of a loved one, a divorce, a family member letting you down, the loss of a child, a broken friendship, or an unexpected trial or hardship, it happens to all of us. There is a normal grieving process for all these heartbreaks. There is shock, denial, anger, sorrow, then peace. We all grieve and process everything differently, and that is okay. As believers in Christ, there must be a time we use these difficulties to grow and continue to move forward in faith.

In the story of Job, he was tried and afflicted in every way possible even down to his children being killed in an accident. He lost all his possessions, his health, and his comfort. When his friends came to visit him, they decided to just stay in pity and sympathize with him. This is something we covered already. Our job as friends is to lovingly support and help our friends out of their despair. Even Job's wife told him to "curse God and die," and his answer was the famous, "Even if he kills me, I will still praise Him." Job passed the heartbreaking tests God gave him, and God gave him double what he had before. Our God is not a God of replacement; He is a God of double portion blessings.

What if Job had given up after the loss of his wealth? What if Job had given up after the loss of his children? He would have missed out on the double portion blessings. Christianity requires the outlook of a bigger picture, a true belief that no matter what we face, God is working all things together for our good. Yes, death can be unfair and untimely, losses can be crippling, and hurt and betrayal can feel heartbreaking and nearly impossible to recover from. But, as believers, we cannot stay in the place of our hurts and betrayal living the pain over again endlessly. God desires for us to heal, strengthen, grow, and progress. We must keep our eyes on Jesus, take the time to heal, but begin to imagine each hardship in life as a test of our faith and outlook.

"Who will separate us from Christ's love? Will we be separated by trouble, or distress, or harassment, or famine, or nakedness, or danger, or sword?... But in all these things we win a sweeping victory through the one who loved us. I'm convinced that nothing can separate us from God's love in Christ Jesus our Lord: not death or life, not angels nor rulers, not present things or future things, not powers or height or depth, or any other thing that is created" (Rom. 8:35, 37-39 CEB).

Whether we go through troubles, distress, harassment, famine, danger, or even the sword, those things cannot separate us from the love of God. His love and purpose are never far away from us. We never exist outside His plan for us. We must begin to heal from our past hurts and remember that God is still in control, even when life hurts and is hard. This is so much easier said than done. It is easy to preach about healing and letting go, but it is hard to truly let resentment go and allow our scars to tell the story of where we have grown from. Your scars do not represent who you are; they simply show where you have come from, where your strength has grown from. We do not have to keep reliving the past traumas of our lives and reliving the pain, resentment, anger, or hurt. There is nothing healing that

KEEP GROWING, EVEN WHEN IT HURTS

comes from rehashing the past. We must take the lessons out of these hardships and use them to strengthen our resolve and outlooks.

James 1:2-4 says, "Consider it a sheer gift, friends, when tests and challenges come at you from all sides. You know that under pressure, your faith-life is forced into the open and shows its true colors. So don't try to get out of anything prematurely. Let it do its work, so you become mature and well-developed, not deficient in any way" (MSG).

I can be honest with you, sisters. When my father died, I had time to prepare before it happened, as he was sick. Even though I was only nine years old, he asked me to heal and be strong from it, so I honored him by already having the mindset of healing. Of course, it hurt. I grieved, I was heartbroken, but I had a goal in the grief to work towards healing. It took years (please do not think it was overnight, sisters). But even amid the most gut-wrenching sobs, I knew this pain was going to make me stronger. I knew I would learn something from this loss. I learned very young that life is short and every day matters. My kids and I have had conversations about if I were to ever pass away suddenly, what would happen, where I would happily be, and that I was not gone and they will see me again. Growth is a mindset, and healing is a goalpost. We must never stay in our pain and choose to sit in it, never finding the lesson in the loss. Sisters, even in the worst pain, we, as Christians, have glorious hope.

Sisters, the deepest, darkest places of your life will be the places God propels you from. You will emerge from the pain and pressure you are in. You will be more refined, polished, and strengthened. Creating diamonds requires an incredible pressure to be put on carbon for the chemical composition to change. This substantial pressure turns regular, nearly worthless carbon into one of the most precious jewels in the world. Think of expensive olive oil. That oil is contained inside a regular olive, but the olive must be pressed with great force to extract the precious oil. Sisters, all the rare and precious things require refinement and pressure to be unveiled. We are the same. The deepest and darkest times in our lives will be the trial that refines and strengthens our characters and outlooks.

I have heard it said when you feel as though you are buried under stress, pressure, and hard times, that is the time that you are actually being planted by God. Before a plant ever shows even a bud on top of the soil, its roots have been unseen but busy, building a deep foundation for the plant. These hard times are when your roots must grow deep in your faith, so that when you come out, you will have dependable and strong roots to continue blossoming with. A tree can only grow as high as its roots are deep. Without strong roots, it does not have the strength needed to hold itself up high. Therefore, your roots of experience, strength, and perseverance must be strong enough to hold up the heights God wants to take you to. The depth of our trials will measure the height of our blessings.

From the loss of my parents, I learned that life is short. My children will tell you, there are days I pack up the car, and we take a day off for a beach day, because I know that tomorrow isn't promised. I do not have a morbid way of living — I promise, but I intentionally interact with every person daily in my path. I intentionally spread joy and I intentionally sow into my own children and kids in my community, because I have learned through my pain to make today count. I learned from my pain to live and love and be intentional with every moment. There is an underlined perseverance, resilience, and strength that I have developed from the loss of my parents.

I am not an orphan. I am the daughter of the King of kings, I am never alone, and I am not weak. I am Holy Spirit-empowered. And sister, so are you. March through your trials sure of who you are and whose you are. Keep your head up and look for the lessons in every heartache. Stand tall and face your troubles; see them as a strengthening for your emotions, outlook, perseverance, and heart. You are never alone; you will conquer every trial in front of you. Your best days are ahead of you, and you are a victor in Christ. Live in your truth today.

KEEP GROWING, EVEN WHEN IT HURTS

DAILY QUESTIONS:

1. What trauma in your life do you need to heal and grow from?

_____

_____

_____

_____

2. How can you begin to progress from the place you are now?

_____

_____

_____

_____

3. How can you change your perspective of future trials to encourage healing?

_____

_____

_____

_____

DAILY PRAYER:

"Lord, thank You for every trial and hardship that You have brought into my life. Help me to embrace every hard time as a time to strengthen and grow in my resilience. Lord, I ask You to help me keep my eyes focused on You and help me to change my perspective of my hardest trials to tests of my faith. God, please show me how to keep moving forward and how to keep healing and progressing in my faith. Lord, please help my scars to start reminding me of the trials You have brought me triumphantly through and help me to realize my resilience and strength. Lord, please help me not to lie in my pain but to get up and keep moving forward. I love You, Lord. Thank You. In Jesus's name. Amen."

DAILY FOCUS:

1. Yes, death can be unfair and untimely, losses can be crippling, and hurt and betrayal can feel heartbreaking and nearly unrecoverable. But, as believers, we cannot stay in the place of our hurt and betrayal, living the pain over again endlessly. God desires for us to heal, strengthen, grow, and progress. We must keep our eyes on Jesus, take the time to heal, but begin to imagine each hardship in life as a test of our faith and outlook.

2. Sisters, the deepest, darkest places of our life will be the place God propels you from. You will emerge from the pain and pressure you are in, more refined, polished, and strengthened. Creating diamonds requires an incredible pressure to be put on carbon for the chemical composition to change. This substantial pressure turns regular nearly worthless carbon into one of the most precious jewels in the world.

3. Your scars do not represent who you are; they simply show where you have come from, where your strength has grown from. We do not have to keep reliving the past traumas of our lives and reliving the pain, resentment, anger, or hurt. We must continue to move onwards and upwards.

Day Thirty-Seven

MARY: FAITHFUL, GENTLE, AND NORMAL MOTHER

> "Pray like Nehemiah, obey like Daniel, lead like Moses, serve like Martha, believe like Mary, fight like David, educate like Paul, build like Noah, love like Jesus."
> CHRISTIANWALLS.COM

THE FIRST TIME WE are introduced to Mary in the Bible, she is described as a young, pure girl who was faithful. There is tremendous strength and resilience in the story of Mary, but there was also grace that mirrors the grace promised to Eve. Imagine being such a young and unmarried girl in a time when pregnancy before marriage was severely judged and shameful. Mary could have told the angel that she was not interested, but instead she chose to be faithful amid a scandalous situation.

Mary held on to her faith instead of giving into shame or fear. Mary trusted God fully, and He led her through her most difficult moments. He made Joseph have a dream and changed his mind about divorcing her. God led them to a prepared place where they could stay safely, so she could give birth. When we trust God explicitly, as Mary did, He promises to guide us through any challenge.

Can you imagine the intense faith and belief that Mary held, when the angel appeared to her and told her she was going to be pregnant and give birth to the Messiah? She could easily have doubted or been dismissive, but she believed in the power of miracles without any proof or explanation of how it would happen. The society we live in today is very cynical. I have heard it said, "If it isn't on social media did it even happen?" I know that is made as a joke, but people today want the experts, scientists, politicians, or a person in power to verify information before they will believe it. God calls us to trust solely in faith, not the "experts." This was a huge issue in 2020 and 2021 when even strong Christians believed in "experts" unquestionably — even if their information was flawed, inconsistent, or nonsensical.

God is not limited to what is earthly possible; our God is limitless. Imagine how this kind of cynicism can be twisted by Satan to control us and what we see and believe in. Mary has the kind of solid blind faith we should all work to have. She did not have the who, what, where, why, or how answers, yet she believed wholeheartedly. Sometimes we feel we need to know exactly how everything will pan out, instead of trusting that when things are of God, we can let Him take care of the details. What we are trying to control, God cannot work in.

Mary chose faith over fear when the angel came to her to tell her about the Messiah. At that pivotal moment she said, "Let it be as you said." She did not think about what society would say, and she did not think about what Joseph would think. She took a HUGE leap of faith and trusted God to work it all out. When we truly trust God to take care of every situation, He will go ahead of us and straighten the path. When Joseph began to doubt Mary (of course, who would blame him if your fiancé you have never touched showed up pregnant), God gave him a supernatural dream so he would know her truth. As humans, we try to convince people of our callings and missions, instead of just allowing God to clear the way and soften hearts and change minds for us. This is such a great lesson for us today. The only one who can convict hearts and truly change minds is God; no amount of nagging, begging, or debating can do what God can do.

MARY: FAITHFUL, GENTLE, AND NORMAL MOTHER

The second thing I love about Mary is the fact that she lost Jesus when He was twelve years old. As mothers, we all have insecurities, doubts, and worries, but could you imagine losing the Messiah? I mean, how do you pray that you find Him?

"God, You know that Messiah You sent me? Is there another one in heaven You can send again in case I can't find Him?"

I am joking, of course. I have had a child wander off in the store, and in that moment, I know how my heart dropped and stomach ached. When I read the story of Mary not being able to find Jesus, only to find Him in the temple teaching the religious leaders, it shows that even with her incredible faith, unwavering strength, and dignity, she was as normal as you or I are. She faltered, made mistakes, and even lost Jesus, but that does not take away from her story; it just adds a normalcy to her story. Sisters, we do not have to be perfect to make a difference for the kingdom. We often read the stories of these incredible women in the Bible and think we can never measure up or be enough. They were normal people, like us, who decided to take a step of faith, and you can do the same.

Remember in the beginning of this study when we said that the grace shown to Eve was mirrored in Mary? What if Eve was scared and gave into shame and low self-worth and never took the step of faith to begin reproducing? There would have been no Mary to give birth to the Messiah who would redeem us all. You see, from Eve's gigantic step of faith came Mary's promise of eternal hope. There are people in the world who God has divine appointments and assignments to fit into our purposes, calling ministries, and vice versa. Sometimes as women, we focus on our personal ministries and not the way we can take a step to further something that someone else has started. We sometimes are assigned to finish or further what they have started for them. Sometimes we need to be satisfied being a small part of something big, instead of a big part of something small. We need to look around and dedicate ourselves to anything that furthers the kingdom, no matter who gets the credit for it. Eve's curse and blessing of crushing the serpent's head came to fruition when Jesus rose from the dead and delivered a crushing blow to Satan. Without Eve's curse there was no promise of Mary and her child, Jesus. The things that seem to be your curses may be another woman's blessings.

Another lesson we can learn from Mary's story is, "She believed and kept these things hidden in her heart." This literally means she had faith in the things God told her, but she stayed quiet about them and strengthened her resolve privately. When God calls us to something, we tend to get extremely excited and begin to tell everyone around us our callings and plans. We need to remember people can only understand on their level of perception, meaning they may never relate to our level of thinking. Oversharing our dreams or callings can open doors for the enemy to use the people around us to begin to discourage us and make us doubt that we can do it.

We need to aim for keeping our callings quiet, to do the inward heart and mind work that is silent and unseen and to build up on resolve and faith. Inner work is usually perspective and mindset turning, and often the most important in our walk. Hidden work is the hardest and most selfless work because there is no recognition, praise, or support for it. Nobody should know everything you are working on in your heart or mind.

Keep your mind open, keep your eyes focused on Jesus, and your heart loving, and you will find every divine encounter and calling meant for you. We read of Mary and think she was all good, then we read of Eve and think she was all bad. Sister, nobody is all of something; everyone has their strengths and weaknesses. I want us to reset our perspective to look for the good in people and call better out of them. Let us set our hearts on having the kind of faith that believes in the divine ability of our limitless God.

Seek God out for your divine callings, keep them in your heart, and strengthen your resolve and faith privately. Change your mindset, perspective, and outlook, and all the silent work needed to walk in what God has called you to. Sisters, have faith like Mary that God will make a way, even if you cannot see an earthly way. God is not held to earthly abilities. He can do all things, and He can move heaven and earth to fulfill every promise in your life. Even if you make a few mistakes (like losing the Messiah), you will still be one of the heroines of the faith.

DAILY QUESTIONS:

1. Have you ever realized what "Mary hid these things in her heart" meant? What does it mean for you and your walk right now?

_____

_____

_____

_____

2. Have you ever "lost the Messiah" or made a big mistake with what God gave you to do? Do you realize there is grace for any mistake?

_____

_____

_____

_____

3. What inner work do you need to work on quietly?

_____

_____

_____

_____

DAILY PRAYER:

"Dear Lord, thank You for a strong and relatable heroine like Mary.

Lord, thank You for her example of pure faith that believes all things even if they seem earthly impossible. Lord, help me to believe in all the callings You have placed in my life, and help me to keep my heart pure and focused on realigning my perspectives and mindsets to Your will. Lord, help me to begin keeping my callings hidden in my heart and doing all the inner hidden work to strengthen my faith and resolve. God, please guide me through any mistakes I make along the way. Keep me focused on You, Lord. I love You. In Jesus's name. Amen."

DAILY FOCUS:

1. As humans, we try to convince people of our callings and missions, instead of just allowing God to clear the way and soften hearts and change minds for us. This is such a great lesson for us today. The only one who can convict hearts and truly change minds is God; no amount of nagging, begging, or debating can do what God can do.
2. Sometimes as women, we focus on our personal ministries and not the way we can take a step to further something that someone else has started. We sometimes are assigned to finish or further what they have started for them. Sometimes we need to be satisfied being a small part of something big, instead of a big part of something small. We need to look around and dedicate ourselves to anything that furthers the kingdom, no matter who gets the credit for it.
3. Oversharing our dreams or callings can open doors for the enemy to use the people around us to begin to discourage us and make us doubt that we can do it. We need to aim for keeping our callings quiet, to do the inward heart and mind work that is silent and unseen to build up on resolve and faith. Inner work is usually perspective and mindset turning, and often the most important in our walk. Hidden work is the hardest and most selfless work because there is no recognition, praise, or support for it. But there is grace, strength, peace, joy, and eternal rewards stored up for it.

Day Thirty-Eight
NO MORE DRAMA

> "Be so busy loving God, loving others and loving your life that you have no time for regret, worry, fear, or drama."
> UNKNOWN

IT SOMETIMES SEEMS LIKE our entire society is hyper focused and feeds off drama. Quite literally, with shows like *Teen Mom*, *The Real Housewives*, *Basketball Wives*, and *The Bachelor*, we seem to love to see people's problems, bad decisions, breakups, gossip, disagreements, and fights. We feed off of the fuel that their lives are worse than ours. It seems everyone follows celebrity gossip and reality stars' lives, and with Twitter and Snapchat and Instagram, we can know what all reality stars are doing, wearing, using, and thinking at any moment. It seems that many are taking celebrity thoughts as fact instead of as their own opinion, which has no bearing on us. The Kardashian family got filthy wealthy off reality TV, so it obviously has a quite large following. But there is a danger in celebrity worship, and we need to remember who is important to our everyday lives.

There is nothing wrong in having things that we enjoy that are not all "church" things. But I believe as Christian women, we must be incredibly careful with what is being fed into our minds and subconscious. There is so much for us to do and accomplish every day. Is drama worth our time, energy, or emotional strength? I thought, *Okay, drama is a relatively new thing. What on earth could the Bible tell us about it?* Boy, was I wrong. So, what does the Bible say about drama?

1 Thessalonians 4:11-12 tells us, "And to aspire to live quietly, and to mind your own affairs, and to work with your hands, as we instructed you; so that you may walk properly before outsiders and be dependent on no one" (ESV).

Philippians 4:8 tells us, "Finally, brothers, whatever is true, whatever is honorable, whatever is just, whatever is pure, whatever is lovely, whatever is commendable, if there is any excellence, if there is anything worthy of praise, let your mind think about these things" (ESV).

Wow, that is conclusive.

I personally believe it is dangerous to keep our minds constantly full of drama about who is dating whom, who said what, who ignored whom, who talked about us, who misunderstood us, who doesn't like whom, and so on. If our minds are so full of all these things, where is the room for God's peace and purpose? Where is the room for joy? God desires for us to live lives that are full of peace. If we are constantly submerged ourselves in all the secular problems, issues, insecurities, and fakeness that surround us, we are limiting the time and energy we can expend on the calling, anointing, and purposes God has called us to do.

Of course, we all like to be entertained and laugh, unwind, and have fun, but there is a certain standard God calls us to live by. He wants our minds focused on exactly what Philippians 4:8 says, "whatever is true, honorable, just, pure, commendable." When you are constantly submerged and surrounded in certain situations or behaviors, it subconsciously becomes normal. Watching or focusing on drama also invites that atmosphere into your spirit and, ultimately, your home. Remember, when Satan comes, he does not come in horns and a red pitchfork; he is clothed in innocent things, such as secular entertainment.

Think back twenty years, if you had told anybody in the '80s or '90s that one day MTV would be a channel full of young insecure teenage girls, having multiple babies with multiple questionable boyfriends, and then living immoral, loud, indecent lives, anybody would have told you it was unfathomable. If you told someone in the 1970s instead of sitcoms, TV would be chock full of cameras following wealthy grown mothers and wives around and filming their constant useless drama, cat fights, and profane arguments, while they live lives with little to no purpose or cause, they would have thought you were crazy. This phenomenon has only become popular in the last twenty or so years.

I believe as Satan seeks to control our minds, time, and lives more he has found ways to keep us entertained and distracted from the "real world." You see when Satan can distract our minds and imbed secularism and loose morals into us through "harmless" entertainment, he has gained a foot across the threshold of our lives. Believe me, Satan's playground is our mind; he strives to control our thoughts and our time. The Bible tells us to, "live quietly and be about our own business" (1 Thess. 4:11).

Another way to steer clear of drama and live a simpler life is to begin to weigh whether certain people in our lives or strangers on social media are worth our time or emotional energy. This is both in real life and online. Even if someone is rude to you or "short" in a store, is it worth your emotional energy to argue your point? Or is it smarter to ignore them, be kind and walk away and keep the same emotional energy you had in the beginning? Does it matter what someone said about you? Does it make sense to justify your opinion to total strangers you will never meet? Do you need to prove your point to friends and family?

I believe sometimes we take on unnecessary and unhealthy dramas that are battles we do not need to deal with. We need to learn to scroll past things on social media we do not agree with and not try to educate or justify to people who may never understand our viewpoints, opinions, or beliefs. A lot of nonbelievers will never understand your points of views because God has granted you spiritual eyes and discernment that the world cannot comprehend. We also need to evaluate if the people we are watering truly want to grow. If we are watering bad ground, nothing will ever blossom. Meaning, if we are hanging around with someone and trying to sow good seeds into them, we need to make sure they are fertile ground for our energy and time to produce a harvest.

I have found it helpful to stop myself and literally ask myself, "Is this the best use of my time?" This question makes me delete a lot of unneeded comments on social media and use my time more wisely. I think we get over involved in earthly things that are not kingdom matters. We can, of course, be interested in earthly things, but we cannot allow them to control our time. Time is the one thing that we need to be more intentional with.

Use all that time and energy into fixing something in your own life, into learning something that will strengthen your own life. Use the extra time to pursue your purpose, to study God's Word, or to hug your children and sow into them. Drama is not worth your time. Start deleting the people off your social media who only post drama. Stop watching mindless television that wastes your time and does not build you up. Stop answering calls for the friend who only calls to gossip, and take yourself out of group chats that are not edifying your values. It will free you as it frees your mind, and you will begin to take back your valuable time. We cannot get wasted time back.

Stay away from getting hurt by "he said, she said" types of issues or gossip. I honestly no longer care who said what about me. If they want to be mature enough to speak to me directly about it, we can discuss it then, but until then I am not going to worry about it. You can waste your mental energy with hypothetical things or even gossip that people tell you. It can make you sad, isolated, or angry, and it will steal your joy. If they did not say it to you, ignore it, and if it is serious enough, address it directly. Start to stand up courageously and be straightforward, direct, kind, and loving. Learn to nip issues when they begin so they do not fester. An example of this is, "I was told that maybe you had commented _____ about me. Is this really how you feel? Please always feel free to come directly to me, and we can talk about it." If this is not feasible, then learn to forgive without the apology, which we already discussed before. Let it go. God is your Defender, and He will vindicate you.

We must elevate our lives and be intentional with our time. Most people waste so much mental energy on reality TV, binge watching, and negative music or movies, then wonder why they are drained, unproductive, stressed, or irritable. What we feed our minds constantly will begin to manifest in our everyday life. As kingdom women, God wants us to use our time, energy, and talents to build the kingdom. Yes, we can relax and unwind, but we need to watch what is going on in our mind and hearts on a consistent basis. The messages are important. Sisters, His time is near, and there is no more time to waste with frivolous activities.

Begin to weigh if you would watch certain things with Jesus (or your pastor), or if you would listen to certain songs with them as well. Weigh if the messages you are hearing constantly are edifying to your goals and values. One of Satan's traps is currently in the Hollywood music and movie industry. There are so many sinful and downright evil themes in current shows, movies, and music, and many believers are not discerning the underlying messages. Let's begin to vet the messages that we are feeding ourselves and our families. You are the gatekeeper of your home; use your discernment to protect your children or spouse. You are a woman of God, a warrior, and an empowered woman. God calls you to higher things. You are not ordinary; your life is extraordinary. Fill your mind and thoughts with extraordinary things.

DAILY QUESTIONS:
1. What are some sources of drama that affect your life?

___

___

___

___

2. How does that drama leave you feeling emotionally?

_____

_____

_____

_____

3. What are specific plans you are going to use to leave the drama behind?

_____

_____

_____

_____

4. Do you need to make a change in the shows you watch or music you listen to?

_____

_____

_____

_____

DAILY PRAYER:
"Lord, please guide me as I identify the drama in my life. God, help my mind to be full and focused on the things You have before me. Please

help me to recognize that useless drama is a way Satan is trying to distract me from the calling You have placed in front of me. Please help me to separate myself from any drama in my life or from watching and focusing on the drama in others' lives. Please help me to use my time in the wisest way to reach the goals You have set for me. Please help me to discern if movies, shows, or music are pleasing to You and help me to separate from anything covertly evil. Please help to focus my thoughts on all that is true, commendable, and honest. Guide me to a clean heart and mind. In Jesus's name. Amen."

DAILY FOCUS:

1. Realize when you are paying attention to drama. Choose to stop. Choose to fill your mind with edifying things.
2. Identify the drama around you. If there is a person or group of people who are a source of drama, reevaluate your need and want to be around them. What you surround yourself with can sneak in.
3. God desires to give you peace and joy. Claim that promise today and begin walking in it. You have the authority and ability to walk away from ANYTHING that is not edifying and building you up.

Day Thirty-Nine

PERSPECTIVE: THERE ARE THREE SIDES TO EVERY STORY

> "I stopped explaining myself when I realized people only understand from their level of perception."
> UNKNOWN

TODAY'S WORLD IS FULL of everyone's outspoken "personal truth," and anyone who does not automatically agree is shut out or shut down. We see a video on social media and assume we are seeing the entire truth, without seeing any other perspective of the beginning or history. We are told by the media why, who, what, when, where, and we assume we understand the entirety of the story. Sisters, we need to stop thinking we know the "truth" and being unwilling to hear other perspectives. The Bible said that there is only one truth. We need to understand that our earthly minds will never see the world as God sees it. We have limited thinking, but God is omnipotent and all-knowing. There are some truths we will never fully understand until we get to heaven. We need to stop being set in our version of the truth and thinking that is the only way to see it.

There is a Christian hip-hop song by Bizzle that my son was listening to. In this song he is answering questions from a secular rapper and speaking in God's perspective about the "heroes" of our time being killed early. Bizzle said, "What if the people you think are heroes were not everything you made them out to be? You made gods out of men who were clay to me."

My son and I had an hour-long conversation about how we only know one side of everyone on earth who is hailed a hero, but God knows the hidden side of every man. It really made me think about all the great tragedies of our time and how things are so much deeper than we will ever truly know or realize. There have to be hidden agendas and conspiracy theories that may be close to the real truth. There is peace in resigning that we will only know some facts, answers, and reasons when we get to heaven. We have earthly minds, so we can only comprehend earthly things. We cannot even begin to comprehend heavenly things.

1 Corinthians 3:19-20 says, "For the wisdom of this world is folly with God. For it is written, 'He catches the wise in their craftiness,' and again, 'The Lord knows the thoughts of the wise, that they are futile'" (ESV).

Psalm 33:13-15 says, "The Lord looks down from heaven and sees the whole human race. From his throne he observes all who live on the earth. He made their hearts, so he understands everything they do" (NLT).

We must realize that envying people of the world, like celebrities, their wealth, or their lifestyles, is not biblical. It is okay to like a movie star or singer, but we must realize they are all human. We cannot begin to hold anybody as idols, or someone to be revered, because to God we are all made from clay. No celebrity should influence you, and you shouldn't aim to imitate any historical hero. You have one goal, and that was and always will be Jesus. Celebrities' lifestyles, wealth, and opinions should not be the basis on which you set your goals or opinions. The only firm foundation for us to build our lives on is Jesus.

No human has ever been or will ever be perfect. Jesus was the only one and He has shown us how to live. We live in a culture where celebrities have obsessive fan clubs who say that they would "die for them."

PERSPECTIVE: THERE ARE THREE SIDES TO EVERY STORY

This is so sinful and worldly. No human being deserves your adoration or worship. Even leading pastors or religious theorists should never be followed 100 percent. We must weigh everything against the Bible.

We see everyone forcefully sharing their opinion on social media, as though it is the only version of truth. We must remember everyone understands things based on their personal experience, perspective, and level of perception. Some people will never understand your point of view because they have never walked through where you have been. Some people's level of perception will never match your mental level, and we insult them and belittle them when they just need time to experience and grow to understand. This is not right to do. The wisest of humans still pale in comparison to the infinite wisdom of God. We must realize we do not know it all, even those most educated here on earth, do not know it all. God understands why each person chooses to do what they do; we can never understand each person as God does. We need to give grace even if they do not deserve it. Do not put your faith in any mere human.

I choose not to display my political or social beliefs publicly, like a bumper sticker or social media posts. If God sends someone who truly seeks to understand my personal outlook and they are open to understanding my perception, I will share it. This is my truth, and it is how I choose to live; it does not mean it is the only way. It is pointless and emotionally exhausting to try to explain or debate your beliefs, values, or feelings and the reasons with people, especially with complete strangers. Nobody can understand until they experience it themselves. Just stop wasting your time explaining and debating. Start silently living your truth. I must not force my opinions and perceptions onto people who have not gone through the same experiences and hardships as me. I heard it said by a police officer that in every car accident there are three perspectives: there's vehicle one's perspective, vehicle two's perspective, and the truth (third perspective). This is true about everything in life, even arguments or disagreements. I won't stay silent or be a doormat for others though — it is a very careful balance of being meek and bold.

We do not need to hide our religious beliefs; we are assigned to be light and love. We are called to motivate and speak life into those around us. If people are drawn to you and ask you what you believe, SHARE IT. Tell them how Jesus has helped you and where He has brought you from. Jesus will bring people to you for you to witness and minister to them. Share your faith. Share God's love and all the things that He has done to give you peace and joy. Your testimony will be someone else's hope.

Now, if you see evil, sin, or danger — be bold and speak against it. If God has given you discernment and you can sense truth being shown to you by the Holy Spirit, do not silence that! Speak it with love, grace, no insults, and firm boldness. We are called to be light. In the light everything is visible; we are not called to hide things under the dark for "peace" sake. There is a huge difference between being a "peacemaker" and a "peacekeeper." Peacekeepers hide and cover for the sake of just keeping the peace. A peacemaker is bold and strong enough to bring dark things to light so that reconciliation of peace can be made. Matthew 5:9 says, "Blessed are the peacemakers for they shall be called the children of God." Notice it doesn't say the "peacekeepers."

Sisters, we will never know the whole truth of anything or anyone in this world, until we reach heaven. We must live out biblical truth quietly and do our best to love God and love people, as Danny Gokey says in his song "Love God Love People." We must try to stop forcing our opinions on others and trying to justify and explain our personal perception and reality. Remember, we do not know if what we think or believe is the truth as God sees it. We need to look at everything on earth through the lens of the Bible and kingdom mentality. We should try to stick to these truths and try to live our life simply, without pushing our opinion on anyone. It is our job to allow the love we shine to attract others to our life and to be a minister of Jesus to others. Jesus's ministry never ostracized or condemned; He always loves people right where they are and pulls them to a higher level of living. Let us aim to begin living this way today.

PERSPECTIVE: THERE ARE THREE SIDES TO EVERY STORY

DAILY QUESTIONS:

1. When have you thought your version of the "truth" was correct?

2. What do you now realize about earthly truths versus heavenly truths?

3. Which celebrity or historical idols do you need to take off the altar of your heart?

4. Has your mind been reset to living quietly and not arguing and debating?

_____

_____

_____

_____

DAILY PRAYER:

"Lord, I thank You for explaining heavenly truths to us and for the peace in knowing You know ALL the truths and I do not. Lord, help me to stop wanting to convince others, even strangers, of my truths. Help me to realize that people can only understand on the level that they have perspective or experiences, and help me to realize some people will never understand my viewpoint or opinion. Help me to let go of hard feelings or resentment and instead find peace that You know my heart and intentions. Lord, help me to live my life by heavenly truths, and not earthly shams. Lord, please help me keep my eyes focused on You and nothing of the earth. In Jesus's name. Amen."

DAILY FOCUS:

1. We only know one side of everyone who earth hails a "hero," but God knows the hidden side of every man. It really made me think about all the great tragedies of our time, and how things are so much deeper than we will ever truly know or realize. There is peace in resigning that we will only know some facts, answers, and reasons when we get to heaven. We have earthly minds, so we can only comprehend earthly things; we cannot even begin to comprehend heavenly things.

2. We must remember everyone understands things based on their personal experience, perspective, and level of perception. Some people will never understand your point of view because they

have never walked through where you have been. Some people's level of perception will never match your mental level, and we insult them and belittle them when they just need time to experience and grow to understand. This is not right to do. The wisest of humans still pale in comparison to the infinite wisdom of God.

3. Sisters, we will never know the whole truth of anything or anyone in this world, until we reach heaven. We must live our truth quietly and do our best to "love God and love people" as Danny Gokey says in his song "Love God Love People." We must try to stop forcing our opinions on others and trying to justify and explain our personal perception and reality. Remember, we do not know if what we think or believe is the absolute truth as God sees it.

Day Forty

TIME IS OF THE ESSENCE

> "I'm no longer looking for the signs of the times.
> I'm listening for the sound of the trumpet."
> TED HILLSIDE

MATTHEW 24:6-8 SAYS, "AND ye shall hear of wars and rumours of wars: see that ye be not troubled: for all these things must come to pass, but the end is not yet. For nation shall rise against nation, and kingdom against kingdom: and there shall be famines, and pestilences, and earthquakes, in diverse places. All these are the beginning of sorrows" (KJV).

2 Timothy 3:1-5 says, "But understand this, that in the last days there will come times of difficulty. For people will be lovers of self, lovers of money, proud, arrogant, abusive, disobedient to their parents, ungrateful, unholy, heartless, unappeasable, slanderous, without self-control, brutal, not loving good, treacherous, reckless, swollen with conceit, lovers of pleasure rather than lovers of God, having the appearance of godliness, but denying its power. Avoid such people" (ESV).

Judging from these verses and descriptions, it would seem we have been living in the end times for some time. With New Age beliefs promising peace without the conviction of sin. With children being told obeying their parents is not necessary, with people chasing their own wants and wealthy celebrities being worshiped as Gods. With people being concerned only for themselves and the belief of "we are all gods." With the drastic move away from morality and godliness. With the push to emasculate men and destroy marriage and the family unit. With the government trying to take over the educational, medical, and moral training for our children. With sin being celebrated and seen as freedom of self-expression. All these things show that we are truly either in the last days or moving quickly toward the last days. I see everything in the news daily, as more signs that we are moving towards that glorious day when Jesus will come back for His Church. It is important that we live as though He could come back at any moment. We must be proactive, not reactive, and play offense, not defense, with the enemy.

In that verse it explains a lot going on in the world, and anyone pointing out the "new world order" direction is labeled as conspiracy theorist. Every "conspiracy theory" has a little touch of truth; many world governments are corrupt and are not of God. Sisters, be aware of the prophecies in Revelation. God tells us the world will move towards a global economy, one world currency, one world order, sustainability used as control, global crisis shams, mass sterilization, and global government. The Bible tells us people will be fearfully gullible and blind sheep following what "government" tells them. Some even being led to murder, riot, and hurt those who do not concede to their false beliefs. Aim to not be sheep to any media, social justice influencers, or political group. Do not blindly follow the well-known pastors. Study the Bible yourself, and ask God for spiritual insight so you can know if you are being misled.

Satan will begin using false prophets to mislead the people of God. Be alert as Revelation tells us to be. Have your spiritual eyes open, discernment heightened, and research the realities (not just what the media tells you). Do any of these things listed remind you of anything in society today? God does not tell us to ignore it silently; He tells us to take the signs in and use more determination to keep invading the culture with biblical truth. This is a war for souls, and we must be on the offense not the defense. It is a fight for every soul!

The reason I emphasize that we are living in the end times is because there needs to be an urgency in us realigning our minds to living God's way so that we can reach the maximum number of souls for Christ. We must take it seriously to reach everyone we can reach with the gospel. It is imperative that we impact every life around us daily so that we can build the kingdom. We must always aim to discern false teaching and false gospels and have a firm foundation of biblical truth. Being grounded in biblical truth is the main way that we can stand out, be a witness, and win souls for Christ. We must aim to take the last forty days to get our house, marriage, and family in order, then to pursue our purpose and impact the culture for Christ!

We need to stop stressing and worrying about the things that do not matter, and we need to start focusing our callings and anointings. We cannot grow to everything we are called to be if we are carrying around unnecessary pain, hurt, resentment, and stress. It is so important to determine what really matters and what does not in an eternal sense. Much of the things that bother and worry us are earthly things that will not last. We should aim to build up our treasures in heaven and our eternal rewards.

Do not waste your energy on earthly matters that do not matter in the kingdom. Do not give into the temptations of meaningless fights and debates that do not matter in the heavenly realm. Let us stop allowing Satan to attack us in anxiety, worry, fear, and anger. That is his attempt to sidetrack us in our purpose. Let us set our mind and energy on the things of heaven, not the things here on earth. Sisters, let us begin to love, guide, and minister to every person we encounter daily. Let us teach our families and children the ways of the Lord, so that if He does not come in our lifetime, they will be able to keep reaching souls for the kingdom. This is not trivial; we are soldiers in the Army of God.

Sisters, we must take advantage of every day and begin to work hard to build up those heavenly rewards, which will survive not only death but the return of Jesus. When He comes back, I do not want to have regret that I did not bring others to the kingdom with me. I do not want to regret that I hid my testimony and did not interact and reach out to every single person I was supposed to. I aim to shine His light every day and lift others out of their past pain so that they will realize the peace that only comes from Jesus. We must strive to be the most potent salt and brightest light here on earth, so that when He returns, we can truly hear Him say, "Well done, good and faithful servant."

Remember, the Bible tells us that no man knows the time and day that Jesus will return; even Jesus does not know the Father's timing. Rest assured, anyone who "predicts" will not be correct. Jesus described the day He will return in the Bible as "suddenly" — that two men are plowing in the field, and one disappears, and one remains behind and confused. We do not want anyone to be left behind on that glorious day. It is imperative we begin reaching everyone with the gospel so that we can all go with Jesus. It should be an exciting thought that Jesus is coming back — it should not scare us. My children are literally excited for the day we will be in heaven; even death doesn't scare them. We should know that our future is secure with Jesus, and we are saved to go ready for the rapture. Our only urgency should be to gather all our loved ones with us, but the only way we will reach others is by quiet examples. We must love people to Jesus. We must not put down or ostracize others; it will not endear them to Jesus.

This is our assignment, sis: "Go out into all the world and preach the gospel." Let us begin to be loving witnesses of God's grace, acceptance, love, and mercy. I long for the day the Lord comes. To include as many people as possible, we should all do our part to gather souls for the kingdom. This is your first job assigned by your Heavenly Father. Do not waste time saying you will do it later; if God has called you to something, begin now. We are living in the definite signs of the end times. Block out all the drama in society, and focus on furthering the kingdom. Do not get hung up on the crisis of the week because a lot of these issues are Satan trying to distract and sidetrack you from your callings. Be strong, follow God's direction, and embrace your callings. Reset your mindset to kingdom over culture and impact this world with its last hope: The Gospel of Jesus Christ! You are a world-changer, a chain-breaker, and an atmosphere-shifter. Walk in that truth today!

DAILY QUESTIONS:

1. Has the thought of the rapture ever scared you?

_____

_____

_____

_____

2. What do you feel is your biggest assignment before the rapture?

_____

_____

_____

_____

3. What do you believe about the signs of the end times and the rapture?

_____

_____

_____

_____

4. How can you reset your mindset to win souls for the kingdom?

_____

_____

_____

_____

DAILY PRAYER:

"Lord, I thank You for the promise that You have made that You will return for Your church one day. God, help me to be excited and on fire to share Your Word and gather as many souls as I can before that day. God, I want to reach as many souls as I can for the kingdom before this miraculous day. Show me all the ways to set my mind on the things of heaven and not on earth. Help me to let go of meaningless earthly matters and to take up the things that matter in the kingdom. God, please show me the ways You desire for me to reach the most people I can for You. God, I long for the rapture to be so glorious with the body of Christ reaching a miraculous amount of people for heaven. Lord, I await Your return excited and ready. In Jesus's name. Amen."

DAILY FOCUS:

1. The reason I emphasize that we are living in the end times is because there needs to be an urgency in us realigning our minds to living God's way so that we can reach the maximum number of souls for Christ. We must take it seriously to reach everyone we can reach with the gospel. It is imperative that we impact every life around us daily so that we can build the kingdom.
2. Do not waste your energy on earthly matters that do not matter in the kingdom. Do not give into the temptations of meaningless fights and debates that do not matter in the heavenly realm. Let us stop allowing Satan to attack us in anxiety, worry, and anger. That

is his attempt to sidetrack us in our purpose. Let us set our mind and energy on the things of heaven, not the things here on earth.

CONCLUSION

CHRISTIAN BLESSING
May the love of God be above you to overshadow you,
beneath you to uphold you,
before you to guide you,
behind you to protect you,
close beside you and within you to make you able for all things,
and to reward your faithfulness with joy and peace
which the world cannot give - neither can it take away.

Sisters, thank you for taking this forty-day life-changing journey with me. I pray that you have or will come to know Jesus as your personal Savior. I pray you will develop a deep and personal friendship with Him. I pray you will choose to abide in His peace and joy every day.

I hope that these last forty days have been eye-opening, realigning, and perspective-changing for you. I pray that God has opened your eyes, mind, and hearts to His peace, joy, and love. Sisters, I pray that God will bless each of you and all those connected to you. I pray that you will realize you are stronger than you know and more equipped than you believe. I hope that you will reach for the stars and awaken to all the blessings and anointings God has for you.

Never accept Satan's lies of who you are and your shortcomings. Instead, I hope this study has drilled into your mind what the Word of God says about you. The Bible says you are equipped, anointed, called, empowered, able, and enough. I hope that you have realized nothing from your past disqualifies you from your divine future. No mistake can hold you back from all the good things God has in store for you.

There is no difficulty that He will take you to that does not match the blessing that He has for you. Remember, He will take you as low as needed to propel you further up than you could imagine. You are a warrior woman of God, you were validated on the cross, and you are worth more than all the precious jewels on earth. You are a daughter of the King of kings, and you are heir to the kingdom of heaven. Never allow the world to tell you anything different. You were created to do great things for the kingdom; stand in that truth today, and start interacting in love with everyone placed in your path. Let us go change the world as strong, validated, and worthy women of God. Stand firm, keep your eyes on Jesus, and do not waver with society.

Colossians 1:9-12 (NLT):

> We ask God to give you complete knowledge of his will and to give you spiritual wisdom and understanding. Then the way you live will always honor and please the Lord, and your lives will produce every kind of good fruit. All the while, you will grow as you learn to know God better and better. We also pray that you will be strengthened with all his glorious power so you will have all the endurance and patience you need. May you be filled with joy, always thanking the Father. He has enabled you to share in the inheritance that belongs to his people, who live in the light.

ABOUT THE AUTHOR

Sara Singh is a wife of seventeen years to her husband Kevin, mother of four active children, and entrepreneur who lives in Orlando, Florida. She works in the real estate/title field and owns her own consulting company. Sara was born in New England and moved to Florida at the age of four. Her mother abandoned her when she was just over a year old, and she lost her dad when he was just twenty-nine years old, and Sara was just nine years old. She was a definite daddy's girl. Sara was raised by her paternal grandparents in Orlando. Her grandparents always kept Sara in church and youth group.

She struggled in school with undiagnosed ADD all her life, and Sara experienced racism at a young age, while living in literal KKK territory. She was beaten up, ran off the road, had her property set on fire, and was even not allowed to ride the school bus because of her skin color. Yet, she realized even this trial was just a lesson in emotional resilience that built emotional strength for the rest of her life. Sara never held ill feelings towards any race because of this history. Instead, she focuses and teaches on the kingdom mentality and seeing people as individuals not as the earthly, divisive labels.

She met her husband at the age of sixteen and knew right away he was the one for her. Her old-fashioned grandparents believed in courtship, and Sara had a promise ring at sixteen, was engaged at the age of eighteen, and was married by twenty. Her marriage was always her source of joy, and her husband is truly her best friend. His family truly took the place in her heart of her lost parents, and she is blessed with what she says are "the best in-laws ever."

Sara's life held a lot of hurt, loss, pain, depression, insecurity, stress, and resentment. She carried much of that into her late twenties. As she had children and refocused into her faith, Sara had a powerful mindset shift as she pressed deeper into Jesus. She realized she could continue carrying around all that baggage and a victim and limited mindset, or she could let it all go and reclaim a victor and limitless mindset. She was depressed, and she had to choose, and she chose the latter. She laid her hurt, pain, and insecurity at the foot of the cross. As she did the hard inner work to shift her mindset, her perspective also changed. She became free from depression, insecurity, hurt, and loss. She realized nobody on earth could validate her worth and that her priceless worth was determined by her Heavenly Father. This led to steadfast peace, emotional resilience, and endless joy, even amid the storms of life.

Sara loves teaching her children from their young ages that they are created and loved by their Heavenly Father. That they are priceless, unique, and created to stand out in the world. That peace is a mindset, and joy is a perspective. She wants to teach all girls and women this same message.

Sara loves the ocean, dolphins, sunsets, and the beach. She enjoys fishing, traveling, swimming, and reading. She most enjoys speaking publicly to youth and women groups about her lessons in her losses and her message that was born out of her messes. She leads a young ladies mentorship group, teaching many of the principles covered in this study. Sara wants to reach as many women as she can with her message of hope, restoration, peace, joy, and redemption. Sara believes God never wastes our pain, and that we must speak about our hurt and losses, because it is our past testimony that gives others hope for their future. She hopes that this work of her heart brings you hope and shifts your mindset drastically.

www.ingramcontent.com/pod-product-compliance
Lightning Source LLC
Chambersburg PA
CBHW070531160426
43199CB00014B/2240